CCH
a Wolters Kluwer business

MW01702884

CCH Accounting for Income Taxes

by Richard R. Petersen, CPA

Highlights

CCH Accounting for Income Taxes provides guidance on the application of FASB Statement No. 109, *Accounting for Income Taxes,* as amended. It also incorporates the various amendments to Statement 109 since 1992, including the guidance contained in FASB Interpretation (FIN) No. 48, *Accounting for Uncertainty in Income Taxes—an Interpretation of FASB Statement No. 109.* This in-depth resource gives professionals indispensable guidance on the complex requirements of Statement 109 and clarifies the implementation issues resulting from applying the statement's criteria. It provides a practical reference tool by selectively combining information from the official text of the FASB, along with information drawn from the AICPA, consensuses of the EITF, SEC Staff Accounting Bulletins, and lessons learned from leading practitioners in the field.

Important Notice for 2008—FASB Proposes Clarification of FIN 48

The 2008 Edition has been updated for the issuance of FIN 48. The guidance in FIN 48 is applicable for fiscal years beginning after December 15, 2006. In other words, a calendar year-end public company would be required to implement the standard effective in its quarter ending March 31, 2007.

ACCOUNTING FOR INCOME TAXES

IMPORTANT NOTICE FOR 2008

As the 2008 edition of *CCH Accounting for Income Taxes* goes to press, the FASB has proposed amending the guidance in FIN 48, which was issued in July 2006. Specifically, FASB Staff Position (FSP) FIN 48-a, "Definition of Settlement in FASB Interpretation No. 48," has been issued for comment until March 28, 2007. The FASB is proposing guidance that would be applicable to companies as they implement FIN 48 for the first time. The proposal addresses how companies should determine whether a tax position is effectively settled for the purpose of recognizing previously unrecognized tax benefits. The proposed FSP: (1) provides examples in the application of FIN 48, (2) clarifies the concept of "settlement," and (3) would amend paragraphs 8, 10, and 12 of FIN 48. The guidance in Appendix I of this publication (in particular, Interpretation FIN 48 10-1) does not reflect the proposed FSP. Accordingly, users should determine whether the FASB finalized its proposal and how any final rule might affect the guidance in Appendix I.

2008 Edition

The 2008 Edition of *CCH Accounting for Income Taxes* contains new Appendix I, *Interpretations of FIN 48, Accounting for Uncertainty in Income Taxes*. This appendix includes material quoted directly from FIN 48, together with the authors' commentary and interpretation. Appendix I contains the following new interpretations:

- FIN 48 5-1, "Unit of Account," which expands on the FASB's view of this concept;
- FIN 48 7-1, "Administrative Practices and Precedents," which describes how a company should evaluate a taxing authority's past administrative practices and precedents when assessing the concept of "more likely than not";

- FIN 48 8-1, "Example of How to Measure the Tax Benefit to Be Recognized Under FIN 48," which provides a numerical example of the measurement of tax benefits;
- FIN 48 8-2, "All Income Tax Uncertainties Need to Be Accounted for Pursuant to FIN 48," which discusses the application of FIN 48 to timing uncertainties of known deductions;
- FIN 48 10-1, "Ultimately Settled Through Negotiation or Litigation," which discusses the appropriate accounting when a taxing authority has completed its examination of a specific period of an enterprise but the parties have not executed a formal closing agreement;
- FIN 48 12-1, "Consideration of Subsequent Events Differs From Statement 5," which discusses whether an enterprise should consider information that occurs after the balance-sheet date but before issuing financial statements when assessing the recognition or measurements of tax positions;
- FIN 48 15-1, "Capitalization of Interest," which discusses whether an enterprise should include interest on unrecognized tax benefits when capitalizing interest costs pursuant to the guidance in FASB Statement No. 34, *Capitalization of Interest;*
- FIN 48 17-1, "Determining the Current Portion of the Liability for Unrecognized Tax Benefits," which discusses how an enterprise should classify a liability related to unrecognized tax benefits in its statement of financial position;
- FIN 48 17-2, "Balance Sheet Classification of Long-Term Liabilities for Unrecognized Tax Benefits," which discusses the presentation of unrecognized tax benefits in the balance sheet;
- FIN 48 18-1, "Interaction Between Net Operating Loss Carryforwards and Liabilities for Unrecognized Tax Benefits," which discusses whether deferred tax assets for net operating loss carryforwards should be based on the filing position or the recognition provisions in FIN 48;
- FIN 48 19-1, "Changing Accounting Policies for Penalties and Interest," which addresses whether the classification of

interest and penalties is subject to the guidance in FASB Statement No. 154, *Accounting Changes and Error Corrections;*

- FIN 48 21-1, "Disclosures Required for Public Companies in Interim Period of Adoption," which discusses the necessary disclosures by a public company when adopting FIN 48;
- FIN 48 21-2, "Amounts Included in the Tabular Rollforward," which addresses the components of the required FIN 48 rollforward analysis;
- FIN 48 21-3, "Effective Tax Rate Disclosure," which discusses the requirement to disclose the total amount of unrecognized tax benefits that, if recognized, would affect the effective tax rate of the enterprise;
- FIN 48 21-4, "Example Disclosure From FIN 48," which refers users to certain guidance in FIN 48; and
- FIN 48 23-1, "Treatment of Subsequent Events at Transition to FIN 48," which discusses the interplay of FIN 48 and FASB Statement No. 5, *Accounting for Contingencies*, at the date of adoption of FIN 48.

Much of the guidance in Interpretation 10-1, "Uncertain Tax Positions," has been moved to the appropriate interpretations in new Appendix I, discussed above.

The 2008 Edition also contains the following added or updated interpretations:

- Revised Interpretation 4-4, "Michigan Single Business Tax," which discusses the repeal of the Michigan single business tax;
- Revised Interpretation 27-1, "Changes in Tax Law," which clarifies the provided guidance;
- Revised Interpretation 35-2, "Exceptions to the General Rule That the Tax Effect of an Item Other Than Income From Continuing Operations Is Computed as the Incremental Tax Effect of That Item," which addresses the presentation of income tax uncertainties related to discontinued operations; and
- Added Interpretation 35-10, "Intraperiod Tax Allocation of Income Tax Uncertainties," which addresses whether

FIN 48 modifies the intraperiod tax allocation provisions of Statement 109.

The section entitled *Recent Developments* was revised to give users a status of projects and related activities at the FASB that may affect the accounting for income taxes.

CCH Learning Center

CCH's goal is to provide you with the clearest, most concise, and up-to-date accounting and auditing information to help further your professional development, as well as a convenient method to help you satisfy your continuing professional education requirements. The CCH Learning Center* offers a complete line of self-study courses covering complex and constantly evolving accounting and auditing issues. We are continually adding new courses to the library to help you stay current on all the latest developments. The CCH Learning Center courses are available 24 hours a day, seven days a week. You'll get immediate exam results and certification. To view our complete accounting and auditing course catalog, go to: **http://cch.learningcenter.com.**

Accounting Research Manager™

For the latest information about income taxes, look to **Accounting Research Manager**, the most comprehensive, up-to-date, and objective online database of financial reporting literature. It includes all authoritative and proposed accounting, auditing, and SEC literature, plus independent, expert-written interpretive guidance.

---

* CCH is registered with the National Association of State Boards of Accountancy (NASBA) as a sponsor of continuing professional education on the National Registry of CPE Sponsors. State boards of accountancy have final authority on the acceptance of individual courses for CPE credit. Complaints regarding registered sponsors may be addressed to the National Registry of CPE Sponsors, 150 Fourth Avenue North, Nashville, TN 37219-2417. Telephone: 615-880-4200.

* CCH is registered with the National Association of State Boards of Accountancy as a Quality Assurance Service (QAS) sponsor of continuing professional education. Participating state boards of accountancy have final authority on the acceptance of individual courses for CPE credit. Complaints regarding QAS program sponsors may be addressed to NASBA, 150 Fourth Avenue North, Suite 700, Nashville, TN 37219-2417. Telephone: 615-880-4200.

With **Accounting Research Manager**, you maximize the efficiency of your research time while enhancing your results. Learn more about our content, our experts, and how you can request a FREE trial by visiting us at **http://www.accountingresearchmanager.com.**

3/07

© 2007 CCH. All Rights Reserved.

2008
CCH ACCOUNTING FOR INCOME TAXES

Interpretations of FASB Statement No. 109,
Accounting for Income Taxes,
as amended

Author: Richard R. Petersen, CPA
Editorial Reviewing Author:
Ronald G. Pippin, CPA

CCH
a Wolters Kluwer business

This publication is designed to provide accurate and authoritative information in regard to the subject matter covered. It is sold with the understanding that the publisher is not engaged in rendering legal, accounting, or other professional services. If legal advice or other professional assistance is required, the services of a competent professional person should be sought.

—From a *Declaration of Principles* jointly adopted by a Committee of the American Bar Association and a Committee of Publishers and Associations

© 2007 CCH. All Rights Reserved.
4025 W. Peterson Ave.
Chicago, IL 60646-6085
1 800 248 3248
http://CCHGroup.com

ISBN: 978-0-8080-9093-9

No claim is made to original government works; however, within this Product or Publication, the following are subject to CCH's copyright: (1) the gathering, compilation, and arrangement of such government materials; (2) the magnetic translation and digital conversion of data, if applicable; (3) the historical, statutory, and other notes and references; and (4) the commentary and other materials.

Printed in the United States of America.

This publication combines material quoted directly from the Financial Accounting Standards Board's (FASB's) Statements of Financial Accounting Standards, including FASB Statement No. 109, *Accounting for Income Taxes*, as amended, FASB Interpretation No. 48, *Accounting for Uncertainty in Income Taxes*, FASB Staff Implementation Guide, *A Guide to Implementation of Statement 109 on Accounting for Income Taxes*, FASB Staff Implementation Guide, *A Guide to Implementation of Statement 115 on Accounting for Certain Investments in Debt and Equity Securities,* and portions of *EITF Abstracts* with commentary and interpretations. FASB publications included in this publication are copyrighted by the Financial Accounting Standards Board, 401 Merritt 7, P.O. Box 5116, Norwalk, CT 06856-5116, and are included in this work by permission. All rights reserved. No portion of the FASB pronouncements in this work may be further reproduced in any format without the written consent of the FASB.

Contents

Preface

In February 1992, the Financial Accounting Standards Board (FASB) issued FASB Statement No. 109, *Accounting for Income Taxes.* In the years since its issuance, the FASB staff has released FASB Staff Implementation Guide, *A Guide to Implementation of Statement 109 on Accounting for Income Taxes,* and the Emerging Issues Task Force (EITF) has dealt with a number of Statement 109 implementation issues, as well. In July 2006, the FASB issued FASB Interpretation (FIN) No. 48, *Accounting for Uncertainty in Income Taxes—an Interpretation of Statement No. 109,* to address financial statement recognition and measurement by an enterprise of a tax position taken or expected to be taken in a tax return.

This publication, *CCH Accounting for Income Taxes,* is organized according to paragraph number within Statement 109, as amended, with verbatim text of the statement set off in a box to distinguish it from the authors' commentary. The book provides the authors' interpretation on areas that have not been specifically addressed by the FASB or that require further explanation. A separate appendix (Appendix I) contains quoted material from FIN 48 together with the authors' interpretation. The analysis in this book is based on discussions with the staffs of the FASB and the Securities and Exchange Commission (SEC), combined with lessons learned from leading accounting practitioners. A glossary (Appendix II) is provided at the end of this publication, as well as an "Index of Accounting Literature Affecting Income Taxes" (Appendix IV), which includes cross-references to the interpretations that either refer to or incorporate the authoritative pronouncement in whole or in part. We also include an appendix (Appendix III) that contains examples reflecting how various U.S. public companies have disclosed the information required by Statement 109 as amended and interpreted (before the issuance of FIN 48).

Practice continues to evolve on many of the issues that are addressed in this book. In addition, various regulatory agencies, such as the SEC, adopt new and different positions from time to time as developments occur. The positions set forth herein represent our understanding of current practice. Given the changing conditions and the complexity of certain issues, users should closely monitor the viewpoints expressed and consult with experts on specific matters, as appropriate. We will continue to update this publication as the need arises.

This publication combines material quoted directly from FASB Statement No. 109, *Accounting for Income Taxes,* as amended, FASB Interpretation No. 48, *Accounting for Uncertainty in Income Taxes,*

FASB Staff Implementation Guide, *A Guide to Implementation of Statement 109 on Accounting for Income Taxes*, FASB Staff Implementation Guide, *A Guide to Implementation of Statement 115 on Accounting for Certain Investments in Debt and Equity Securities*, and portions of *EITF Abstracts* with our commentary and interpretation. Quoted material is reprinted with permission of the FASB.

FASB documents included in this publication are copyrighted by the Financial Accounting Standards Board, 401 Merritt 7, P.O. Box 5116, Norwalk, Connecticut, 06856-5116, U.S.A. Copies of the complete documents are available from the FASB.

About the Authors

Lead Author

Richard R. Petersen

Richard R. Petersen is a co-founder and Managing Director of Financial Reporting Advisors LLC (FRA). Based in Chicago, Illinois, FRA provides consulting services related to accounting and SEC reporting, and litigation support services.

Previously, Richard was a partner with Arthur Andersen LLP in its Professional Standards Group (PSG). In this role, he consulted with clients and engagement teams on complex financial reporting matters and authored interpretive guidance on topics, such as consolidations, income taxes, leases, and revenue recognition, for Andersen's worldwide practice. He also represented the firm before various standards setters, including the FASB, the SEC, and the AICPA.

Richard has served as the chair or member of various Emerging Issues Task Force working groups on a wide array of topics, such as consolidation, leases, income taxes, and revenue recognition. He also was a member of the AICPA Task Force on Reorganization that developed AICPA Practice Bulletin No. 11, *Accounting for Preconfirmation Contingencies in Fresh-Start Reporting*. Richard is currently a member of the AICPA's Accounting Standards Executive Committee (AcSEC).

From 1988 to 1990, Richard was a Practice Fellow at the FASB. He was the project manager for the reconsideration of FASB Statement No. 96, *Accounting for Income Taxes*, and FASB Statement No. 101, *Regulated Enterprises—Accounting for the Discontinuation of Application of FASB Statement No. 71*. He also worked on issues related to business combinations and leveraged buyouts.

Richard received his Bachelor of Science in Business Administration from the University of Nebraska at Lincoln. He is a licensed Certified Public Accountant in Nebraska and Illinois and is a member of the AICPA and the Illinois CPA Society.

Editorial Reviewing Author

Ronald G. Pippin

Managing Director, Accounting Research Manager

Ron authors and oversees the maintenance of the SEC content on the Accounting Research Manager (ARM) database as well as a significant portion of the accounting content on ARM. Among other responsibilities at ARM, Ron reviews the completeness of the content for this publication, *CCH Accounting for Income Taxes*.

Ron has 20 years of public accounting experience, including six years as an audit partner with Arthur Andersen. He also served as the senior technical accounting officer at a Chicago-based Fortune 50 firm for 10 years. Before Ron joined CCH, a Wolters Kluwer business, he worked in Andersen's Professional Standards Group (commonly known as the "national office"), where he consulted on technical accounting matters and contributed to the authoring and maintenance of ARM's accounting content. Wolters Kluwer purchased ARM from Andersen in 2001.

Ron is a CPA, a graduate of the University of Colorado in Boulder, and a member of Financial Executives International, the AICPA, and the Illinois Society of CPAs.

SECTION I
INTERPRETATIONS

SECTION I
INTERPRETATIONS

CONTENTS

PARAGRAPHS 1–2: INTRODUCTION

EXCERPT FROM OFFICIAL TEXT

INTRODUCTION

1. This Statement addresses financial accounting and reporting for the effects of **income taxes**[1] that result from an enterprise's activities during the current and preceding years.
2. FASB Statement No. 96, *Accounting for Income Taxes*, which was issued in December 1987, superseded APB Opinion No. 11, *Accounting for Income Taxes*. The effective date of Statement 96 was delayed to fiscal years that begin after December 15, 1992. In March 1989, the Board began consideration of requests to amend Statement 96 to (a) change the criteria for recognition and measurement of deferred tax assets and various other requirements of Statement 96 and (b) reduce complexity. This Statement is the result of that reconsideration.

---

[1] Words that appear in the glossary are set in boldface type the first time they appear. [Editorial Note: The glossary is reproduced in this publication as Appendix II.]

PARAGRAPHS 3–5: SCOPE

EXCERPT FROM OFFICIAL TEXT

Scope

3. This Statement establishes standards of financial accounting and reporting for income taxes that are currently payable and for the tax consequences of:

   a. Revenues, expenses, gains, or losses that are included in **taxable income** of an earlier or later year than the year in which they are recognized in financial income
   b. Other **events** that create differences between the tax bases of assets and liabilities and their amounts for financial reporting
   c. Operating loss or tax credit **carrybacks** for refunds of taxes paid in prior years and **carryforwards** to reduce taxes payable in future years.

   This Statement supersedes Statement 96 and supersedes or amends other accounting pronouncements listed in Appendix D.

4. The principles and requirements of this Statement are applicable to:

   a. Domestic federal (national) income taxes (U.S. federal income taxes for U.S. enterprises) and foreign, state, and local (including franchise) taxes based on income
   b. An enterprise's[2] domestic and foreign operations that are consolidated, combined, or accounted for by the equity method
   c. Foreign enterprises in preparing financial statements in accordance with U.S. generally accepted accounting principles.

---

[2] The term *enterprise* is used throughout this Statement because accounting for income taxes is primarily an issue for business enterprises. However, the requirements of this Statement apply to the activities of a not-for-profit organization that are subject to income taxes.

INTERPRETATION

4-1. [Not Used]

4-2. Not-for-Profit Entities: Tax on Investment Income

Question: Certain not-for-profit entities that generally are exempt from income tax are required to pay taxes on investment income. For example:

- Not-for-profit foundations that make certain minimum distributions are generally exempt from federal income taxes. However, such foundations are subject to an excise tax on their net investment income.
- Voluntary employee beneficiary organizations for employees not covered by collective bargaining agreements pay federal income tax on net investment income.

Does Statement 109 require such entities to provide for deferred taxes for differences between the financial reporting and tax bases of investment securities (e.g., basis differences caused by carrying investment securities at market value for financial reporting purposes)?

Response: Yes. The taxes described previously are taxes "based on income" and are therefore within the scope of Statement 109. Basis differences related to investment securities should be treated as temporary differences. Deferred taxes should be recognized and the need for a valuation allowance (if any deductible temporary differences or loss carryforwards exist) should be evaluated as with any deferred tax asset.

4-3. Mexican Profit-Sharing Arrangements

Question: Mexican law requires enterprises to pay employees a specified percentage of an amount that is based on adjusted taxable income. In effect, this is a mandated employee profit-sharing plan with annual contributions based on a computation that begins with taxable income. Are such employee profit-sharing payments an "income tax" and as such governed by Statement 109?

Response: No. These employee profit-sharing payments technically are not taxes because the amounts are not payable to the government. However, the required profit-sharing arrangement has the same economic effect on an enterprise as an income tax, including deferred consequences from existing basis differences (i.e., the recovery of assets and the settlement of liabilities at their financial reporting carrying amounts inherently have tax consequences and profit-sharing consequences).

We believe, and understand that the SEC staff agrees, Statement 109 is generally the appropriate model for the recognition of the deferred profit-sharing consequences caused by existing basis differences. The only exception to the Statement 109 model relates to the recognition of deferred profit-sharing assets. Because any assets recognized for deferred profit-sharing consequences are not literally deferred tax assets, we believe it would be inappropriate to recognize such assets based only on expectations of future income. We think the amount recognized as an asset for deferred profit-sharing consequences should be limited to the amount realizable assuming future break-even operating results for financial reporting purposes (in effect, the Statement 96 model for recognition of assets).

4-4. Michigan Single Business Tax

Question: The Michigan single business tax is based on an amount that is computed by adding payroll costs to, and subtracting construction expenditures from, income for the period. In many situations, the payroll and construction expenditures components may be more significant than the income component. Is the Michigan single business tax a "tax on income" and as such governed by Statement 109?

Response: Yes. Although the state tax law in Michigan clearly states that the tax is not an income tax, the starting point for the tax is income for the period and therefore meets the Statement 109 definition of a "tax on income." Although interperiod tax allocation is required for the Michigan single business tax, general practice indicates some diversity in the financial statement classification of the provision for this tax. This diversity arises because enterprises may show losses for both financial reporting and U.S. federal income tax purposes and still have a Michigan single business tax liability due to the payroll component of the base computation. Thus, enterprises may elect to classify this tax: (*a*) as income tax expense, (*b*) partially as income tax expense and partially as general expense, or (*c*) as general expense.

On August 9, 2006, the Michigan legislature approved a voters' initiative to repeal the Michigan single business tax for tax years beginning after December 31, 2007. Previously, the Michigan single business tax was scheduled to be repealed for tax years beginning after December 31, 2009. Pursuant to the guidance in paragraph 27 of Statement 109, the effect on deferred tax assets and liabilities of this change in tax law should be reflected in the period the change in tax law is enacted. If the state of Michigan enacts a new tax that meets the definition of an income tax, the effect on deferred tax assets and liabilities of that new tax should be reflected in the period of its enactment.

4-5. Texas State Franchise Tax

(Editorial Note: In May 2006, the state of Texas enacted legislation that, effective in 2007, significantly modifies its franchise tax. In this interpretation, we refer to the 2006 tax as a franchise tax and the 2007 and later tax as a "margin tax." The first two questions in this interpretation address the franchise tax. The remaining questions address the margin tax.)

Question: The state of Texas requires companies to pay a franchise tax based on the greater of two amounts: (1) a percentage of net taxable capital (.25% for 2006) or (2) a percentage of taxable income (4.5% for 2006). Is the Texas state franchise tax a "tax on income?"

Response: The Texas state franchise tax is an income tax only to the extent that the total tax exceeds the capital-based tax in a given year.

The EITF addressed the application of Statement 96 to the Texas state franchise tax in EITF Issue No. 91-8, "Application of FASB Statement No. 96 to a State Tax Based on the Greater of a Franchise Tax or an Income Tax." The FASB staff added the following paragraphs to the status section of Issue 91-8 as a result of the issuance of Statement 109:

> Two basic principles of Statement 109 are to recognize a current tax liability or asset for the estimated taxes payable or refundable on tax returns for the current year and a deferred tax liability or asset for the estimated future tax effects attributable to temporary differences and carryforwards. A deferred tax liability or asset is measured using the enacted tax rate(s) expected to apply to taxable income in the periods in which the deferred tax liability or asset is expected to be settled or realized.
>
> Under the consensus for Issue 91-8, the Texas tax is an income tax only to the extent that the tax exceeds the capital-based tax in a given year. Accordingly, under Statement 109 deferred taxes are recognized for temporary differences that will reverse in future years for which annual taxable income is expected to exceed 5.555% (.25% of net taxable capital/4.5% of taxable income) of expected net taxable capital . . . .

Question: How should the Texas state franchise tax be computed?

Response: The measurement of deferred taxes under Statement 109 is based on an incremental concept. That is, in theory, deferred tax liabilities and assets should be measured based on the incremental tax liability or benefit that will be caused by the reversal of existing temporary differences. Primarily to reduce the complexity of accounting for income taxes, the FASB decided to measure deferred tax liabilities and assets using a tax rate convention—the enacted tax rate(s) expected to apply to taxable income in the periods in which the deferred tax liability or asset is expected to be settled or realized. When measurement of the deferred tax effect of a temporary difference is unclear, the underlying theory of Statement 109 suggests that one consider existing temporary differences to be the last dollars of taxable income in the periods in which the temporary differences reverse.

To apply that approach to the Texas franchise tax, one would first determine the portion of existing temporary differences that is expected to reverse in periods when the expected income tax exceeds the expected capital-based tax. State deferred taxes would then be computed by multiplying *that portion* of the temporary differences by the statutory income tax rate (currently 4.5%). Another approach is to view the Texas franchise tax as a graduated tax rate situation (see paragraph 18 of Statement 109 for the graduated tax rate exception to the general measurement rule). Under this approach, the portion of taxable income covered by the capital-based tax would be treated as income subject to a zero income tax rate. We believe the second approach is less desirable because it is inconsistent with the expected economic effect of the reversal of the temporary differences.

To illustrate the two approaches, assume that an enterprise has $100 of taxable temporary differences that are expected to reverse in the same future year. In that future year, the enterprise expects to have taxable income of $1,000 (including the reversal of the $100 of taxable temporary differences), the enacted state tax rate on income is 4.5%, and the capital-based tax is estimated to be $10. Total tax in that year is therefore expected to be $45 ($1,000 × 4.5%) and the preferable method of computing today's deferred tax liability would result in a deferred tax liability of $4.50 ($100 × 4.5%). The alternative approach would result in a deferred tax liability of $3.50 ([($45 – $10)/$1,000] × $100).

The same thought process also applies to computing deferred tax assets. Companies that, absent the reversal of existing temporary differences, would not be paying an income tax would not have a deferred state tax asset for deductible temporary differences or net operating loss (NOL) carryforwards.

The Texas law also provides that taxpayers may elect a limited credit against future income tax liabilities. In essence, that credit is based on the amount of temporary differences that existed at the date of the law change priced at the income tax rate of 4.5% (and then spread over 20 years). However, the franchise tax rate is increased for any company that elects to claim that credit. That credit is not a carryforward and therefore we believe it should not be recognized as a deferred tax asset. (Deferred taxes should only be recognized for temporary differences and carryforwards.

This credit is more akin to a "special deduction." See Interpretations 18-4 and 18-5 for examples of the treatment of special deductions.) Regardless, the credit could only be recognized if the enterprise *expects* to claim the credit and then any tax benefit recognized should be reduced by the additional franchise tax that will be payable in future years as a result of claiming the credit.

Question: Beginning in 2007, the state of Texas will require enterprises to pay a tax based on their "taxable margin." The taxable margin is the lesser of: (*a*) 70% of revenue or (*b*) 100% of revenue less (i) the cost of goods sold or (ii) compensation. The taxpayer annually elects whether to deduct the cost of goods sold or compensation. Is the Texas state margin tax a "tax on income?"

Response: Because it is expected that most enterprises will pay tax based on 100% of revenues less either the cost of goods sold or compensation, we believe the Texas state margin tax is a "tax based on income" and is therefore within the scope of Statement 109.

Question: In what period should enterprises recognize any effect on their Texas state deferred tax assets and liabilities from the new tax legislation?

Response: Paragraph 27 of Statement 109 requires that the effect of changes in tax law and rates be reflected in the interim period the change in tax law or rates is enacted. In the case of the Texas margin tax, the effect should be reflected in the period that includes May 18, 2006 (the date the legislation was enacted).

Question: In general, how does the change in tax law and rates affect Texas state deferred tax assets and liabilities?

Response: The revised tax system changes both the tax rate (in general, .5% of taxable margin for enterprises engaged in retail or wholesale trade and 1.0% of taxable margin for all other enterprises) and the amount of some temporary differences. Temporary differences are existing differences between financial reporting and tax bases of assets and liabilities that are expected to have a tax consequence when the financial reporting bases of the assets or liabilities are recovered or settled, respectively. Although the revised tax system does not change the tax bases of any assets or liabilities, it does change, for some basis differences, whether the basis difference is expected to have a future tax consequence. The portion of the basis differences that is expected to reverse after 2006 and that is not expected to have a tax consequence when it reverses is, effective May 18, 2006, no longer a temporary difference.

4-6. Accounting for Investments in Non-Consolidated Tax-Advantaged Limited Partnerships (Such as Investments in Affordable Housing Projects)

Question: The return to investors from investments in certain types of limited partnerships may be driven primarily by the tax credits generated by the limited partnership. For example, to encourage investments in affordable housing projects, the Omnibus Budget Reconciliation Act of 1993 (Internal Revenue Code [IRC] Section 42) made permanent the affordable housing tax credit. The pass through of such credits from the limited partnership to the investor may be the primary source for the investor's return of and on its investment in the limited partnership. The same may be true of investments in limited partnerships that generate, for example, historic rehabilitation tax credits (IRC Section 47) or tax credits for the domestic production of oil or gas from nonconventional sources (IRC Section 29). Should an investor with a noncontrolling interest in such a limited partnership account for its investment as the purchase of tax benefits or as a traditional investment in a limited partnership?

Response: The EITF addressed this topic in EITF Issue No. 94-1, "Accounting for Tax Benefits Resulting from Investments in Affordable Housing Projects," and concluded that generally an investor in such a limited partnership should account for its investment as a traditional investment in a limited partnership. The EITF also decided that it was not appropriate to recognize the tax benefits to be received from a limited partnership investment in a qualified affordable housing project prior to their inclusion in the investor's tax return.

Issue 94-1 allows an entity that invests in a qualified affordable housing project through a limited partnership to *elect* to account for the investment using the effective yield method if all of the following conditions are met:

- The availability (but not necessarily the realization) of the tax credits allocable to the investor is guaranteed by a creditworthy entity through a letter of credit, a tax indemnity agreement, or another similar arrangement;
- The investor's projected yield based solely on the cash flows from the guaranteed tax credits is positive; and
- The investor is a limited partner in the affordable housing project for both legal and tax purposes and the investor's liability is limited to its capital investment.

Under the effective yield method, the investor recognizes tax credits as they are allocated and amortizes the initial cost of the investment to provide a constant effective yield over the period that tax credits are allocated to the investor. The effective yield is the internal rate of return on the investment, based on the cost of the investment and the guaranteed tax credits allocated to the investor. Any expected residual value of the investment should be excluded from the effective yield calculation.

Under the effective yield method, the tax credit allocated, net of the amortization of the investment in the limited partnership, is recognized in the income statement as a component of income taxes attributable to continuing operations. Any other tax benefits received should be accounted for pursuant to Statement 109. For a limited partnership investment in a qualified affordable housing project not accounted for using the effective yield method, the EITF reached a consensus that the investment should be accounted for in accordance with American Institute of Certified Public Accountants (AICPA) Statement of Position (SOP) 78-9, *Accounting for Investments in Real Estate Ventures.*

SOP 78-9 generally requires the use of the equity method of accounting unless: (*a*) the limited partner's interest is so minor as to give the partner virtually no influence over partnership operating and financial policies or (*b*) the investor controls the limited partnership. The SEC staff's interpretation of that guidance in SOP 78-9 is that investments in limited partnerships "of more than 3 to 5 percent [are] more than minor." This SEC staff's view is documented in *EITF Abstracts*, Topic D-46, "Accounting for Limited Partnership Investments."

An investor using the cost method for affordable housing partnerships should amortize any excess of the carrying amount of the investment over its estimated residual value during the periods when tax credits are allocated to the investor. This annual amortization should be based on the proportion of tax credits received in the current year to total tax credits to be allocated to the investor. An investor that controls the limited partnership should consolidate the limited partnership.

The EITF also decided in Issue 94-1 that a liability should be recognized for delayed equity contributions that are: (*a*) unconditional and legally binding or (*b*) contingent on a future probable event.

The SEC staff believes that it would be inappropriate to further extend the effective yield method of accounting to other analogous situations. We believe the effective yield method discussed in Issue 94-1 should be applied only to investments in limited partnerships in which: (*a*) the pass through of tax credits to the investor is the primary source for the investor's return of its investment in the limited partnership and (*b*) all of the criteria contained in Issue 94-1 are met. Investments in limited partnerships that generate historic rehabilitation tax credits (IRC Section 47) and tax credits for the domestic production of oil or gas from nonconventional sources (IRC Section 29) may meet these criteria.

FASB Interpretation (FIN) No. 46 (Revised December 2003), *Consolidation of Variable Interest Entities,* requires enterprises that will absorb a majority of a variable interest entity's (VIE's) expected losses or is entitled to receive a majority of a VIE's residual returns to consolidate that VIE. Tax related cash flows generally are not considered when developing expected loss and expected residual return calculations. However, we understand that tax credits generated by affordable housing project VIEs should be considered when developing expected loss and expected residual return calculations.

4-7. Taxes Assessed on Dividends

Question: Some tax jurisdictions or systems outside of the United States assess a tax on enterprises based on dividends distributed. For example, the French tax system utilizes a tax credit (referred to as the "precompte mobilier" or "precompte") at the shareholder level to eliminate or mitigate the double taxation that would otherwise apply to a dividend. The precompte is a tax paid by the French corporation at the time of a dividend distribution that is equal to the difference between a tax based on the regular corporation tax rate applied to the amount of the declared dividend and taxes previously paid by the corporation on the income being distributed. In addition, if a French corporation pays a dividend from earnings that have been retained for more than five years, the corporation loses the benefit of any taxes previously paid in the computation of the precompte.

Should a tax that is assessed on an enterprise based on dividends distributed, such as the precompte tax, be recorded as an increase in income tax expense or be considered a withholding of tax for the recipient of the dividend and recorded in equity as part of the dividend paid to shareholders?

Response: The EITF addressed this question in EITF Issue No. 95-9, "Accounting for Tax Effects of Dividends in France in Accordance with FASB Statement No. 109." The EITF reached a consensus that a tax that is assessed on an enterprise based on dividends distributed is, in effect, a withholding tax for the benefit of recipients of the dividend and should be recorded in equity only if both of the following conditions are met:

- The tax is payable by the corporation if and only if a dividend is distributed to shareholders. The tax does not reduce future income taxes the corporation would otherwise pay.
- Shareholders receiving the dividend are entitled to a tax credit at least equal to the taxes paid by the corporation and that credit is realizable either as a refund or as a reduction of taxes otherwise due, regardless of the tax status of the shareholders.

If either or both of the previous conditions are not met, the tax assessed on dividends distributed should be treated as part of the enterprise's normal tax expense.

Question: When should taxes that are assessed on an enterprise based on dividends distributed be recognized for financial reporting purposes?

Response: The timing of recognition of taxes that are assessed on an enterprise based on dividends distributed depends on whether the tax is determined to be an income tax on the enterprise or a withholding of tax for the recipient of the dividend. If the tax is an income tax on the enterprise, we believe the income tax expense should be recognized in the period the financial reporting income is earned. The EITF addressed a similar situation in EITF Issue No. 93-16, "Application of FASB Statement No. 109 to Basis Differences within Foreign Subsidiaries That Meet the Indefinite Reversal Criterion of APB Opinion No. 23" (see Interpretation 31-8). Issue 93-16 addresses a situation in which certain amounts are not taxable to the enterprise until those amounts are distributed to shareholders through dividends or liquidation of the enterprise and concludes that those amounts, even though characterized as a component of equity for tax purposes, should be considered taxable temporary differences under Statement 109.

If the tax is a withholding of tax for the recipient of the dividend, it should be recognized in the period that the dividend is declared.

EXCERPT FROM OFFICIAL TEXT

> 5. This Statement does not address:
>
> a. The basic methods of accounting for the U.S. federal investment tax credit (ITC) and for foreign, state, and local investment tax credits or grants. (The deferral and flow-through methods as set forth in APB Opinions No. 2 and No. 4, *Accounting for the "Investment Credit,"* continue to be acceptable methods to account for the U.S. federal ITC.)
>
> b. Discounting (Paragraph 6 of APB Opinion No. 10, *Omnibus Opinion—1966*, addresses that subject.)
>
> c. Accounting for income taxes in interim periods (other than the criteria for recognition of tax benefits and the effect of enacted changes in tax laws or rates and changes in valuation allowances). (APB Opinion No. 28, *Interim Financial Reporting*, and other accounting pronouncements address that subject.)

INTERPRETATION

5-1. Changes in Valuation Allowances During Interim Periods

Question: Are changes in the valuation allowance during interim periods discrete events or should the changes be reflected as adjustments of the estimated effective tax rate for the year?

Response: How changes in the valuation allowance during interim periods should be reflected depends on the reason for the change. The guidance on this question is contained in the amendments to APB Opinion No. 28, *Interim Financial Reporting*, and FASB Interpretation (FIN) No. 18, *Accounting for Income Taxes in Interim Periods*, in Appendix D of Statement 109. The following outline summarizes the guidance in Opinion 28 and FIN 18, as amended, on changes in valuation allowances in interim periods:

- Increase in valuation allowance from the beginning of the year:
  - *Due to a change in judgment about future years.* Treat as a discrete item in the interim period in which the change in judgment occurs.
  - *Due to increases in deductible temporary differences and carryforwards arising from "ordinary" income or loss during the current year.* Include in the computation of the effective tax rate.

— *Due to increases in deductible temporary differences and carryforwards arising from significant, unusual, or infrequently occurring items, discontinued operations, or extraordinary items during the current year.* Treat as a discrete item in the interim period in which those events occur.

- Decrease in the valuation allowance from the beginning of the year:

— *Due to a change in judgment about future years.* Treat as a discrete item in the interim period in which the change in judgment occurs.

— *Due to realization of a previously unrecognized benefit as a result of "ordinary" income in the current year.* Include in the computation of the effective tax rate. Based on discussions with the FASB staff, "realization" in this context should be interpreted to be recognizable for financial reporting, not necessarily realized on the tax return.

— *Due to realization from significant, unusual, or infrequently occurring items; discontinued operations; or extraordinary items during the current year.* Treat as a discrete item in the interim period in which those events occur.

Changes in valuation allowances in interim periods become complex when several of the previous items occur in the same reporting period. Consider Example 5-1A.

Example 5-1A

Assume the current tax rate is 40% and that Enterprise had a $24 valuation allowance against a $40 deferred tax asset as of January 1, 20X0 (Enterprise has a $100 net operating loss [NOL] carryforward and no temporary differences). The valuation allowance was required because Enterprise expects $40 of income in 20X0 ($40 × 40% = $16; the net deferred tax asset) and concluded existing negative evidence precluded it from considering any income beyond 20X0 in establishing its valuation allowance. Enterprise then reports $10 of pretax book income (no permanent items are expected in 20X0) in the first quarter of 20X0. The net asset of $16 should be written off over 20X0 using Enterprise's effective tax rate (40%). That is, if the assessment of the future does not change, Enterprise would have no net deferred tax asset at the end of 20X0. Accordingly, Enterprise should write off $4 of the deferred tax asset in the first quarter of 20X0.

If Enterprise now expects income in periods beyond 20X0 (i.e., there is a "change in circumstances that causes a change in judgment about the realizability of the deferred tax asset"), the valuation allowance could be reduced (which would reduce tax expense for

Continued on page 27

Continued from page 26

the quarter). However, that reduction is treated as a discrete event and is dependent on Enterprise's specific facts and circumstances.

If none of the deferred tax asset is written off in the first quarter in this example (i.e., $10 of pretax income and no tax expense is reported in the first quarter), Enterprise is implicitly writing off $4 of deferred tax asset and then reducing the valuation allowance by the same amount (because Enterprise's judgment about the amount of future income has implicitly changed), which may or may not be appropriate in Enterprise's facts and circumstances.

5-2. Changes in a Valuation Allowance in Interim Periods Subsequent to an Acquisition, Quasi Reorganization, or Fresh-Start Accounting

Question: Assume Company A acquired Company B in 20X0. As part of the purchase accounting, a valuation allowance was recognized for all of Company B's net operating loss (NOL) carryforward. Accordingly, if this tax asset is recognized in a future period (by a reduction in the valuation allowance), the benefit will be applied: (*a*) first to reduce to zero any goodwill related to the acquisition, (*b*) second to reduce to zero other noncurrent intangible assets related to the acquisition, and (*c*) third to reduce income tax expense. Because of large quarterly swings in profit and other uncertainties, Company A cannot reliably estimate an effective tax rate for 20X1. Therefore, it will treat each interim period as a separate period and calculate the required provision accordingly (pursuant to footnote 7 to FASB Interpretation (FIN) No. 18, *Accounting for Income Taxes in Interim Periods*). If goodwill is credited in an early quarter, is it acceptable to debit goodwill if losses are incurred in a subsequent quarter?

Response: In the unusual case in which an effective rate cannot be estimated at the beginning of the year, we believe it is acceptable to record adjustments, both positive and negative, to goodwill in interim periods. The objective should be that the financial statements for the annual period are properly stated in accordance with Statement 109. Consider Example 5-2A.

Example 5-2A

Example assumptions:

Company's preacquisition NOL at January 1, 20X1, is $100, all of which is offset by a valuation allowance.

Continued on page 28

Continued from page 27

Company has book income (no temporary differences) of $50 in the first quarter of 20X1, but cannot reasonably estimate results (and therefore an effective tax rate) for the remainder of the year.

Subsequently, Company incurs a book loss of $30 in the second quarter.

Company has a tax rate of 40% in all periods.

The following entries would be made in the first and second quarters:

First Quarter		
Tax provision ($50 × 40%)	$20	
Goodwill		$20
Second Quarter		
Goodwill	$12	
Tax benefit ($30 × 40%)		$12

We believe this approach would be acceptable *only* within a year. (See Interpretation 35-7 for a discussion of a similar issue.)

This same approach would be appropriate for quasi reorganizations and entities following "fresh-start" accounting under AICPA Statement of Position (SOP) 90-7, *Financial Reporting by Entities in Reorganization Under the Bankruptcy Code*. Paragraph 39 of Statement 109 indicates that the tax benefits of deductible temporary differences and carryforwards as of the date of a quasi reorganization ordinarily are reported as a direct addition to contributed capital if the tax benefits are recognized in future years (see Interpretation 39-1 for an exception to the above). Accordingly, in the previous example, the credit to goodwill in the first quarter and the debit to goodwill in the second quarter would be to a capital account. For fresh-start accounting under SOP 90-7, tax benefits realized from reductions in the valuation allowance established as part of the fresh-start opening balance sheet should first reduce "reorganization value in excess of amounts allocable to identifiable assets" (similar to goodwill) and other intangibles until exhausted and thereafter be reported as a direct addition to paid-in-capital. Accordingly, in the previous example, the credits/debits to goodwill would be to reorganization value in excess of amounts allocable to identifiable assets.

PARAGRAPHS 6–15: OBJECTIVES AND BASIC PRINCIPLES

EXCERPT FROM OFFICIAL TEXT

Objectives and Basic Principles

6. One objective of accounting for income taxes is to recognize the amount of taxes payable or refundable for the current year. A second objective is to recognize **deferred tax liabilities and assets** for the future **tax consequences** of events[3] that have been recognized in an enterprise's financial statements or tax returns.

7. Ideally, the second objective might be stated more specifically to recognize the expected future tax consequences of events that have been recognized in the financial statements or tax returns. However, that objective is realistically constrained because (a) the tax payment or refund that results from a particular tax return is a joint result of all the items included in that return, (b) taxes that will be paid or refunded in future years are the joint result of events of the current or prior years and events of future years, and (c) information available about the future is limited. As a result, attribution of taxes to individual items and events is arbitrary and, except in the simplest situations, requires estimates and approximations.

8. To implement the objectives in light of those constraints, the following basic principles (the only exceptions are identified in paragraph 9) are applied in accounting for income taxes at the date of the financial statements:

    a. A tax liability or asset is recognized based on the provisions of FASB Interpretation No. 48, *Accounting for Uncertainty in Income Taxes,* for the estimated taxes payable or refundable on tax returns for the current and prior years.

    b. A deferred tax liability or asset is recognized for the estimated future tax effects attributable to **temporary differences** and carryforwards.

    c. The measurement of current and deferred tax liabilities and assets is based on provisions of the enacted tax law; the

Continued on page 30

Continued from page 29

effects of future changes in tax laws or rates are not anticipated.

d. The measurement of deferred tax assets is reduced, if necessary, by the amount of any tax benefits that, based on available evidence, are not expected to be realized.

9. The only exceptions in applying those basic principles are that this Statement:

   a. Continues certain exceptions to the requirements for recognition of deferred taxes for the areas addressed by APB Opinion No. 23, *Accounting for Income Taxes—Special Areas*, as amended by this Statement (paragraphs 31–34)

   b. Provides special transitional procedures for temporary differences related to deposits in statutory reserve funds by U.S. steamship enterprises (paragraph 32)

   c. Does not amend accounting for leveraged leases as required by FASB Statement No. 13, *Accounting for Leases*, and FASB Interpretation No. 21, *Accounting for Leases in a Business Combination* (paragraphs 256–258)

   d. Prohibits recognition of a deferred tax liability or asset related to goodwill (or the portion thereof) for which amortization is not deductible for tax purposes (paragraph 30)

   e. Does not amend Accounting Research Bulletin No. 51, *Consolidated Financial Statements*, for income taxes paid on intercompany profits on assets remaining within the group, and prohibits recognition of a deferred tax asset for the difference between the tax basis of the assets in the buyer's tax jurisdiction and their cost as reported in the consolidated financial statements

   f. Prohibits recognition of a deferred tax liability or asset for differences related to assets and liabilities that, under FASB Statement No. 52, *Foreign Currency Translation*, are remeasured from the local currency into the functional currency using historical exchange rates and that result from (1) changes in exchange rates or (2) indexing for tax purposes.

---

[3] Some events do not have tax consequences. Certain revenues are exempt from taxation and certain expenses are not deductible. In the United States, for example, interest earned on certain municipal obligations is not taxable and fines are not deductible.

INTERPRETATION

9-1. Safe Harbor Leases

Question: The Economic Recovery Act of 1981 allowed certain tax benefits to be transferred via leases (safe harbor leases). Safe harbor leases were structured in the form of a lease for tax purposes but, in substance, were *solely* the sale and purchase of tax benefits because the leases did not contain any element of financing from the buyer-lessor to the seller-lessee, nor did the buyer-lessor have any interest in the residual value of the leased property. Changes in the tax law generally eliminated the transfer of tax benefits via safe harbor leases after 1983. However, some safe harbor leases entered into before that date still exist. Does Statement 109 affect an enterprise's current accounting for the purchase of tax benefits under safe harbor leases?

Response: The effect that Statement 109 has on current accounting for the purchase of tax benefits under safe harbor leases depends on a number of factors. The FASB issued two exposure drafts (EDs) on accounting for safe harbor leases—one in 1981 and one in 1982. Due to the change in the tax law, however, a final statement was never issued. The 1981 ED was silent on the accounting required by the change in tax law or other significant assumptions. In EITF Issue No. 86-44, "Effect of a Change in Tax Law on Investments in Safe Harbor Leases," the EITF addressed how to account for the effect of a change in tax law on investments in safe harbor leases. That guidance was dependent on how the buyer-lessor previously had been accounting for the investment. The EITF reached a consensus that for safe harbor leases accounted for under the 1981 ED, it is appropriate to account for the effect of a change in tax law either prospectively or by recalculating the safe harbor lease from its inception and including a catch-up adjustment in income in the year in which the tax law is enacted, similar to a leveraged lease.

The 1982 ED explicitly addressed the accounting for a change in tax law and required the investor to recalculate the investment balance from the inception of the lease to determine the income effect of the change. As a result, the EITF reached a consensus that if the investor accounted for the safe harbor lease under the 1982 ED, the lease should be recalculated from inception in accordance with the 1982 ED and the difference between the amounts originally recorded and the recalculated amounts should be included in income in the period in which the change in tax law is enacted.

The EITF did not address safe harbor leases accounted for using a method other than the methods contained in the 1981 and 1982 EDs.

We believe that the cumulative catch-up method is preferable and should be used for these leases as well. Prior to the adoption of Statement 109, as a less preferable alternative, the prospective method may be used for these investments.

Unlike leveraged leases, safe harbor leases are not explicitly excluded from Statement 109. The prospective method is not appropriate for investors that have adopted the liability method of accounting for income taxes because the prospective method is based on the deferred method of accounting for income taxes under Opinion 11, under which no adjustments are made to deferred taxes for changes in tax rates. Investors that have elected the prospective method and have adopted Statement 109 should adjust the deferred tax balance to conform to the liability method. On the other hand, although not specifically excluded from the scope of Statement 109, we believe the cumulative catch-up method is based on the leveraged lease model and investors that use the cumulative catch-up method need not adjust the deferred tax balance to conform to the liability method.

9-2. Identified Intangible Assets That Are Not Amortizable for Tax Purposes

Question (from FASB Staff Implementation Guide, Question 16):

> Paragraph 30 states that deferred taxes shall not be provided for temporary differences related to positive goodwill for which amortization is not deductible for tax purposes or unallocated negative goodwill. Should temporary differences related to intangible assets (for example, customer lists and trademarks) be handled in the same manner?

Response (from FASB Staff Implementation Guide, Question 16):

> No. A deferred tax liability or asset should be recognized for temporary differences related to intangible assets other than goodwill in accordance with the recognition and measurement requirements of Statement 109. Goodwill recognized in a business combination accounted for as a purchase is a residual—it is the excess of purchase price over the assigned values of the identifiable net assets acquired. Other intangible assets such as customer lists and trademarks are not residuals and are not included among the exceptions (which include goodwill) to comprehensive recognition of deferred taxes identified in paragraph 9.

9-3. Computation of Deferred Taxes Related to Identified Intangible Assets That Are Not Amortizable for Tax Purposes

Question: Interpretation 9-2 indicates that an identified intangible asset that cannot be amortized for tax purposes (e.g., if it is concluded that the identified intangible asset has an "indeterminate" life) is not exempt from deferred tax accounting. How should such identified intangible assets be treated when computing deferred taxes?

Response: Identified intangible assets that are not amortizable for tax purposes should be treated the same as any other non-goodwill asset when identifying temporary differences and quantifying deferred tax assets and liabilities. Consider Example 9-3A.

Example 9-3A

Assume Financial Institution acquires a portfolio of credit card receivables. The total amount paid for the portfolio is $110 and the face amount of the receivables is $100. Assume that the amount paid in excess of the face amount of the receivables ($10) relates to the credit card relationships and is not amortizable for tax purposes. On Day 1, the book and tax basis of the credit card relationship is $10 and there is no temporary difference and therefore no deferred tax asset or liability. However, at the end of Financial Institution's fiscal year, the book basis of the credit card relationships has been reduced through amortization to $8, but the tax basis remains at $10. A $2 deductible temporary difference now exists and (assuming a 40% tax rate) a gross deferred tax asset of $.80 should be recognized. If a valuation allowance is not required for that deferred tax asset, Financial Institution's effective tax rate is not affected by the book amortization of the credit card relationship intangible asset because the recognition of the deferred tax asset offsets the increase in current tax expense.

It may be difficult to conclude that a valuation allowance is not needed related to a deferred tax asset caused by an identified intangible asset that is not amortizable for tax purposes. Statement 109 uses a "more-likely-than-not" standard for the determination of a valuation allowance. Such a standard makes valuation allowance decisions dependent on the specific enterprise's facts and circumstances and makes it difficult to generalize. Nevertheless, in general, there is greater uncertainty about the realization of deferred tax assets created by identified intangible assets that are not amortizable for tax purposes than about the realization of most other deferred tax assets. The timing of the future tax deduction related to such a deferred tax asset is usually uncertain, but is typically not expected to occur in the foreseeable future—both of which create uncertainty about the ultimate realization of the deferred tax assets. However, in situations in which the identified intangible asset giving rise to the underlying deductible temporary difference is expected to eventually be sold, it may be possible to conclude that the sale of that asset will provide the needed future taxable income to realize the deferred tax asset. This should be the case if the fair value of the identified intangible asset is expected to be equal to, or in excess of, the tax basis of the identified intangible asset at the date of the expected sale of the asset.

Since 1993, most purchased intangible assets are amortizable in the United States and therefore this issue is not applicable to most intangible assets in the U.S. tax jurisdiction.

Question: How does one distinguish between intangible assets that are not amortizable for tax purposes and tax goodwill that is not amortizable for tax purposes?

Response: In a "taxable" business combination (i.e., a business combination in which the tax bases of assets acquired and liabilities assumed are established based on an allocation of the purchase price rather than carrying forward the tax bases of assets and liabilities of the acquired enterprise), it is sometimes difficult to distinguish such intangible assets (e.g., the amount assigned to core deposits in the acquisition of a financial institution) from tax goodwill. We believe a key distinction between such intangible assets and tax goodwill is the event(s) that would allow for a tax deduction. Goodwill is a residual amount that relates to the value of the enterprise as a whole and, in a jurisdiction that does not allow a tax deduction for amortization of goodwill, a tax deduction for goodwill is generally only allowed when substantially the entire business that was acquired is sold or abandoned. However, an identified intangible asset that is not amortizable for tax purposes should be deductible for tax purposes on the occurrence of some event(s) short of the sale or abandonment of the business. Stated another way, if a portion of the purchase price will not be deductible for tax purposes until substantially all of the business is sold or abandoned, that amount is probably goodwill for tax purposes. Statement 109 precludes deferred tax accounting for basis differences related to goodwill for which amortization is not deductible for tax purposes.

Question: Assume that a portion of the purchase price ($100) is allocated to a customer related intangible asset for financial reporting and tax purposes and the enterprise expects the intangible asset will be amortizable for tax purposes on a straight-line basis over 10 years (the same life as is used for financial reporting purposes). Further assume that three years later the enterprise settles the allocation of purchase price and subsequent years' tax returns by agreeing with the taxing authority that the $100 is not amortizable for tax purposes. The enterprise pays $12 of tax (tax effect of three years of amortization at a 40% tax rate). How should the settlement be accounted for?

Response: The deferred tax accounting for the effects of the tax settlement depends on the answers to two questions (one factual question and one judgmental question):

1. *Factual question*: Is the $100 goodwill or an identified intangible asset that is not amortizable for tax purposes?
2. *Judgmental question*: If the $100 represents an identified intangible asset that is not amortizable for tax purposes, is a valuation allowance needed for the related deferred tax asset?

Assume the $100 is goodwill for tax purposes. The enterprise now has a $70 *taxable* temporary difference (i.e., the enterprise has an asset that has a $70 basis for financial reporting and no basis for tax purposes) and should accrue a deferred tax *liability* of $28. (The enterprise also has a $100 basis difference related to goodwill for which the amortization is not deductible for tax purposes, but is precluded by Statement 109 from treating that basis difference as a temporary difference.) Based on EITF Issue No. 93-7, "Uncertainties Related to Income Taxes in a Purchase Business Combination" (see Interpretation 30-9), the tax effects of the change in the allocation of purchase price for tax purposes should be charged to goodwill and amortized on a prospective basis over the remaining life of the goodwill. Therefore, $40 is added to goodwill ($12 of current tax + $28 of deferred tax) and the only effect on the current period's income is the recognition of any interest or penalty or both that had not been accrued previously.

Assume the $100 is an identified intangible asset that is not amortizable for tax purposes and that no valuation allowance is needed for the deferred tax asset. The enterprise now has a deductible temporary difference of $30 (i.e., the enterprise has an asset that has a $70 basis for financial reporting purposes and a $100 basis for tax purposes) and should recognize a deferred tax asset of $12. Therefore, the net tax effect is zero (the $12 of current tax expense is offset by the $12 of deferred tax benefit) and the only effect on the current period's income is the recognition of any interest or penalty or both that had not been accrued previously.

Assume the $100 is an identified intangible asset that is not amortizable for tax purposes and that a valuation allowance is needed for the deferred tax asset. The enterprise still has a deductible temporary difference of $30 and should recognize a gross deferred tax asset of $12. However, the gross deferred tax asset is offset by a $12 valuation allowance. Therefore, in addition to recognition of any interest or penalty that had not been accrued previously, the enterprise has a net tax effect of $12 that is reflected in the current period's income (the $12 of current tax expense). Issue 93-7 does not apply in this situation because the allocation of purchase price for tax purposes has not changed.

9-4. Reorganization Value in Excess of Amounts Allocable to Identified Assets

Question: For enterprises that follow fresh-start accounting on emerging from Chapter 11 bankruptcy, AICPA Statement of Position (SOP) 90-7, *Financial Reporting by Entities in Reorganization Under the Bankruptcy Code,* provides for the recognition of an asset identified as "reorganization value in excess of amounts allocable to identified assets" in certain circumstances. Should that asset be treated as goodwill for Statement 109 purposes?

Response: Yes. Paragraph 6 of FASB Statement No. 142, *Goodwill and Other Intangible Assets,* states:

> This Statement, including its transition provisions, applies to . . . the excess reorganization value recognized by entities that adopt fresh-start reporting in accordance with AICPA Statement of Position 90-7, *Financial Reporting by Entities in Reorganization Under the Bankruptcy Code.* That excess reorganization value shall be reported as goodwill and accounted for in the same manner as goodwill.

(See Interpretation 37-3 for guidance on the subsequent recognition of tax benefits existing at the date of emerging from bankruptcy.)

9-5. Applicability of Paragraph 9(f) of Statement 109 to U.S. GAAP Financial Statements of Non-U.S. Companies, Including Financial Statements of Non-U.S. Companies Operating in Highly Inflationary Economies

Question: Some non-U.S. companies elect to prepare their primary financial statements in accordance with U.S. generally accepted accounting principles (GAAP). Paragraph 9(f) of Statement 109:

> . . . [p]rohibits recognition of a deferred tax liability or asset for differences related to assets and liabilities that, under FASB Statement No. 52, *Foreign Currency Translation,* are remeasured from the local currency into the functional currency using historical exchange rates and that result from (1) changes in exchange rates or (2) indexing for tax purposes.

The SEC allows non-U.S. companies to prepare their financial statements in any currency that their management believes is appropriate. In other words, non-U.S. companies are allowed to choose their reporting currency. However, non-U.S. companies must determine their functional currency using the guidance in Statement 52.

Does paragraph 9(f) of Statement 109 apply to financial statements of non-U.S. companies operating in highly inflationary economies that prepare their primary financial statements in accordance with U.S. GAAP?

Response: The basis on which the financial statements of non-U.S. companies are prepared determines if paragraph 9(f) of Statement 109 applies. Non-U.S. companies operating in highly inflationary economies that elect to prepare their primary financial statements in accordance with U.S. GAAP are allowed, in filing financial statements with the SEC, to prepare either: (*a*) price-level adjusted financial statements in the local highly inflationary currency, for example, by following the guidance in Accounting Principles Board (APB) Statement No. 3, *Financial Statements Restated for General Price-Level Changes,*[1] or (*b*) financial statements in a stable currency, such as the U.S. dollar, and apply the remeasurement principles of Statement 52.

Price-Level-Adjusted Financial Statements

In EITF Issue No. 93-9, "Application of FASB Statement No. 109 in Foreign Financial Statements Restated for General Price-Level Changes," the EITF concluded that Statement 109 requires an enterprise preparing price-level-adjusted financial statements to treat all

[1] In 1993, AcSEC rescinded all of the APB statements, including APB Statement 3, with the issuance of AICPA Statement of Position (SOP) 93-3, *Rescission of Accounting Principles Board Statements.* However, SOP 93-3 provides that comprehensive price-level adjusted financial statements prepared following the guidance in APB Statement 3 are acceptable for companies operating in highly inflationary economies.

differences between financial reporting bases and tax bases of assets and liabilities (that will result in taxable or deductible amounts in future years when the reported amounts of the assets and liabilities are recovered or settled, respectively) as temporary differences. Accordingly, paragraph 9(f) of Statement 109 does not apply to such financial statements, regardless of whether a "convenience translation" of the financial statements to U.S. dollars is provided.

Continuing with the conclusions reached in Issue 93-9, the EITF also reached the following consensus:

> [T]he deferred tax expense or benefit should be calculated as the difference between (1) deferred tax assets and liabilities reported at the end of the current year, determined in accordance with the above paragraph, and (2) deferred tax assets and liabilities reported at the end of the prior year, remeasured to units of current general purchasing power at the end of the current year. The remeasurement of deferred tax assets and liabilities at the end of the prior year is reported together with the remeasurement of all other assets and liabilities as a restatement of beginning equity.

The following is an extract from Issue 93-9 (Exhibit 93-9A):

> A company has one asset, a nonmonetary asset that is not depreciated for financial reporting or tax purposes. The local currency is FC. Units of current purchasing power are referred to as CFC. The enacted tax rate is 40 percent. The asset had a price-level-adjusted financial reporting amount of CFC350 and an indexed basis for tax purposes of CFC100 at December 31, 19X2, both measured using CFC at December 31, 19X2. The company has a taxable temporary difference of CFC250 (CFC350 – CFC100) and a related deferred tax liability of CFC100 (CFC250 × 40 percent) using CFC at December 31, 19X2.
>
> General price levels increase by 50 percent in 19X3, and indexing allowed for 19X3 for tax purposes is 25 percent. At December 31, 19X3, the asset has a price-level-adjusted financial reporting amount of CFC525 (CFC350 × 150 percent) and an indexed basis for tax purposes of CFC125 (CFC100 × 125 percent), using CFC at December 31, 19X3. The company has a taxable temporary difference of CFC400 (CFC525 – CFC125) and a related deferred tax liability of CFC160 (CFC400 × 40 percent) at December 31, 19X3, using CFC at December 31, 19X3. The deferred tax liability at December 31, 19X2 is restated to units of current general purchasing power as of December 31, 19X3. The restated December 31, 19X2 deferred tax

liability is CFC150 (CFC100×150 percent). For 19X3, the difference between CFC160 and CFC150 is reported as deferred tax expense in income from continuing operations. The difference between the deferred tax liability of CFC100 at December 31, 19X2 and the restated December 31, 19X2 deferred tax liability of CFC150 is reported in 19X3 as a restatement of beginning equity.

The following is a tabular presentation of this example:

	19X2		**19X3**
Financial reporting basis	CFC350	× 1.50	CFC525
Tax basis	CFC100	× 1.25	CFC125
Temporary difference	CFC250		CFC400
Tax rate	× .40		× .40
Deferred tax liability, end of year	CFC100		CFC160
Deferred tax liability (restated), beginning of year	CFC100	× 1.50	CFC150
Deferred tax expense			CFC 10

Statement 52 Approach

Non-U.S. companies that follow the Statement 52 approach prepare their financial statements as if they were preparing financial statements for a "shell" U.S. company that wholly owns the non-U.S. company. For non-U.S. companies operating in highly inflationary economies, their functional currency would be different from their local currency and they would be required to remeasure nonmonetary assets and liabilities from the local currency into their functional currency at historical exchange rates. Accordingly, paragraph 9(f) would apply to such financial statements.

Question: Does paragraph 9(f) of Statement 109 apply to financial statements of non-U.S. companies operating in economies that are not highly inflationary and prepare their primary financial statements in U.S. dollars and in accordance with U.S. GAAP?

Response: Typically, no. Non-U.S. companies operating in economies that are not highly inflationary that elect to prepare their primary financial statements in accordance with U.S. GAAP are allowed, in filing financial statements with the SEC, to prepare financial statements in U.S. dollars by applying the remeasurement principles of Statement 52.

As stated previously, non-U.S. companies that follow the Statement 52 approach prepare their financial statements as if they were preparing financial statements for a shell U.S. company that wholly owns the non-U.S. company. If the non-U.S. company's local currency is its functional currency, paragraph 9(f) of Statement 109 would not apply as none of its assets and liabilities would be remeasured from the local currency into its functional currency using historical exchange rates. That is, all of its assets and liabilities would be translated at the current balance sheet exchange rate, all of the revenues and expenses would be translated at the exchange rate existing at the time of the transactions (usually at an average exchange rate for the year), and all of the translation effects of exchange rate changes would be included as a separate component of equity. Because all of the asset and liabilities would be translated at the current exchange rate, paragraph 9(f) of Statement 109 would not apply to such financial statements.

However, if the non-U.S. company's functional currency is not its local currency (e.g., if its functional currency is the U.S. dollar), it would be required to remeasure nonmonetary assets and liabilities from the local currency into its functional currency at historical exchange rates. Accordingly, paragraph 9(f) of Statement 109 would apply to such financial statements.

9-6. Nonmonetary Assets and Liabilities of Foreign Operations for Which the Local Currency Is Not the Functional Currency

Question: Paragraph 9(f) of Statement 109:

> ...[p]rohibits recognition of a deferred tax liability or asset for differences related to assets and liabilities that, under FASB Statement No. 52, *Foreign Currency Translation,* are remeasured from the local currency into the functional currency using historical exchange rates and that result from (1) changes in exchange rates or (2) indexing for tax purposes.

Does paragraph 9(f) apply only to operations in highly inflationary economies?

Response: No. Paragraph 9(f) applies to all foreign operations in which the functional currency is other than the local currency.

Question: How are temporary differences computed related to assets and liabilities that, under Statement 52, are remeasured from the local currency into the functional currency using historical exchange rates?

Response: Temporary differences for such assets and liabilities are determined by comparing the local currency (LC) historical cost basis (on a U.S. generally accepted accounting principles [GAAP] financial reporting basis, ignoring any price-level adjustments that may have been made to the local currency records) to the local currency historical cost tax basis (ignoring the effect of any indexing of the basis for tax purposes). Note that the tax basis absent indexing will probably need to be computed from scratch—prior to Statement 109, there was no need to maintain records of such amounts. Deferred taxes are provided for those temporary differences using the local country tax law and then are remeasured into U.S. dollars using the current exchange rate. Tax deductions received due to indexing of the bases of assets for tax purposes are treated as permanent differences and recognized in the periods the increased deductions are received. Example 9-6A is an illustration of paragraph 9(f).

Example 9-6A

Example assumptions:

The property is acquired on January 1, Year 1. The property has a five-year life for financial reporting purposes, but is depreciated over three years for tax purposes, both on a straight-line basis.

Property cost is LC450.

Exchange rate on January 1, Year 1 is LC15 = U.S. $1.

Inflation rate is 80% per year and currency devaluation is 100% per year.

The reporting currency is the U.S. dollar, the local economy is highly inflationary, and therefore the functional currency is the U.S. dollar.

Income tax rate in the local country is 40%. Property is indexed for inflation for tax purposes.

Computation of Deferred Taxes at the End of Year 2

Property-historical cost	LC450
Accumulated depreciation	LC180
Net book value per books	LC270
Net tax basis (ignoring indexing)	LC150
Temporary difference	LC120
Tax rate	40%
Deferred tax liability—LC	LC48
Remeasured at current exchange rates (LC60 = U.S. $1)	U.S. $0.80

Question: Does the previous response mean there will be a "catch-up" adjustment needed for deferred tax liabilities at the time the economy ceases to be highly inflationary and the functional currency of the foreign operation changes from the reporting currency to the local currency?

Response: Yes. The EITF has addressed the pretax accounting issue and the tax accounting issue in two separate EITF pronouncements. In EITF Issue No. 92-4, "Accounting for a Change in Functional Currency When an Economy Ceases to Be Considered Highly Inflationary," the EITF concluded that enterprises should restate the local (now functional) currency accounting bases of assets and liabilities at that time by translating the reporting currency bases of those assets and liabilities to the local currency at the current exchange rate.

In EITF Issue No. 92-8, "Accounting for the Income Tax Effects under FASB Statement No. 109 of a Change in Functional Currency When an Economy Ceases to Be Considered Highly Inflationary," the EITF concluded that the deferred taxes associated with temporary differences that arise from a change in functional currency when an economy ceases to be considered highly inflationary should be reflected as an adjustment to the cumulative translation adjustment component of shareholders' equity. Once the economy ceases to be considered highly inflationary, temporary differences will be computed by comparing the new local (now functional) currency book basis to the actual (indexed) tax basis.

Question: How should an enterprise account for a change in a subsidiary's functional currency from the local currency to the reporting currency when the economy in which the subsidiary operates becomes highly inflationary?

Response: The FASB staff addressed both the pretax and the tax accounting for such a situation in *EITF Abstracts*, Topic D-56, "Accounting for a Change in Functional Currency and Deferred Taxes When an Economy Becomes Highly Inflationary." Regarding the pretax accounting, the FASB staff concludes that translation adjustments for prior periods should not be removed from equity and the translated amounts for nonmonetary assets and liabilities should become the accounting basis for those assets and liabilities.

Because there is no change to the pretax carrying amounts of the subsidiary's assets and liabilities at the time the economy in which it operates becomes highly inflationary, temporary differences do not change and there should be no adjustment to the subsidiary's deferred tax assets and liabilities. Prospectively, paragraph 9(f) of Statement 109 applies and prohibits recognition of deferred tax benefits that result for indexing for tax purposes assets and liabilities that are remeasured into the reporting currency using historical exchange rates. Deferred tax benefits that were recognized for indexing prior to the change in functional currency to the reporting currency are eliminated when the related indexed amounts are realized as deductions for tax purposes.

9-7. Inflationary Profits Tax in Countries With Hyperinflation

Question: Prior to 1998, the Brazilian economy was highly inflationary and therefore U.S. enterprises with operations in Brazil used the U.S. dollar as the functional currency for their Brazilian operations. Paragraph 9(f) of Statement 109:

> ...[p]rohibits recognition of a deferred tax liability or asset for differences related to assets and liabilities that, under FASB Statement No. 52, *Foreign Currency Translation*, are remeasured from the local currency into the functional currency using historical exchange rates and that result from (1) changes in exchange rates or (2) indexing for tax purposes.

This interpretation was written to address the periods in which the Brazilian economy was highly inflationary and has been retained to provide guidance for analogous situations that may arise in other countries.

Brazil indexes certain assets for tax purposes and also imposes an "inflationary profits" tax. In simplified terms, the "inflationary profit" is computed by indexing certain assets and equity and including in taxable income the excess of the increase in assets due to indexing over the increase in equity due to indexing. Therefore, the more equity the enterprise has outstanding, the lower the inflationary profit (because not all assets are indexed and there are monetary corrections reflected for certain monetary assets and liabilities, it is also possible for this computation to result in an inflationary loss). If the net result is an increase in taxable income, the taxpayer has the option to defer recognizing that increase in taxable income (the taxpayer has different options about the time period in which the inflationary profit will be included in taxable income).

Should the future tax consequences of the inflationary profits for which recognition in taxable income has been deferred until future periods be treated as a long-term tax liability or should the inflationary profits be treated as a temporary difference resulting from indexing for tax purposes?

Response: We believe the preferable accounting is to treat the tax associated with deferred inflationary profits as a long-term tax liability (i.e., recognize the liability and tax expense in the period the inflationary profit occurs). However, a reasonable argument can be made that the deferred inflationary profit is a temporary difference resulting from indexing and we believe that treatment is an acceptable alternative treatment (i.e., do not recognize the liability in the period the inflationary profit occurs in accordance with paragraph 9(f)). Whichever alternative an enterprise elects to follow should be applied consistently period to period. A change from one alternative to the other would be a change in accounting principle.

A somewhat related question arises with net operating loss (NOL) carryforwards in Brazil (NOL carryforwards are indexed for tax purposes in Brazil). We believe enterprises that treat the deferred inflationary profits as a temporary difference resulting from indexing (and therefore do not recognize the related tax liability) should recognize as a gross deferred tax asset the amount of the NOL carryforward as originally reported in the tax return and not recognize any increases in that deferred tax asset caused by subsequent indexing for tax purposes until realized. That deferred tax asset is subject to the usual Statement 109 assessment for realizability (a more-likely-than-not standard).

9-8. Effect of a Change in an Important Assumption on the Accounting for Leveraged Leases

Question: Statement 109 does not amend the accounting for leveraged leases as prescribed by FASB Statement No. 13, *Accounting for Leases.* What literature addresses the accounting for changes in important assumptions, including income tax related assumptions, for a leveraged lease?

Response: Paragraph 46 of Statement 13 provides that, when an important assumption changes, the rate of return and the allocation of income shall be recalculated from the inception of the lease and the change in the recalculated net investment shall be recognized as a gain or loss in the period in which the assumption is changed.

FASB Technical Bulletin (FTB) No. 79-16 (Revised), *Effect of a Change in Income Tax Rate on the Accounting for Leveraged Leases*, states that the lessor's income tax rate is an important assumption in accounting for a leveraged lease. FASB Staff Position (FSP) FAS 13-2, "Accounting for a Change or Projected Change in the Timing of Cash Flows Relating to Income Taxes Generated by a Leveraged Lease Transaction," amends Statement 13 and adds the timing of the cash flows relating to income taxes generated by a leveraged lease as an important assumption. Accordingly, changes or expected changes in the timing of cash flows related to income taxes will cause the leveraged lease to be recalculated with the change in the recalculated net investment being recognized as a gain or loss in the period in which the assumption is changed. FSP FAS 13-2 is effective for fiscal years beginning after December 15, 2006.

(See interpretations of paragraph 46 in the publication, *CCH Accounting for Leases*, for guidance on when and how to recalculate a leveraged lease.)

Temporary Differences

EXCERPT FROM OFFICIAL TEXT

Temporary Differences

10. **Income taxes currently payable**[4] for a particular year usually include the tax consequences of most events that are recognized in the financial statements for that year. However, because tax laws and financial accounting standards differ in their recognition and measurement of assets, liabilities, equity, revenues, expenses, gains, and losses, differences arise between:

    a. The amount of taxable income and pretax financial income for a year

    b. The tax bases of assets or liabilities[4a] and their reported amounts in financial statements

---

4 References in this Statement to income taxes currently payable and (total) **income tax expense** are intended to include also **income taxes currently refundable** and (total) **income tax benefit**, respectively.

4a Interpretation 48 provides guidance for computing the tax bases of assets and liabilities for financial reporting purposes.

INTERPRETATION

10-1. Uncertain Tax Positions

Question: There are different aspects of income tax reporting that create uncertainty concerning what amount, if any, will ultimately be owed to a taxing authority for a particular period. For example, there could be uncertainty about: (*a*) the period in which an expenditure is deductible for tax purposes, (*b*) whether certain expenditures qualify as credits against income tax liabilities, or (*c*) whether a tax return should be filed in a specific tax jurisdiction. Enterprises must decide what position they will take on these issues when they file their tax returns. How should such uncertainties affect accounting for income taxes?

Response: The FASB issued FASB Interpretation (FIN) No. 48, *Accounting for Uncertainty in Income Taxes,* in July 2006. FIN 48 is effective for fiscal years beginning after December 15, 2006, and requires that the cumulative earnings effect of applying the provisions of FIN 48 be reported as an adjustment to the opening balance of retained earnings.

FIN 48 provides that enterprises should recognize a benefit from a tax position taken in a tax return (or expected to be taken in a tax return) in their financial statements when it is more likely than not that the tax position will be sustained on examination by the relevant taxing authority. In making this assessment, enterprises should consider all of the facts, circumstances, and information available at the balance-sheet date and should presume the tax position will be examined by the taxing authority on its individual technical merits. The benefit recognized from a tax position that meets the more-likely-than-not criterion should be the largest amount that is greater than 50% likely of being realized on ultimate settlement with a taxing authority that has full knowledge of all of the relevant information.

No financial statement benefit should be recognized for tax positions that fail to meet the more-likely-than-not criterion. Tax positions that initially fail the more-likely-than-not criterion should be subsequently recognized in the first interim period in which: (*a*) the tax position meets that criterion, (*b*) the tax matter is resolved with the taxing authority, or (*c*) the statute of limitations for the tax position expires. Similarly, an enterprise should derecognize a previously recognized tax position in the first interim period in which it is no longer more likely than not that the tax position would be sustained on examination. Refer to Appendix I for more detailed interpretive guidance regarding FIN 48.

EXCERPT FROM OFFICIAL TEXT

11. An assumption inherent in an enterprise's statement of financial position prepared in accordance with generally accepted accounting principles is that the reported amounts of assets and liabilities will be recovered and settled, respectively. Based on that assumption, a difference between the tax basis of an asset or a liability and its reported amount in the statement of financial position will result in taxable or deductible amounts in some future year(s) when the reported amounts of assets are recovered and the reported amounts of liabilities are settled. Examples follow:

   a. *Revenues or gains that are taxable after they are recognized in financial income.* An asset (for example, a receivable from an installment sale) may be recognized for revenues or gains that will result in future taxable amounts when the asset is recovered.

   b. *Expenses or losses that are deductible after they are recognized in financial income.* A liability (for example, a product warranty liability) may be recognized for expenses or losses that will result in future tax deductible amounts when the liability is settled.

   c. *Revenues or gains that are taxable before they are recognized in financial income.* A liability (for example, subscriptions received in advance) may be recognized for an advance payment for goods or services to be provided in future years. For tax purposes, the advance payment is included in taxable income upon the receipt of cash. Future sacrifices to provide goods or services (or future refunds to those who cancel their orders) will result in future tax deductible amounts when the liability is settled.

   d. *Expenses or losses that are deductible before they are recognized in financial income.* The cost of an asset (for example, depreciable personal property) may have been deducted for tax purposes faster than it was depreciated for financial reporting. Amounts received upon future recovery of the amount of the asset for financial reporting will exceed the remaining tax basis of the asset, and the excess will be taxable when the asset is recovered.

   e. *A reduction in the tax basis of depreciable assets because of tax credits.*[5] Amounts received upon future recovery of the amount of the asset for financial reporting will exceed the remaining tax basis of the asset, and the excess will be taxable when the asset is recovered.

Continued on page 48

Continued from page 47

f. *ITC accounted for by the deferral method.* Under Opinion 2, ITC is viewed and accounted for as a reduction of the cost of the related asset (even though, for financial statement presentation, deferred ITC may be reported as deferred income). Amounts received upon future recovery of the reduced cost of the asset for financial reporting will be less than the tax basis of the asset, and the difference will be tax deductible when the asset is recovered.

g. *An increase in the tax basis of assets because of indexing whenever the local currency is the functional currency.* The tax law for a particular tax jurisdiction might require adjustment of the tax basis of a depreciable (or other) asset for the effects of inflation. The inflation-adjusted tax basis of the asset would be used to compute future tax deductions for depreciation or to compute gain or loss on sale of the asset. Amounts received upon future recovery of the local currency historical cost of the asset will be less than the remaining tax basis of the asset, and the difference will be tax deductible when the asset is recovered.

h. *Business combinations.* There may be differences between the assigned values and the tax bases of the assets and liabilities recognized in a business combination. Those differences will result in taxable or deductible amounts when the reported amounts of the assets and liabilities are recovered and settled, respectively.

12. Examples (a)–(d) in paragraph 11 illustrate revenues, expenses, gains, or losses that are included in taxable income of an earlier or later year than the year in which they are recognized in pretax financial income. Those differences between taxable income and pretax financial income also create differences (sometimes accumulating over more than one year) between the tax basis of an asset or liability and its reported amount in the financial statements. Examples (e)–(h) in paragraph 11 illustrate other events that create differences between the tax basis of an asset or liability and its reported amount in the financial statements. For all eight examples, the differences result in taxable or deductible amounts when the reported amount of an asset or liability in the financial statements is recovered or settled, respectively.

13. This Statement refers collectively to the types of differences illustrated by those eight examples and to the ones described in paragraph 15 as *temporary differences.* Temporary differences that will result in taxable amounts in future years when the related asset or liability is recovered or settled are often referred to in this

Continued on page 49

Continued from page 48

Statement as **taxable temporary differences** (examples (a), (d), and (e) in paragraph 11 are taxable temporary differences). Likewise, temporary differences that will result in deductible amounts in future years are often referred to as **deductible temporary differences** (examples (b), (c), (f), and (g) in paragraph 11 are deductible temporary differences). Business combinations (example (h)) may give rise to both taxable and deductible temporary differences.

---

5 The Tax Equity and Fiscal Responsibility Act of 1982 provided taxpayers with the choice of either (a) taking the full amount of Accelerated Cost Recovery System (ACRS) deductions and a reduced tax credit (that is, investment tax credit and certain other tax credits) or (b) taking the full tax credit and a reduced amount of ACRS deductions.

INTERPRETATION

13-1. Deferred State Income Taxes Give Rise to a U.S. Federal Temporary Difference

Question (from FASB Staff Implementation Guide, Question 7):

State income taxes are deductible for U.S. federal income tax purposes. Does a deferred state income tax liability or asset give rise to a temporary difference for purposes of determining a deferred U.S. federal income tax liability or asset?

Response (from FASB Staff Implementation Guide, Question 7):

Yes. A deferred state income tax liability or asset gives rise to a temporary difference for purposes of determining a deferred U.S. federal income tax asset or liability, respectively. The pattern of deductible or taxable amounts in future years for temporary differences related to deferred state income tax liabilities or assets should be determined by estimates of the amount of those state income taxes that are expected to become payable or recoverable for particular future years and, therefore, deductible or taxable for U.S. federal tax purposes in those particular future years.

13-2. Accounting for Temporary Differences in Monetary Assets and Liabilities Caused by Changes in Currency Exchange Rates When a Company's Functional Currency Is Different From Its Local (Tax Reporting) Currency

Question: Some foreign tax jurisdictions include currency gains and losses related to U.S. dollar denominated debt or receivables in determining taxable income or loss. When a company's functional currency is the U.S. dollar for its operations in such a foreign jurisdiction, the tax effect of those currency gains and losses is a permanent item in the company's effective tax rate reconciliation (i.e., there is no pretax gain or loss as the debt or receivable is denominated in the company's functional currency, but there will be a taxable gain or loss as currency exchange rates change over time). What accounting, if any, should be performed when the currency exchange rate has changed since the time the foreign operation issued its U.S. dollar denominated debt or established its U.S. dollar denominated receivable?

Response: The tax effect of a change in currency exchange rates should be recognized in the period the currency exchange rate changes. Paragraph 9(f) of Statement 109 only applies to nonmonetary assets and liabilities because of the reference in that paragraph to remeasurement at historical exchange rates. Monetary items, such as debt and receivables, are not remeasured at historical exchange rates.

If the foreign tax jurisdiction includes only realized currency gains and losses in the determination of taxable income or loss (i.e., the gains or losses only enter the determination of taxable income in the period the debt is extinguished or the receivable is collected), a question arises about what should be performed for financial reporting purposes at a period end after the U.S. dollar denominated debt has been issued (or receivable has been established), the currency exchange rate has changed, and the debt has not yet been paid off (or the receivable has not yet been collected)? In such a situation, a temporary difference exists in the foreign jurisdiction (i.e., if the debt would be paid off at its carrying amount at the balance-sheet date or the receivable collected at its carrying amount at the balance-sheet date, there would be a tax consequence in the foreign jurisdiction) and therefore a deferred tax asset (assuming no issues with a valuation allowance) or deferred tax liability should be recognized. The effect of recognizing such a deferred tax asset or liability would be to create a permanent item in the company's effective tax rate in the period the change in the currency exchange rate occurs.

If the foreign tax jurisdiction includes unrealized currency gains and losses in the determination of taxable income or loss (i.e., the gains or losses enter the determination of taxable income in the period the currency exchange rate changes regardless of whether the debt has been extinguished or the receivable has been collected), there is no question about what should be performed for financial reporting purposes at a period end after the U.S. dollar denominated debt is issued (or the receivable is established), the currency exchange rate has changed, and the debt has not yet been paid off (or the receivable has not yet been collected). In such a situation, no temporary difference exists (i.e., if the debt is paid off at its carrying amount at the balance-sheet date or the receivable is collected at its carrying amount at the balance-sheet date, there would be no additional tax consequence—the tax consequence of the change in the currency exchange rate is already included in the computation of the current period's taxable income) and therefore no deferred tax asset or deferred tax liability should be recognized.

In summary, regardless of whether the foreign jurisdiction recognizes currency gains and losses on a realized or unrealized basis, the permanent item from the currency gain or loss affects the company's effective tax rate in the period that the currency exchange rate changes.

EXCERPT FROM OFFICIAL TEXT

14. Certain basis differences may not result in taxable or deductible amounts in future years when the related asset or liability for financial reporting is recovered or settled and, therefore, may not be temporary differences for which a deferred tax liability or asset is recognized. One example under current U.S. tax law is the excess of cash surrender value of life insurance over premiums paid. That excess is a temporary difference if the cash surrender value is expected to be recovered by surrendering the policy, but is not a temporary difference if the asset is expected to be recovered without tax consequence upon the death of the insured (there will be no taxable amount if the insurance policy is held until the death of the insured).

INTERPRETATION

14-1. Basis Differences of Regulated Investment Companies, Cooperatives, and Similar Enterprises

Question: Certain enterprises that meet the applicable criteria under the U.S. Internal Revenue Code are allowed a tax deduction for all distributed earnings (e.g., regulated investment companies and real estate investment trusts) or all patronage dividends paid in money, qualified written notices of allocation, and property (e.g., exempt cooperatives). Should such enterprises provide deferred taxes for basis differences that, on reversal, are not expected to have a tax consequence to the enterprise itself due to expected future tax deductions of the type described in the preceding sentence?

Response: No. The Basis for Conclusions to Statement 109 (paragraph 145) states, "The Board believes that a tax deduction received for the payment of dividends (exclusive of dividends paid on unallocated shares held by an ESOP) represents, in substance, an exemption from taxation of an equivalent amount of earnings." Therefore, a basis difference that is expected to be part of a tax deduction related to the distribution of earnings is a basis difference that, in substance, is related to tax-exempt earnings. A basis difference that has no future tax consequence (a rare situation) is not a temporary difference and no deferred taxes should be provided.

The previous rationale should not be applied to other types of future deductions (i.e., future deductions other than those derived from the distribution of earnings). Paragraph 231 of Statement 109 states that the tax benefit of statutory depletion and other types of "special" deductions should not be anticipated for purposes of offsetting a deferred tax liability for taxable temporary differences. (See Interpretations 18-4 and 18-5 for a further discussion of the accounting for the tax effects of special deductions.)

14-2. Determining if a Basis Difference Is a Taxable Temporary Difference

Question: Paragraph 289 of Statement 109 defines a temporary difference as:

> A difference between the tax basis of an asset or liability computed pursuant to FASB Interpretation No. 48, *Accounting for Uncertainty in Income Taxes,* and its reported amount in the financial statements that will result in taxable or deductible amounts in future years when the reported amount of the asset or liability is recovered or settled, respectively.

Statement 109 goes on to state:

> Some events recognized in financial statements do not have tax consequences. Certain revenues are exempt from taxation and certain expenses are not deductible. Events that do not have tax consequences do not give rise to temporary differences.

What criteria should be used to determine if an existing unfavorable book/tax basis difference is a taxable temporary difference?

Response: Almost all unfavorable book/tax basis differences are taxable temporary differences. However, there are exceptions to that general rule. Paragraph 14 of Statement 109 gives one such exception. Under current U.S. tax law, the excess of cash surrender value of life insurance over premiums paid is not a taxable temporary difference if the cash surrender value is expected to be recovered without tax consequence on the death of the insured. Another exception is contained in paragraph 33 of Statement 109, which provides:

> An excess of the amount for financial reporting over the tax basis of an investment in a . . . domestic subsidiary . . . is not a taxable temporary difference if the tax law provides a means by which the reported amount of that investment can be recovered tax-free and the enterprise expects that it will ultimately use that means.

We believe it is appropriate to conclude there will be no future tax consequence from the reversal of an existing unfavorable book/tax basis difference only if *all* of the following conditions are met:

- The strategy to eliminate the existing book/tax basis difference is prudent and feasible;
- The company expects to execute the strategy;
- The execution of the strategy is substantially within the company's control (e.g., the company does not need other than perfunctory approval from a lender or regulator to execute the strategy);
- There is no significant cost to the strategy;
- It is probable the strategy will be successful; and
- The strategy eliminates, not just defers, the tax consequence of the existing book/tax basis difference.

14-3. Accounting for the Effects of Temporary Differences During a Tax Holiday

Question: The taxing authorities in some jurisdictions sometimes grant "tax holidays" for a finite period of time to specific taxpayers, usually to encourage a particular investment. Such taxpayers may have book/tax basis differences in that tax jurisdiction at the time the tax holiday is granted or book/tax basis differences may be created during the term of the tax holiday. What accounting, if any, should be performed for book/tax basis differences during a tax holiday?

Response: Book/tax basis differences that will reverse after the end of the tax holiday meet the definition of a temporary difference and deferred tax assets and liabilities should be recognized for those temporary differences. Book/tax basis differences that will reverse during the tax holiday can be viewed as either: (*a*) not meeting the definition of a temporary difference as the reversal of that book/tax basis difference is expected to have no future tax consequence or (*b*) temporary differences that are subject to a zero tax rate. Under either view, no deferred tax asset or liability is recognized for book/tax basis differences expected to reverse during the tax holiday.

Consider Example 14-3A.

Example 14-3A

Enterprise is granted a tax holiday at the time it completes the construction of a new facility that has a useful life of 20 years. Under the tax holiday, Enterprise will not be required to pay income taxes on any taxable income earned during the next five years. However,

Continued on page 55

Continued from page 54

> Enterprise is required to use an accelerated depreciation method for tax purposes. As a result, Enterprise, assuming it uses the straight-line method for books, will have a higher book basis than tax basis in the facility at the end of Year 1 (and all subsequent year ends during the tax holiday). That book/tax basis difference will reverse after the end of the tax holiday. Accordingly, that book/tax basis difference is a taxable temporary difference and a deferred tax liability (and deferred tax expense) should be recognized by the enterprise during the first year of the tax holiday.

Paragraphs 183 and 184 of Statement 109 discuss one specific question with respect to tax holidays. Should an enterprise that has been granted a tax holiday recognize a tax asset related to the expected future tax savings to be realized from the tax holiday? The FASB concluded that enterprises should not recognize an asset for the expected future tax savings from a tax holiday. However, Statement 109 does not explicitly discuss the accounting for book/tax basis differences during a tax holiday and therefore enterprises should apply the principles of Statement 109, as discussed previously, to the effects of the tax holiday.

14-4. Accounting for the Tax Consequences of the Medicare Prescription Drug, Improvement and Modernization Act of 2003

Question: In May 2004, the FASB issued FASB Staff Position (FSP) FAS 106-2, "Accounting and Disclosure Requirements Related to the Medicare Prescription Drug, Improvement and Modernization Act of 2003," which superseded FSP FAS 106-1 of the same title. This FSP provides guidance on the accounting for the tax-free subsidy that, pursuant to the act, will be received by sponsors of single-employer defined benefit postretirement health care plans that meet certain criteria. Because the effect of the subsidy will be recognized for financial reporting purposes in different periods than the subsidy is realized (i.e., received in cash), the subsidy will affect an enterprise's book/tax basis difference that exists related to its other postretirement benefits (OPEB) obligation, calculated under FASB Statement No. 106, *Employers' Accounting for Postretirement Benefits Other Than Pensions*. How should an enterprise that is eligible for the tax-free subsidy determine the temporary difference related to its OPEB obligation?

Response: FSP FAS 106-2 provides:

> In the periods in which the subsidy affects the employer's accounting for the plan, it shall have no effect on any

> plan-related temporary difference accounted for under Statement 109 because the subsidy is exempt from federal taxation. That is, the measure of any temporary difference shall continue to be determined as if the subsidy did not exist.

We believe that enterprises should view their OPEB related book/tax basis difference as being composed of two separate book/tax differences—one related to the gross amount of the OPEB obligation before the effect of the subsidy and one related to the federal subsidy. The book/tax basis difference related to the OPEB obligation would be a temporary difference as the future settlement of that liability would have a tax consequence. The book/tax basis difference related to the federal subsidy would not be a temporary difference as the future realization of that benefit would not have a tax consequence.

Determining the amount of the two separate book/tax basis differences will likely require enterprises to compute, on a continuing basis, what their OPEB obligation would have been without the federal subsidy. The difference between an enterprise's actual OPEB obligation and what its OPEB obligation would have been absent the federal subsidy is the amount of the book/tax basis difference related to the federal subsidy.

14-5. Corporate Owned Life Insurance

Question: Enterprises sometimes purchase life insurance covering the lives of employees with the enterprise named as the beneficiary. Pursuant to the guidance in FASB Technical Bulletin (FTB) No. 85-4, *Accounting for Purchases of Life Insurance,* enterprises recognize as an asset the amount that could be realized under the insurance contract as of the date of the financial statement (i.e., the cash surrender or contract value of the policy). Under U.S. tax law, the tax basis of the life insurance policy is the cumulative amount of premiums paid. If the asset (i.e., the cash surrender value of the life insurance policy) is realized by surrendering the policy, a taxable gain or loss occurs for the difference between the amount received on surrendering the life insurance policy and the tax basis of the life insurance policy. If the asset is realized on the death of the insured, there is no tax consequence.

Is the excess of cash surrender value of life insurance over premiums paid a temporary difference?

Response: Whether the excess of cash surrender value of life insurance over premiums paid is a temporary difference depends on the manner in which the enterprise expects to realize its investment in the life insurance policy. Paragraph 14 of Statement

109 recognizes that the excess of cash surrender value of life insurance over premiums paid may or may not be a temporary difference depending on the company's intentions. The excess is a temporary difference if the cash surrender value is expected to be recovered by surrendering the policy, but is not a temporary difference if the asset is expected to be recovered without tax consequence on the death of the insured.

EXCERPT FROM OFFICIAL TEXT

> 15. Some temporary differences are deferred taxable income or tax deductions and have balances only on the income tax balance sheet and therefore cannot be identified with a particular asset or liability for financial reporting. That occurs, for example, when a long-term contract is accounted for by the percentage-of-completion method for financial reporting and by the completed-contract method for tax purposes. The temporary difference (income on the contract) is deferred income for tax purposes that becomes taxable when the contract is completed. Another example is organizational costs that are recognized as expenses when incurred for financial reporting and are deferred and deducted in a later year for tax purposes. In both instances, there is no related, identifiable asset or liability for financial reporting, but there is a temporary difference that results from an event that has been recognized in the financial statements and, based on provisions in the tax law, the temporary difference will result in taxable or deductible amounts in future years.

INTERPRETATION

15-1. Temporary Differences Caused by a Change in Tax Law

Question (from FASB Staff Implementation Guide, Question 5):

A change in tax law may require a change in accounting method for tax purposes, for example, the uniform cost capitalization rules required by the Tax Reform Act of 1986. For calendar-year taxpayers, inventories on hand at the beginning of 1987 are revalued as though the new rules had been in effect in prior years. That initial catch-up adjustment is deferred and taken into taxable income over not more than four years. Does the deferral of the initial catch-up adjustment for a change in accounting method for tax purposes give rise to a temporary difference?

Response (from FASB Staff Implementation Guide, Question 5):

Yes. The uniform cost capitalization rules required by the Tax Reform Act of 1986 initially give rise to two temporary differences.

One temporary difference is related to the additional amounts initially capitalized into inventory for tax purposes. As a result of those additional amounts, the tax basis of the inventory exceeds the amount of the inventory for financial reporting. That temporary difference is considered to result in a deductible amount when the inventory is expected to be sold.[3] Therefore, the excess of the tax basis of the inventory over the amount of the inventory for financial reporting as of December 31, 1986[4] is considered to result in a deductible amount in 1987 when the inventory turns over. As of subsequent year-ends, the deductible temporary difference to be considered would be the amount capitalized for tax purposes and not for financial reporting as of those year-ends.

The other temporary difference is related to the deferred income for tax purposes that results from the initial catch-up adjustment. As stated above, that deferred income likely will be included in taxable income over four years. Ordinarily, the reversal pattern for this temporary difference should be considered to follow the tax pattern and would also be four years. This assumes that it is expected that inventory sold will be replaced. However, under the tax law, if there is a one-third reduction in the amount of inventory for two years running, any remaining balance of that deferred income is included in taxable income for the second year. If such inventory reductions are expected, then the reversal pattern will be less than four years.

---

3 This assumes that the inventory is not measured on a LIFO basis; temporary differences related to LIFO inventories reverse when the inventory is sold and not replaced as provided in paragraph 228.

4 Paragraph 27 of Statement 109 requires recognition of the effect of a change in tax law or rate in the period that includes the enactment date. The Tax Reform Act of 1986 was enacted in 1986. Therefore, under the requirements of Statement 109, the effects are recognized in a calendar-year enterprise's 1986 financial statements.

15-2. Family-Owned Farming Businesses

Question (from FASB Staff Implementation Guide, Question 6):

The Omnibus Budget Reconciliation Act of 1987 requires family-owned farming businesses to use the accrual method of accounting for tax purposes. The initial catch-up adjustment to change from the cash to the accrual method of accounting is deferred. It is included in taxable income if the business ceases to be family owned (for example, it goes public). It also is included in taxable income if gross receipts from farming activities in future years drop below certain 1987 levels as set forth in the tax law. Does the deferral of the initial catch-up adjustment for that change in accounting method for tax purposes by family-owned farming businesses give rise to a temporary difference?

Response (from FASB Staff Implementation Guide, Question 6):

Yes. The entire amount of the catch-up adjustment is a temporary difference. An assumption inherent in an enterprise's statement of financial position is that the reported amounts of assets and liabilities will be recovered and settled. Under Statement 109, deferred tax liabilities may not be eliminated or reduced because an enterprise may be able to delay the settlement of those liabilities by delaying the events that would cause taxable temporary differences to reverse. Accordingly, the deferred tax liability is recognized. If the events that trigger the payment of the tax are not expected in the foreseeable future, the reversal pattern of the related temporary difference is indefinite and the deferred tax liability should be classified as noncurrent.

PARAGRAPHS 16–34: RECOGNITION AND MEASUREMENT

EXCERPT FROM OFFICIAL TEXT

Recognition and Measurement

16. An enterprise shall recognize a deferred tax liability or asset for all temporary differences[6] and operating loss and tax credit carryforwards in accordance with the provisions of paragraph 17. **Deferred tax expense or benefit** is the change during the year in an enterprise's deferred tax liabilities and assets.[7] For deferred tax liabilities and assets acquired in a purchase business combination during the year, it is the change since the combination date. Total income tax expense or benefit for the year is the sum of deferred tax expense or benefit and income taxes currently payable or refundable.

---

6 Refer to paragraph 9. A deferred tax liability shall be recognized for the temporary differences addressed by Opinion 23 in accordance with the requirements of this Statement (paragraphs 31–34) and that Opinion, as amended.

7 Paragraph 230 addresses the manner of reporting the transaction gain or loss that is included in the net change in a deferred foreign tax liability or asset when the reporting currency is the functional currency.

16-1. Accounting for Temporary Differences and Carryforwards Acquired Other Than in a Business Combination

Question: Paragraph 30 of Statement 109 provides guidance on how to account for differences between the financial reporting basis and tax basis of a group of assets acquired in a business combination. How should such differences between financial reporting and tax bases be accounted for if the group of assets acquired is not a business?

Response: In EITF Issue No. 98-11, "Accounting for Acquired Temporary Differences in Certain Purchase Transactions That Are Not Accounted for as Business Combinations," the EITF addressed how differences between financial reporting and tax bases should be accounted for if the group of assets acquired is not a business. The EITF concluded: (*a*) such differences between financial reporting and tax bases of acquired assets should not result in immediate income statement recognition and (*b*) the accounting for such acquisitions of groups of assets should follow the accounting for a business combination, with the following exceptions:

- Goodwill cannot be recognized.
- Any excess of fair value of asset acquired over consideration paid remaining after reducing all noncurrent assets (other than financial assets, assets held for disposal, and deferred tax assets) to zero should be classified as a deferred credit. The deferred credit is not a temporary difference under Statement 109.
- The deferred credit should be amortized to income tax expense in proportion to the realization of the tax benefits that gave rise to the deferred credit. The deferred credit should not be classified as part of deferred tax liabilities or as an offset to deferred tax assets.
- If a valuation allowance is subsequently recognized for a deferred tax asset that, when originally recognized, gave rise to a deferred credit, a proportionate share of any remaining unamortized deferred credit should be recognized as an offset to income tax expense.
- Any subsequent unfavorable adjustments of tax uncertainties that exist at the time of or arise in connection with the acquisition should be recognized in income. (See Interpretations 10-1 and 10-2, together with Appendix I, for guidance regarding the effect of tax uncertainties on the recognition of tax benefits generally.)

The EITF concluded that the same accounting model should be used to account for the net tax benefit resulting from the purchase of future tax benefits from a third party that is not a government acting in its capacity as a taxing authority.

The EITF also observed that paragraph 9(e) of Statement 109 applies to intercompany transactions between members of a consolidated enterprise. Consequently, for acquisitions of tax benefits that result from intercompany transactions, the guidance in paragraph 9(e) should be applied, which results in the deferral of the seller's net tax expense and prohibits recognition of a deferred tax asset for the difference between the tax basis of assets in the buyer's tax jurisdiction and the financial reporting basis of those assets.

Question: How should an enterprise account for the acquisition of tax benefits directly from a government acting in its capacity as a taxing authority?

Response: The EITF concluded that transactions directly between an enterprise and a government (in its capacity as a taxing authority) should be recognized directly in income in the same manner that an enterprise accounts for changes in tax laws, rates, and other elections under Statement 109.

Annual Computation of Deferred Tax Liabilities and Assets

EXCERPT FROM OFFICIAL TEXT

Annual Computation of Deferred Tax Liabilities and Assets

17. Deferred taxes shall be determined separately for each tax-paying component (an individual entity or group of entities that is consolidated for tax purposes) in each tax jurisdiction. That determination includes the following procedures:

a. Identify (1) the types and amounts of existing temporary differences and (2) the nature and amount of each type of operating loss and tax credit carryforward and the remaining length of the carryforward period

b. Measure the total deferred tax liability for taxable temporary differences using the applicable tax rate (paragraph 18)

c. Measure the total deferred tax asset for deductible temporary differences and operating loss carryforwards using the applicable tax rate

d. Measure deferred tax assets for each type of tax credit carryforward

e. Reduce deferred tax assets by a **valuation allowance** if, based on the weight of available evidence, it is *more likely than not* (a likelihood of more than 50 percent) that some portion or all of the deferred tax assets will not be realized. The valuation allowance should be sufficient to reduce the deferred tax asset to the amount that is more likely than not to be realized.

INTERPRETATION

17-1. Separate Computations for Each Tax Jurisdiction

Question (from FASB Staff Implementation Guide, Question 3):

Does Statement 109 require separate deferred tax computations for each state or local tax jurisdiction?

Response (from FASB Staff Implementation Guide, Question 3):

If deferred tax assets or liabilities for a state or local tax jurisdiction are significant, Statement 109 requires a separate deferred tax computation when there are significant differences between the tax laws of that and other tax jurisdictions that apply to the enterprise. In the United States, however, many state or local income taxes are based on U.S. federal taxable income, and aggregate computations of deferred tax assets and liabilities for at least some of those state or local tax jurisdictions might be acceptable. In assessing whether an aggregate calculation is appropriate, matters such as differences in tax rates or the loss carryback and carryforward periods in those state or local tax jurisdictions should be considered. Also, the provisions of paragraph 42 about offset of deferred tax liabilities and assets of different tax jurisdictions should be considered. In assessing the significance of deferred tax expense for a state or local tax jurisdiction, it is appropriate to consider the deferred tax consequences that those deferred state or local tax assets or liabilities have on other tax jurisdictions, for example, on deferred federal income taxes.

EXCERPT FROM OFFICIAL TEXT

18. The objective is to measure a deferred tax liability or asset using the enacted tax rate(s) expected to apply to taxable income in the periods in which the deferred tax liability or asset is expected to be settled or realized. Under current U.S. federal tax law, if taxable income exceeds a specified amount, all taxable income is taxed, in substance, at a single flat tax rate. That tax rate shall be used for measurement of a deferred tax liability or asset by enterprises for which graduated tax rates are not a significant factor. Enterprises for which graduated tax rates are a significant factor shall measure a deferred tax liability or asset using the average graduated tax rate applicable to the amount of estimated annual taxable income in the periods in which the deferred tax liability or asset is estimated to be settled or realized (paragraph 236). Other provisions of enacted tax laws should be considered when determining the tax rate to apply to certain types of temporary differences and carryforwards (for example, the tax law may provide for different tax rates on ordinary income and capital gains). If there is a phased-in change in tax rates, determination of the applicable tax rate requires knowledge about when deferred tax liabilities and assets will be settled and realized.

INTERPRETATION

18-1. Scheduling Reversal Patterns of Existing Temporary Differences

Question (from FASB Staff Implementation Guide, Question 1):

When is it necessary to schedule reversal patterns of existing temporary differences?

Response (from FASB Staff Implementation Guide, Question 1):

Under FASB Statement No. 109, *Accounting for Income Taxes*

a. Deferred taxes are classified as current or noncurrent based on the classification of the related asset or liability. Therefore, scheduling is required only for deferred taxes not related to a specific asset or liability.

b. Deferred tax assets are recognized without reference to offsetting, and then an assessment is made about the need for a valuation allowance. Paragraph 21 lists four possible sources of taxable income that may be available to realize such deferred tax assets. In many cases it may be possible to determine without scheduling that expected future taxable income (paragraph 21 (b)) will be adequate to eliminate the need for a valuation allowance. Disclosure of the amounts and expiration dates (or a reasonable aggregation of expiration dates) of operating loss and tax credit carryforwards is required only on a tax basis and does not require scheduling.
c. The adoption of a tax rate convention for measuring deferred taxes when graduated tax rates are a significant factor will, in many cases, eliminate the need for scheduling. In addition, alternative minimum tax (AMT) rates and laws are a factor only in considering the need for a valuation allowance for a deferred tax asset for AMT credit carryforwards. When there is a phased-in change in tax rates, however, scheduling will often be necessary. Refer to paragraphs 234–239 of Statement 109.

Under Statement 109, a general understanding of reversal patterns is, in many cases, relevant in assessing the need for a valuation allowance. Judgment is crucial in making that assessment. The amount of scheduling, if any, that will be required will depend on the facts and circumstances of each situation.

Because of cost-benefit considerations, the Board has chosen not to specify in detail how the reversal patterns for each class of temporary differences should be treated. In many cases there is more than one logical approach.

The following concepts, however, underlie the determination of reversal patterns for existing temporary differences under Statement 109:

a. "The particular years in which temporary differences result in taxable or deductible amounts generally are determined by the timing of the recovery of the related asset or settlement of the related liability" (paragraph 228).
b. "The tax law determines whether future reversals of temporary differences will result in taxable and

deductible amounts that offset each other in future years" (paragraph 227).

Minimizing complexity is an appropriate consideration in selecting a method for determining reversal patterns. The methods used for determining reversal patterns should be systematic and logical. The same method should be used for all temporary differences within a particular category[2] of temporary differences for a particular tax jurisdiction. Different methods may be used for different categories of temporary differences. If the same temporary difference exists in two tax jurisdictions (for example, U.S. federal and a state tax jurisdiction), the same method should be used for that temporary difference in both tax jurisdictions. The same method for a particular category in a particular tax jurisdiction should be used consistently from year to year. A change in method is a change in accounting principle under APB Opinion No. 20, *Accounting Changes.*

[2] Two examples of a category of temporary differences are those related to (a) liabilities for deferred compensation and (b) investments in direct financing and sales-type leases.

18-2. Losses of a Foreign Branch

Question: A U.S. company is taxed currently on the earnings of a foreign branch in its U.S. federal tax return. The branch generally pays taxes in the foreign jurisdiction in which it operates as well. The foreign taxes paid generate foreign tax credits (FTCs) that, subject to certain limitations, can be utilized to offset the U.S. federal tax on foreign source income. If a foreign branch of a U.S. company incurs a loss in a given year, is it possible to record the benefit of the loss in the United States, as well as in the foreign jurisdiction?

Response: No. Example 18-2A demonstrates the appropriate accounting a foreign branch of a U.S. company should use when it incurs a loss in a given year.

Example 18-2A

Example assumptions:

There are no temporary differences at the beginning or end of the year.

The tax rate is 40% in U.S. federal and foreign jurisdiction A and is 30% in foreign jurisdiction B.

Continued on page 69

Continued from page 68

There is no carryback ability for operating losses or FTCs, but provisions exist in the tax law of each jurisdiction that allow for carryforwards.

The assumption and calculation of U.S. federal tax:

U.S. domestic income	$600
Foreign Branch A income	400
Foreign Branch B loss	(100)
Worldwide income	$900
U.S. federal tax rate	40%
U.S. federal tax prior to FTC	$360

The calculation of FTC availability:

	Net Foreign Source Income	Foreign Tax Paid
Branch A	$400	$160
Branch B	(100)	0
Total foreign source income/taxes paid	$300	$160
Divided by worldwide income	900	
FTC limitation%	33%	
U.S. federal tax	$360	
FTC limitation%	33%	
FTC limitation	$120	

This results in $120 of FTC being able to be utilized in the current year in the United States with a $40 FTC carryforward.

The calculation of U.S. provision (prior to FTC carryforward):

Tax prior to FTC	$360
FTC utilized	(120)
Total U.S. federal tax	$240

Assuming that it is more-likely-than-not that the United States will be able to realize the $40 FTC carryforward *and* Branch B will be able to realize its $100 tax net operating loss (NOL) carryforward, the following provisions (benefits) would be recorded:

Currently Payable	
U.S. federal	$240
Foreign (Branch A)	160
	400
Deferred Taxes	
U.S. FTC carryforward	(40)
Foreign NOL (Branch B)	0
	(40)
Total tax provision	$360

Continued on page 70

Continued from page 69

The Branch B foreign NOL is reflected at zero in the previous analysis because it provides no net future benefit to Company as a whole. To illustrate that point, assume that Branch B earns $100 next year and all other operations break even for book and tax. With the NOL carryforward, Company pays no tax in the foreign jurisdiction, no tax in the United States (because of the NOL carryforward, there is no FTC generated in the current year but the FTC carryforward is used to offset the U.S. income taxes otherwise due on the $100 of income), and charges off its $40 deferred tax asset for the FTC carryforward utilized for a total of $40 of tax expense related to that $100 of income. Without the NOL carryforward, Company pays $30 of tax in the foreign jurisdiction and uses $10 of its FTC carryforward for a total of $40 of tax expense related to that $100 of income. With or without the foreign NOL carryforward, Company, in total, recognizes the same amount of income tax expense on future income. Therefore, the foreign NOL carryforward provides no net future benefit.

However, if the tax rate in Branch B's tax jurisdiction is higher than the U.S. federal tax rate, there is an incremental benefit to the foreign NOL carryforward that, assuming the NOL carryforward is realizable (on a more-likely-than-not basis), should be recognized. Assume the same facts as above except that the tax rate in Branch B's jurisdiction is 50%. In that situation, the foreign NOL carryforward has an incremental benefit of $10 that should be recognized in the deferred tax computation. With the NOL carryforward, Company pays no tax in the foreign jurisdiction, no tax in the United States (because of the NOL carryforward, there is no FTC generated in the current year but the FTC carryforward is used to offset the U.S. income taxes otherwise due on the $100 of income), and charges off its $40 deferred tax asset for the FTC carryforward utilized for a total of $40 of tax expense related to that $100 of income. Without the NOL carryforward, Company pays $50 of tax in the foreign jurisdiction and no tax in the United States (net of the FTC) for a total of $50 of tax expense related to that $100 of income. Therefore, the foreign NOL carryforward that exists at the end of the current year provides a net $10 of future benefit that should be recognized in the deferred tax computation.

Example 18-2A has been greatly simplified to illustrate the interaction of foreign branch losses and FTCs. In actual situations, factors, such as the U.S. federal alternative minimum tax, carryback provisions, allocation of costs to foreign source income, and so forth, should be considered.

18-3. State Apportionment Factors

Question: Some states apportion a corporation's taxable income based on the ratio of the corporation's income, property, and payroll within the state tax jurisdiction to the corporation's total income, property, and payroll. How should temporary differences be apportioned to such states when computing deferred taxes?

Response: The apportionment factors expected to apply in future years (based on currently enacted tax law) should be used when computing deferred state taxes. Generally, these would be the apportionment factors used in the current year, adjusted for known changes.

18-4. Percentage Depletion

Question: A deduction for depletion is allowed in determining the taxable income from natural resources. A special method of computing the depletion deduction for tax purposes, known as percentage depletion, may be applied to some types of natural resources. Percentage depletion is generally a percentage of gross income from the property, limited to a percentage of taxable income from the property. The tax basis of the natural resource is reduced by the depletion deduction (cost or percentage). However, percentage depletion deductions are still allowed after the tax basis of the natural resource is reduced to zero. Is a basis difference that is caused by taking a percentage depletion deduction for natural resources a temporary difference?

Response: Any basis difference related to natural resources (whether caused by cost or percentage depletion) is a temporary difference and a deferred tax liability should be recognized for that temporary difference using the enacted regular tax rate. Therefore, there will not be a net decrease in the total income tax provision until the period in which a tax deduction is received that is not offset by an increase in a taxable temporary difference (i.e., when the tax basis of the asset has been reduced to zero and a tax deduction continues to be allowed). In essence, any deduction allowed *after* the tax basis has been reduced to zero is treated as a permanent difference in the year in which the deduction is taken on the tax return.

The treatment of percentage depletion under Statement 109 is significantly different than its treatment under Statement 96. That difference in treatment is due to the "tax rate convention" used by Statement 109 to price deferred tax assets and liabilities. (See paragraphs 231 and 232 of Statement 109.)

18-5. Small Life Insurance Companies

Question: Small life insurance companies (defined in the Internal Revenue Code as, in general, life insurance companies with less than

$500 million in total assets at year end) receive a deduction equal to 60% of their taxable income. How should deferred taxes be computed for an insurance company that meets the definition of a "small life insurance company?"

Response: The deferred tax computation for a small life insurance company is no different than for any other taxable enterprise. Any temporary differences should be measured using the enacted regular tax rate (i.e., 34% or 35% for U.S. federal tax purposes). If graduated tax rates are significant, the average graduated tax rate expected to apply to the amount of estimated annual taxable income in the periods in which the deferred tax liability or asset is estimated to be settled or realized should be used. Consider Example 18-5A.

Example 18-5A

Assume the tax law provides that the first $20 of taxable income is subject to tax at a 30% rate and all income over $20 is taxed at a 34% rate. Small Company expects $100 of taxable income prior to the small insurance company deduction in the future year in which all its temporary differences are expected to reverse. Small Company's enacted regular tax rate in this example is 34% and its average graduated regular tax rate is 32%. That rate is computed as follows:

> The expected tax in the year of reversal of the temporary difference of $12.80 ($20 × 30% + $20 × 34%) is divided by the expected taxable income in the year of reversal of the temporary difference ($100 – $60).

In this situation, Small Company should measure its temporary differences (taxable and deductible) using a 32% tax rate.

In addition, small life insurance companies eligible for the special deduction should consider the effect that deduction will have on the amount of future taxable income that is expected to be available when assessing the realizability of existing deferred tax assets.

The treatment of the small life insurance deduction under Statement 109 is significantly different than its treatment under Statement 96. That difference in treatment is due to the "tax rate convention" used by Statement 109 to price deferred tax assets and liabilities. (See paragraphs 231 and 232 of Statement 109.)

18-6. Canadian Crown Royalties and Resource Allowance

Question: Canadian taxation of the natural resource industry has evolved over a number of years resulting both from disagreements between federal and provincial governments over taxation rights and from general political revenue producing initiatives. Prior to May 6, 1974, taxpayers were allowed to deduct in computing Canadian federal taxable income, the royalties, taxes, and other payments made to provincial governments in respect to their resource activities. Following a sharp increase in the price of oil and natural gas in 1973 and 1974, the provincial governments increased the level of the royalties being charged. The federal government believed this action by the provincial governments resulted in an erosion of the federal tax base and, effective May 6, 1974, the federal government amended the provisions of the Canadian Income Tax Act to disallow all provincial and other crown levies on the production of natural resources as a deduction from Canadian federal taxable income. At the same time, the federal government implemented a new tax deduction called the "resource allowance." This allowance was originally intended to mitigate the non-deductibility of the provincial and other crown levies in the computation of Canadian federal taxable income. The resource allowance is calculated as a percentage of "adjusted resource profits." Generally, adjusted resource profits include gross revenues, less certain non-crown royalty payments, production costs, depreciation on production related tangible assets, and production related general and administrative costs.

Should future resource allowance deductions or future non-deductible crown royalty payments (or both) be considered when computing deferred taxes related to the Canadian federal tax jurisdiction?

Response: We believe that preferably neither future resource allowance deductions nor future non-deductible crown royalty payments should be considered when computing deferred taxes related to the Canadian federal tax jurisdiction. We believe the resource allowance is similar to both percentage depletion (see Interpretation 18-4) and the small life insurance deduction (see Interpretation 18-5) allowed under the U.S. Internal Revenue Code. Statement 109 specifically addresses both of those deductions and enterprises are precluded from including those future deductions in the computation of deferred taxes.

Pretax effects of royalty payments will be recognized in future periods for financial reporting purposes as the cost is incurred. Those costs do not create differences between the financial reporting and tax bases of assets or liabilities and do not enter into the determination of taxable income in a period different than recognized for financial reporting purposes. Therefore, there is no deferred tax accounting required related to future non-deductible royalty payments.

Less desirably, because these items are not specifically addressed by Statement 109 and because the approach seems to more closely mirror the economics of the tax law, both the future resource allowance deductions and future non-deductible crown royalty payments could be considered when computing deferred taxes related to the Canadian federal tax jurisdiction. We believe it would not be acceptable to consider only the future resource allowance deductions and not the future crown royalty payments when computing deferred taxes.

18-7. Effect of Changes in the Estimated Graduated Tax Rate

Question: Enterprises for which graduated rates are a significant factor should measure a deferred tax liability or asset using the average graduated tax rate applicable to the amount of estimated taxable income in the periods in which the deferred tax liability or asset is estimated to be settled or realized. If an enterprise has deferred tax liabilities or assets whose tax effects have been recognized other than through the income statement (e.g., recognized as part of a business combination [paragraph 30] or recognized as a component of shareholders' equity [paragraph 36]) and the enterprise's estimate of the appropriate graduated rate changes in the future (because of changes in the estimate of taxable income in some future year), how should the adjustment of the deferred tax liability or asset be recognized?

Response: Consistent with the treatment of changes in tax laws or rates and increases in valuation allowances for such items, we believe that the effect of the change in the estimated graduated rate should be included in income from continuing operations in the period of the change in estimate. Intraperiod tax allocation does not apply to this situation because there is no "pretax" effect (i.e., the temporary difference did not change, just the estimate of its tax effect).

(See Interpretation 37-5 for the subsequent accounting for items that are originally recognized in shareholders' equity, but ultimately will be charged or credited to the income statement, e.g., unrealized gains and losses resulting from applying FASB Statement No. 115, *Accounting for Certain Investments in Debt and Equity Securities.*)

18-8. Measuring Deferred Taxes When Different Tax Rates Are Applied to Distributed and Undistributed Earnings

Question: Some tax jurisdictions or systems outside of the United States tax corporate income at different rates depending on whether that income is distributed to shareholders. (See Interpretation 4–7 for guidance on accounting for additional taxes assessed at the time dividends are distributed, i.e., for tax systems in which the total tax rate is higher for distributed earnings than undistributed earnings). Other tax systems tax undistributed earnings at a higher rate than distributed earnings. In some such tax systems (e.g., Germany prior to 2001), enterprises that later pay dividends from previously undistributed earnings receive a tax credit or refund equal to the difference between the tax computed at the "undistributed rate" and the tax computed at the "distributed rate" in effect the year the dividend is distributed.

In a tax system in which the tax rate applied to undistributed earnings is higher than the tax rate applied to distributed earnings, should the tax effects of temporary differences be measured using the distributed or the undistributed tax rate in the enterprises' separate financial statements?

Response: The tax effects of temporary differences should be measured using the undistributed tax rate. The EITF addressed this question in EITF Issue No. 95-10, "Accounting for Tax Credits Related to Dividend Payments in Accordance with FASB Statement No. 109." The EITF reached a consensus that the tax benefit from the tax credits that will be realized when the previously taxed income is distributed should be recognized as a reduction of income tax expense in the period that the tax credits are included in the enterprise's tax return. Based on that consensus, the enterprise should measure the tax effects of its temporary differences using the undistributed tax rate.

In 2003, the AICPA International Practices Task Force addressed the accounting for the tax system in Taiwan. In Taiwan, corporate taxable income is currently subject to a 25% tax. In addition, a 10% tax is assessed on taxable income that is not distributed before the end of the following year. The AICPA International Practices Task Force concluded that Issue 95-10 applied to enterprises subject to the Taiwan tax system and therefore temporary differences in the Taiwan tax system should be measured at the undistributed income tax rate (i.e., 35%).

Question: How should the parent of a foreign subsidiary that is subject to such a tax system account in its consolidated financial statements for the tax benefit from the tax credits that will be realized when the foreign subsidiary's previously taxed income is distributed to the parent?

Response: The answer depends on whether the parent applies the indefinite reversal criteria of APB Opinion No. 23, *Accounting for Income Taxes—Special Areas,* to the undistributed earnings of this foreign subsidiary. The EITF addressed this issue in EITF Issue No. 95-20, "Measurement in the Consolidated Financial Statements of a Parent of the Tax Effects Related to the Operations of a Foreign Subsidiary That Receives Tax Credits Related to Dividend Payments." If the parent is not applying the indefinite reversal criteria of Opinion 23, the temporary differences within the foreign subsidiary should be measured based on the distributed tax rate and a tax asset should be recognized for the future tax credit or refund that will be received when dividends are paid from previously taxed earnings. If the parent is applying the indefinite reversal criteria of Opinion 23, accounting in consolidation should be the same as the foreign subsidiary's accounting in its separate financial statements (i.e., the temporary differences within the foreign subsidiary should be measured based on the undistributed tax rate and a tax asset should not be recognized for the future tax credit or refund that will be received when dividends are paid from previously taxed earnings).

18-9. Qualified Production Activities

Question: The American Jobs Creation Act of 2004 (2004 Tax Act) provides for a tax deduction on qualified production activities. The deduction is computed as a percentage of the lesser of: (*a*) qualified production activities income, as defined in the 2004 Tax Act or (*b*) taxable income less utilization of any net operating loss carryforwards. The deduction is then limited to 50% of wages paid. Should the effect of this provision of the 2004 Tax Act be accounted for as a special deduction or as a tax rate reduction?

Response: The effect of the 2004 Tax Act provision should be accounted for as a special deduction. The FASB staff issued FASB Staff Position (FSP) FAS 109-1, "Application of FASB Statement No. 109, *Accounting for Income Taxes,* to the Tax Deduction on Qualified Production Activities Provided by the American Jobs Creation Act of 2004," in December 2004 and concluded that the qualified production activities deduction had characteristics similar to the special deductions illustrated in paragraph 231 of Statement 109.

As a result, enterprises will recognize the benefit from the qualified production activities deduction each year as the deduction is claimed on their tax returns. The FASB staff also observed in FSP FAS 109-1 "that the special deduction should be considered by an enterprise (*a*) measuring deferred tax assets when graduated tax rates are a significant factor and (*b*) assessing whether a valuation allowance is necessary as required by paragraph 232 of Statement 109." FSP FAS 109-2 includes an example to assist users in the application of this standard.

EXCERPT FROM OFFICIAL TEXT

19. In the U.S. federal tax jurisdiction, the applicable tax rate is the regular tax rate, and a deferred tax asset is recognized for alternative minimum tax credit carryforwards in accordance with the provisions of paragraph 17(d) and (e) of this Statement. If alternative tax systems exist in jurisdictions other than the U.S. federal jurisdiction, the applicable tax rate is determined in a manner consistent with the tax law after giving consideration to any interaction (that is, a mechanism similar to the U.S. alternative minimum tax credit) between the two systems.

20. All available evidence, both positive and negative, should be considered to determine whether, based on the weight of that evidence, a valuation allowance is needed. Information about an enterprise's current financial position and its results of operations for the current and preceding years ordinarily is readily available. That historical information is supplemented by all currently available information about future years. Sometimes, however, historical information may not be available (for example, start-up operations) or it may not be as relevant (for example, if there has been a significant, recent change in circumstances) and special attention is required.

INTERPRETATION

20-1. Deferred Tax Assets Resulting From OPEB Liabilities

Question: Due to the nature of other postretirement benefit (OPEB) liabilities (i.e., liabilities recognized under FASB Statement No. 106, *Employers' Accounting for Postretirement Benefits Other Than Pensions*), are there any special provisions to consider when determining the need for a valuation allowance for the deferred tax assets that relate to OPEB liabilities?

Response: No. The temporary difference that results from OPEB liabilities is the same as any other temporary difference and there is no "special treatment" for that temporary difference. For enterprises that adopted Statement 106 on a cumulative catch-up basis, the temporary difference could be significant. Additionally, a large portion of this temporary difference may not result in tax deductions for many years. Accordingly, the use of tax carrybacks and the offsetting of taxable temporary differences will be limited in most cases and the assessment of realizability may be based primarily on expectations of future income.

20-2. Temporary Differences Related to Mexican Inventories

Question: Under the Mexican income tax law in effect from 1987 to 2004, purchases, labor, and overhead related to inventory were deductible when incurred. As a result, enterprises had a taxable temporary difference in the amount of the inventory book balance (tax basis of the inventory was zero). In transitioning to this law (prior law was to deduct the cost of sales when the inventory was sold), enterprises were allowed a tax deduction for the inventory on hand at December 31, 1986, or December 31, 1988, whichever was lower. However, that deduction was amortized into taxable income over a 30-year period beginning in 1992. In assessing the realizability of the deferred tax asset (deferred costs on the tax basis balance sheet related to the change in accounting for tax purposes), can the deferred tax liability (resulting from the inventory basis difference) be netted against the deferred tax asset?

Response: No. The deferred tax liability relating to the current expensing for tax purposes of purchases, labor, and overhead cannot necessarily be used to justify realization of the deferred tax asset as these are two distinct temporary differences that will be realized at two different points in time. The taxable temporary difference will usually be settled in the following year (assuming an inventory turnover of at least one time) while the deductible temporary difference will be realized over a 30-year period.

Mexican tax law was amended in late 2004 such that, effective in 2005, enterprises will be allowed a deduction for cost of sales and will no longer be allowed to immediately deduct inventory purchases and related conversion costs. The value of inventory on hand as of December 31, 2004, computed in accordance with tax regulations, less the unamortized amount of inventory costs from the transition to the prior tax law (i.e., the remaining unamortized amount described above that was being amortized over a 30-year period for tax purposes), will be recognized as an increase to taxable income on a ratable basis over a 4- to 12-year period. Accordingly, enterprises will no longer have a taxable temporary difference for the entire amount of their inventory for financial reporting purposes, but will have a taxable temporary difference for the net "transition" amount that will be amortized into taxable income over a 4- to 12-year period.

20-3. Limitations on Future Events Anticipated When Assessing the Realizability of Deferred Tax Assets

Question: Are there any future events that should *not* be considered when assessing the realizability of deferred tax assets?

Response: In general, enterprises should consider all currently available information about the future when assessing the realizability of deferred tax assets. The following is a listing of exceptions to that general rule—future events that should not be considered when assessing the realizability of deferred tax assets:

- Changes in tax law or rates (paragraph 27 of Statement 109);
- Changes in tax status (paragraph 28 of Statement 109);
- Business combinations. Paragraph 266 requires that any reduction in an acquiring enterprise's valuation allowance be accounted for as part of the business combination (see Interpretation 30-2). Therefore, it would not be appropriate for the acquiring enterprise to anticipate the business combination in order to reduce a valuation allowance otherwise required. We believe increases in valuation allowances caused by business combinations likewise should not be anticipated, but should be recognized as part of tax expense in the period of the business combination;
- Net losses expected in future years. Paragraph 185 of Statement 109 prohibits anticipation of tax losses in future years;
- Forgiveness of indebtedness. We believe that anticipating future income from forgiveness of indebtedness for purposes of reducing an otherwise required valuation allowance is inappropriate. Paragraph 11 of Statement 109 states, "[A]n assumption inherent in an enterprise's statement of financial position prepared in accordance with generally accepted accounting principles is that the reported amounts of assets and liabilities will be recovered and settled, respectively." Therefore, we believe it is not acceptable under Statement 109 to assume that a liability will be settled for an amount other than the amount the liability is reported at in the enterprise's statement of financial position;
- Events dependent on future market conditions or otherwise not within the enterprise's control. Statement 109 differentiates between certain basis differences based on the enterprise's control over the events that will cause the reversal of the basis difference. For example, an excess of the amount for financial reporting over the tax basis of an investment in a domestic subsidiary may or may not be a taxable temporary difference (paragraph 33 of Statement 109). However, an excess of the amount for financial reporting over the tax basis of an investment in a 50%-or-less-owned investee is always a taxable temporary difference (paragraph 32 of Statement 109). The difference between those two situations is the amount of control the investor has over the manner in which the basis difference will reverse. Admittedly, Statement 109 is

not symmetrical in its treatment of deferred tax liabilities and assets (i.e., anticipated future income is considered in assessing the need for a valuation allowance for deferred tax assets, but anticipated future losses cannot be considered in the assessment of deferred tax liabilities). However, we believe that future events that are dependent on future market conditions, such as a future initial public offering, or otherwise not within the enterprise's control, usually should not be anticipated.

20-4. Valuation Allowance: Recognizing Impairment of Deferred Tax Assets Compared With Impairment of Long-Lived Intangible Assets

Question: Assume that an enterprise has a significant long-lived intangible asset from a prior business combination that is being amortized over some lengthy period (e.g., 20 years) and also has a deferred tax asset related to the same business operation as the intangible asset. Would it be inconsistent to recognize a valuation allowance for some or all of the deferred tax asset and not recognize an impairment of the intangible asset?

Response: Not necessarily. Although a forecast of the enterprise's future performance may be used in both impairment tests, the impairment test itself is different for each evaluation. FASB Statement No. 144, *Accounting for the Impairment or Disposal of Long-Lived Assets,* requires recognition of an impairment of a long-lived intangible asset when the expected undiscounted future cash flows resulting from that asset are less than the carrying value recorded on the balance sheet. Statement 109 requires recognition of a valuation allowance on a deferred tax asset when it is "more-likely-than-not" (defined as a greater than 50% likelihood) that a benefit from the tax deduction will not be realized through some source of future taxable income (see paragraph 21 of Statement 109). Because enterprises generally must generate future earnings to realize a benefit from deferred tax assets but must only "breakeven" before interest expense in the future to conclude its carrying amount of a long-lived intangible asset is not impaired, it is possible to conclude from the same forecast that the intangible asset is not impaired and yet the company does not expect to generate sufficient taxable income to avoid recording a valuation allowance for some or all of its deferred tax assets.

The SEC staff has stated that assumptions used in forecasts made for purposes of assessing if an impairment of long-lived intangible assets has occurred should be consistent with the assumptions used in forecasts made for purposes of assessing if deferred tax valuation allowances are necessary. For example, the SEC staff has objected to a registrant's accounting when the registrant developed cash flow projections for purposes of applying the provisions of FASB Statement No. 121, *Accounting for the Impairment of Long-Lived Assets and for Long-Lived Assets to Be Disposed Of*, (the predecessor to Statement 144) using one set of assumptions and utilized a second, more conservative set of assumptions for purposes of determining if deferred tax valuation allowances were necessary. We believe this SEC staff view is unchanged with the issuance of Statement 144.

In addition, forecasts of future income are only one type of evidence that needs to be considered when assessing the need for a valuation allowance on deferred tax assets. In some situations, negative evidence, such as cumulative losses in recent years, will outweigh the positive evidence provided by the forecasts of future income and a valuation allowance will be required in spite of forecasts of future income (see Interpretation 23-2).

EXCERPT FROM OFFICIAL TEXT

21. Future realization of the tax benefit of an existing deductible temporary difference or carryforward ultimately depends on the existence of sufficient taxable income of the appropriate character (for example, ordinary income or capital gain) within the carry-back, carryforward period available under the tax law. The following four possible sources of taxable income may be available under the tax law to realize a tax benefit for deductible temporary differences and carryforwards:

    a. Future reversals of existing taxable temporary differences
    b. Future taxable income exclusive of reversing temporary differences and carryforwards
    c. Taxable income in prior carryback year(s) if carryback is permitted under the tax law
    d. **Tax-planning strategies** (paragraph 22) that would, if necessary, be implemented to, for example:

        (1) Accelerate taxable amounts to utilize expiring carryforwards
        (2) Change the character of taxable or deductible amounts from ordinary income or loss to capital gain or loss
        (3) Switch from tax-exempt to taxable investments.

    Evidence available about each of those possible sources of taxable income will vary for different tax jurisdictions and, possibly, from year to year. To the extent evidence about one or more sources of taxable income is sufficient to support a conclusion that a valuation allowance is not necessary, other sources need not be considered. Consideration of each source is required, however, to determine the amount of the valuation allowance that is recognized for deferred tax assets.

INTERPRETATION

21-1. Sources of Taxable Income

Question: Paragraph 21 lists four sources of taxable income that may be available to enable realization of a deferred tax asset. Is there any particular order in which these sources should be considered?

Response: Of the four sources listed in paragraph 21, two—"future reversals of existing taxable temporary differences" (source a.) and "carryback to open years" (source c.)—are amenable to objective verification. The other two sources—"future taxable income exclusive of reversing temporary differences and carryforwards" (source b.) and "tax-planning strategies" (source d.) represent future events and therefore are more subjective. Paragraph 25 states that the weight given to the potential effect of positive evidence "should be commensurate with the extent to which it can be objectively verified." Those sources of taxable income that are objectively verifiable should be considered first and, to the extent those sources will generate sufficient taxable income of the right character in the appropriate timeframe, there is no need to evaluate the likelihood of other future taxable income. The timing of the taxable income must coincide with the timing of the deductions and other benefits that comprise the deferred tax asset (see Interpretation 21-2 for scheduling of future originating and reversing temporary differences). The taxable income must also be of the appropriate character (e.g., capital or ordinary). In some situations, a tax-planning strategy may be needed in order to alter the timing or character of the future taxable income. The existence of such a qualifying strategy (source d.) provides more objectively determinable evidence of realizability and therefore is given more weight than a forecast of future taxable income from future events (source b.).

21-2. Scheduling Future Originating and Reversing Temporary Differences

Question (from FASB Staff Implementation Guide, Question 2):

> Paragraph 229 of Statement 109 states that future originating temporary differences for existing depreciable assets and their subsequent reversals are a factor to be considered when assessing the likelihood of future realization of a tax benefit for existing deductible temporary differences and carryforwards. Should future originating and reversing depreciation and other types of temporary differences always be scheduled for purposes of determining the need for a valuation allowance for deferred tax assets relating to existing deductible temporary differences and carryforwards?

Response (from FASB Staff Implementation Guide, Question 2):

> Not necessarily. Paragraph 21 lists four possible sources of taxable income that may be available to realize a future

tax benefit for deductible temporary differences and carryforwards. One source is future taxable income exclusive of reversing temporary differences and carryforwards. Future originating temporary differences and their subsequent reversal are implicit in estimates of future taxable income. Where it can be easily demonstrated that future taxable income will more likely than not be adequate to realize future tax benefits of existing deferred tax assets, scheduling of reversals of existing taxable temporary differences would be unnecessary.

In other cases it may be easier to demonstrate that no valuation allowance is needed by considering the reversal of existing taxable temporary differences. Even in that case, the extent of scheduling will depend on the relative magnitudes involved. For example, if existing taxable temporary differences that will reverse over a long number of future years greatly exceed deductible differences that are expected to reverse over a short number of future years, it may be appropriate to conclude, in view of the 15-year carryforward period for net operating losses, that realization of future tax benefits for the deductible differences is thereby more likely than not without the need for scheduling.

21-3. Scheduling of Tax Contingencies

Question (from FASB Staff Implementation Guide, Question 4):

An enterprise may have a basis under the tax law for claiming certain deductions, such as repair expenses on its income tax returns. However, the enterprise may have recognized a liability (including interest) for the probable disallowance of those tax deductions that, if disallowed, would be capitalized for tax purposes and then would be deductible in later years. How should these items be considered if scheduling of future taxable or deductible differences is necessary?

Response (from FASB Staff Implementation Guide, Question 4):

Accrual of a liability for probable disallowance of expenses, such as repairs, has the effect of implicitly capitalizing those expenses for tax purposes. Those capitalized expenses are considered to result in deductible amounts in the later years in which allowable deductions (such as depreciation expense) are expected for tax purposes. If the liability for probable disallowance is based on an overall evaluation of various exposure areas, scheduling should reflect the evaluations made in determining the liability for probable disallowance that was recognized.

Upon disallowance of those expenses, taxable income of the year for which the expenses are disallowed is higher. That increase provides a source of taxable income (paragraph 21(c)) for purposes of assessing the need for a valuation allowance for deductible temporary differences. Similarly, taxable income for years after the disallowance will be lower because of annual deductions attributable to those capitalized amounts.

A deductible amount for the accrued interest is scheduled for the future year in which that interest is expected to become deductible as a result of settling the underlying issue(s) with the tax authority.

21-4. AMT Credit Carryforwards and Valuation Allowances

Question: Alternative minimum tax (AMT) credit carryforwards can be carried forward for an indefinite period of time. Given the indefinite carryforward period, if an enterprise is currently profitable, are there any circumstances in which a valuation allowance may be needed for AMT credit carryforwards?

Response: Yes. The length of carryforward period and the current profitability of the enterprise are important factors, but not the only factors, to consider when assessing the need for a valuation allowance. For example, an AMT credit carryforward may be of no future benefit to a profitable enterprise that, simply by the nature of its business (e.g., oil and gas exploration), has historically generated more AMT credit carryforwards than it has been able to use. Such an enterprise may conclude that existing AMT credit carryforwards, more likely than not, will provide no future benefit to the enterprise. In order to conclude otherwise, the enterprise must reasonably expect its future mix of taxable income to be different than it has been in the past (changes in tax law cannot be anticipated). Such a conclusion would need to be evaluated for reasonableness based on that enterprise's specific facts and circumstances.

21-5. Consideration of Deferred Tax Liabilities Related to Investments in Leveraged Leases When Assessing the Need for a Valuation Allowance for Deferred Tax Assets

Question: Statement 109 does not amend the accounting for leveraged leases required by FASB Statement No. 13, *Accounting for Leases,* and therefore temporary differences related to leveraged leases are exempt from the requirements of Statement 109. Accordingly, the recognition and measurement of deferred taxes related to such temporary differences continue to be governed by Statement 13. In assessing the need for a valuation allowance for deferred tax assets, paragraph 21(a) of Statement 109 requires enterprises to consider the future taxable income related to the future reversal of existing taxable temporary differences. Is it appropriate to consider leveraged lease-related taxable temporary differences (and the resultant deferred tax credits recognized under Statement 13) when assessing the need for a valuation allowance for deferred tax assets? If so, how should the differences in measurement of deferred taxes between Statement 13 and Statement 109 be handled?

Response: It is appropriate to consider leveraged lease-related taxable temporary differences and deferred tax credits when assessing the need for a valuation allowance for deferred tax assets. Statement 109 (paragraphs 256 to 258) provides for the integration of the results of income tax accounting for leveraged leases with the other results of accounting for income taxes under Statement 109. As the example in paragraph 258 illustrates, the focus is on the amount of the leveraged lease-related taxable temporary difference (which represents the future taxable income inherent in the existing financial reporting carrying amount of the leveraged lease), not on the amount of deferred tax credit recognized under Statement 13. Consider Example 21-5A.

Example 21-5A

Assume: (*a*) Enterprise has a deductible temporary difference of $120,000 that, absent consideration of a leveraged lease-related taxable temporary difference, does not meet the more-likely-than-not criterion for recognition, (*b*) the tax rate for all future periods is 40%, (*c*) the leveraged lease-related taxable temporary difference is $100,000, and (*d*) the leveraged lease-related taxable temporary difference reverses over approximately the same time period as the deductible temporary difference. Enterprise's gross deferred tax asset would be $48,000 ($120,000 × 40%), its valuation allowance would be $8,000 ([$120,000 – $100,000] × 40%), and its net deferred tax asset would be $40,000 regardless of whether deferred tax credits recognized under Statement 13 related to the leverage lease are $30,000 or $50,000.

For business combinations involving leveraged leases, FASB Interpretation (FIN) No. 21, *Accounting for Leases in a Business Combination*, requires that the tax effect of any difference between the assigned value and the tax basis of a leveraged lease at the date of a business combination *not* be accounted for as a deferred tax credit (i.e., the investment in the acquired leveraged lease is recorded "net of tax" and no deferred tax balance is established). These tax effects are included in unearned and deferred income and are not available to offset deferred tax assets when evaluating the need for a valuation allowance. However, leveraged lease-related temporary differences that arise after the date of a business combination should be integrated into the Statement 109 computations as described previously. Further, the excess of the appreciated value of a net investment in a leveraged lease over its tax basis might provide positive evidence to support a conclusion that a valuation allowance is not needed when there is negative evidence.

21-6. Consideration of "Held-to-Maturity" Securities When Assessing the Need for a Valuation Allowance for Deferred Tax Assets

Question: When assessing the need for a valuation allowance for deferred tax assets, enterprises are required to consider all possible sources of future income. Should an enterprise consider the future income that could be generated by either: (*a*) selling appreciated "held-to-maturity" securities or (*b*) selling tax-exempt held-to-maturity securities and investing the proceeds in taxable securities when assessing the need for a valuation allowance?

Response: No. Paragraph 71 of FASB Statement No. 115, *Accounting for Certain Investments in Debt and Equity Securities*, states that securities that may need to be sold to implement tax-planning strategies should be classified as available-for-sale, not held-to-maturity. Therefore, neither the unrealized appreciation of securities classified as held-to-maturity nor a tax-planning strategy to convert tax-exempt securities classified as held-to-maturity to taxable securities should be considered in assessing the need for a valuation allowance. However, it would be acceptable to assume the proceeds received on *maturity* of securities classified as held-to-maturity will be reinvested in taxable debt securities (if the enterprise so intends to invest the proceeds) when assessing the likelihood of sufficient future taxable income to utilize existing deferred tax assets.

21-7. RAP/GAAP Differences for Financial Institutions

Question: Do any of the four U.S. federal banking and thrift regulatory agencies (i.e., Office of the Comptroller of the Currency, Board of Governors of the Federal Reserve System, Federal Deposit Insurance Corporation, or Office of Thrift Supervision) prescribe accounting for deferred taxes for regulatory accounting principles (RAP) purposes that differs from Statement 109?

Response: No. However, the four federal banking and thrift regulatory agencies each have issued rules that, for capital adequacy computational purposes, limit the amount of future taxable income financial institutions can anticipate when assessing the need for a valuation allowance for deferred tax assets. However, those rules do not affect an institution's reporting on call reports or reporting in accordance with generally accepted accounting principles.

In general, those rules limit a financial institution's net deferred tax asset for capital adequacy computational purposes to the lesser of: (*a*) the amount of deferred tax asset that is expected to be realized within one year of the quarter-end report date, based on the institution's estimate of future taxable income for that year or (*b*) 10% of Tier 1 capital before the deduction of any disallowed purchased servicing rights, purchased credit card relationships, credit-enhancing interest-only strips, nonfinancial equity investments, and deferred tax assets. When determining the limit, institutions are to assume that all temporary differences reverse fully within the next year (such an assumption allows institutions to offset deductible and taxable temporary differences without regard to actual reversal patterns and allows for the maximum possible deferred tax asset based on carryback to open tax years). There is no limitation on recognition of deferred tax assets based on offsetting deferred tax liabilities or carryback to open tax years. The previous computations should be done separately for each tax jurisdiction.

EXCERPT FROM OFFICIAL TEXT

> 22. In some circumstances, there are actions (including elections for tax purposes) that (a) are prudent and feasible, (b) an enterprise ordinarily might not take, but would take to prevent an operating loss or tax credit carryforward from expiring unused, and (c) would result in realization of deferred tax assets. This Statement refers to those actions as *tax-planning strategies.* An enterprise shall consider tax-planning strategies in determining the amount of valuation allowance required. Significant expenses to implement a tax-planning strategy or any significant losses that would be recognized if that strategy were implemented (net of any recognizable tax benefits associated with those expenses or losses) shall be included in the valuation allowance. Refer to paragraphs 246–251 for additional guidance.

INTERPRETATION

22-1. Elections for Tax Purposes That Qualify as Tax-Planning Strategies

Question (from FASB Staff Implementation Guide, Question 25):

Paragraph 22 indicates that tax-planning strategies include elections for tax purposes. What are some examples of those elections?

Response (from FASB Staff Implementation Guide, Question 25):

The following are some examples of elections under current U.S. federal tax law that, if they meet the criteria for tax-planning strategies, should be considered in determining the amount, if any, of valuation allowance required for deferred tax assets:

a. The election to file a consolidated tax return.
b. The election to claim either a deduction or a tax credit for foreign taxes paid.
c. The election to forego carryback and only carry forward a net operating loss.

22-2. Alternative Tax-Planning Strategies

Question (from FASB Staff Implementation Guide, Question 26):

An enterprise might identify several qualifying tax-planning strategies that would either reduce or eliminate the need for a valuation allowance for a deferred tax asset. For example, assume that an enterprise's required valuation allowance would be reduced $5,000 based on strategy A, $7,000 based on strategy B, and $12,000 based on both strategies. May that enterprise recognize the effect of one of those strategies in the current year and postpone recognition of the effect of the other strategy to a later year?

Response (from FASB Staff Implementation Guide, Question 26):

No. The enterprise should recognize the effect of both tax-planning strategies and reduce the valuation allowance by $12,000 at the end of the current year. Paragraph 22 of Statement 109 states that "An enterprise shall consider tax-planning strategies in determining the amount of valuation allowance required." Strategies that meet the criteria set forth in paragraph 22 should be considered in determining the required valuation allowance.

22-3. Reasonable Effort to Identify Tax-Planning Strategies

Question (from FASB Staff Implementation Guide, Question 27):

Because the effects of known qualifying tax-planning strategies must be recognized (refer to Interpretation 22-2), must management make an extensive effort to identify all tax-planning strategies that meet the criteria for tax-planning strategies?

Response (from FASB Staff Implementation Guide, Question 27):

Management should make a reasonable effort to identify those qualifying tax-planning strategies that are significant. Management's obligation to apply qualifying tax-planning strategies in determining the amount of valuation allowance required is the same as its obligation to apply the requirements of other standards for financial accounting and reporting. However, if there is sufficient evidence that taxable income from one of the other sources of taxable income listed in paragraph 21 will be adequate to eliminate the need for any valuation allowance, a search for tax-planning strategies is not necessary.

22-4. Changing the Timing or Character of Future Taxable Income

Question: The objective of some tax-planning strategies is to change the timing or character of taxable items in order to realize deferred tax assets. This could involve accelerating taxable amounts to utilize expiring carryforwards or changing the character of a taxable amount from ordinary to capital. What are some examples of qualifying tax-planning strategies that achieve these objectives?

Response: An example of a qualifying tax-planning strategy that affects the timing of taxable amounts is the sale and leaseback of property that would be performed, if necessary, to utilize a net operating loss carryforward before the carryforward expires. The sale and leaseback of the property at book value triggers taxable income from accelerated depreciation previously taken for tax purposes, thereby moving taxable income from future periods (i.e., periods when book depreciation will exceed tax depreciation) to the current period. (See Interpretation 22-5 for a discussion of the implications of a sale and leaseback of appreciated operating assets.)

Altering the character of a taxable item in many tax jurisdictions, including the United States, is more difficult. For example, in the United States, a capital loss can be offset only against a capital gain. Because most sources of taxable income produce ordinary income, it is not uncommon for an entity with a capital loss carryforward to seek a qualifying tax-planning strategy that will convert ordinary income into capital gains. These types of situations are very fact specific and the identification of qualifying tax-planning strategies, if any, requires consultation with experienced tax personnel.

22-5. Using the Sale of Appreciated Operating Assets as a Tax-Planning Strategy

Question: Paragraphs 246 to 251 of Statement 109 give general guidance about tax-planning strategies (prudent, feasible, substantially within the enterprise's control, and so forth). How is that guidance applied to a tax-planning strategy involving the sale of an appreciated operating asset?

Response: The guidance about tax planning strategies in paragraphs 246 to 251 of Statement 109 should be applied very carefully.

First, the sale may not be "substantially within the enterprise's control" if the asset has been pledged as collateral and the enterprise needs the approval of the lender to sell the asset (if the lender's approval is considered "perfunctory," however, the sale would be substantially within the enterprise's control).

Second, the strategy must be something the enterprise really would do, if needed, to utilize a tax benefit before it expires. It is helpful to think of this requirement in terms of economic compulsion. That is, although the sale of an enterprise's main manufacturing facility would generate a sufficient gain to utilize the deferred tax asset in question, the enterprise is probably economically compelled to continue to own and operate that asset. A sale and leaseback of an operating asset is one way to trigger a tax gain, but still retain the use of the critical facility. However, a sale and leaseback transaction only extends the time period for utilization of a deferred tax asset by substituting one deferred tax asset for another deferred tax asset. It does not actually reduce net deferred tax assets. Consider Example 22-5A.

Example 22-5A

Enterprise with a $100 net operating loss (NOL) carryforward sells and leases back an asset. The asset has a carrying value of $60 for financial reporting and $20 for tax purposes (and therefore Enterprise has a taxable temporary difference of $40 for a "net" uncovered NOL carryforward of $60) and is sold for $120. The tax gain on the sale ($100) utilizes the NOL carryforward, but a deductible temporary difference of $60 (the deferred gain for financial reporting purposes; $120 – $60) is created.

In essence, the NOL carryforward is "freshened" and Enterprise has a longer time horizon to realize its deferred tax asset. That longer time horizon would be included in the assessment of the need for a valuation allowance and may or may not reduce the amount of valuation allowance otherwise needed.

Finally, paragraph 24 (b) of Statement 109 prohibits "cherry picking" of appreciated assets. That is, the enterprise cannot consider appreciation of a specific asset in an amount greater than the excess of appreciated asset value over the financial reporting basis of the enterprise's net assets.

22-6. The Effect of Uncertainty on Tax-Planning Strategies

Question: Do tax-planning strategies need to meet a minimum threshold of likelihood of being sustained if challenged by taxing authorities in order to be considered when assessing the need for a deferred tax asset valuation allowance?

Response: Yes. Paragraph 8 of FASB Interpretation (FIN) No. 48, *Accounting for Uncertainty in Income Taxes,* requires that a tax-planning strategy be more likely than not of being sustained on examination by the relevant taxing authority in order to be considered when assessing the need for a deferred tax asset valuation allowance. Enterprises should presume the tax-planning strategy will be examined by the taxing authority on its individual technical merits when assessing whether the tax planning strategy is more likely than not of being sustained.

EXCERPT FROM OFFICIAL TEXT

23. Forming a conclusion that a valuation allowance is not needed is difficult when there is negative evidence such as cumulative losses in recent years. Other examples of negative evidence include (but are not limited to) the following:

    a. A history of operating loss or tax credit carryforwards expiring unused

    b. Losses expected in early future years (by a presently profitable entity)

    c. Unsettled circumstances that, if unfavorably resolved, would adversely affect future operations and profit levels on a continuing basis in future years

    d. A carryback, carryforward period that is so brief that it would limit realization of tax benefits if (1) a significant deductible temporary difference is expected to reverse in a single year or (2) the enterprise operates in a traditionally cyclical business.

INTERPRETATION

23-1. Definition of Cumulative Losses in Recent Years

Question: In evaluating the need for a valuation allowance, one of the pieces of negative evidence to be considered is "cumulative losses in recent years." Does Statement 109 define that term?

Response: No. The FASB concluded that the additional complexity that would inevitably result from a rigid definition of the term "cumulative losses" would exceed any benefits derived (paragraphs 100 to 103 of Statement 109).

We believe cumulative losses should be defined as pretax losses inclusive of income or loss from discontinued operations, extraordinary items, and so forth. The time period for "recent years" is deliberately vague and judgment should be used to determine the appropriate period. Generally, recent years would be considered to be the three-year period ending with the current reporting date. However, break-even or marginal cumulative profitability in those three years is not sufficient to conclude that cumulative losses in recent years are not a problem. For example, a company that has lost money in five of the past six years but was sufficiently profitable in the immediately prior year to break even on a three-year basis typically would be considered to have cumulative losses in recent years.

23-2. Significance of Cumulative Losses in Recent Years

Question: How much weight should be given to "cumulative losses in recent years" when evaluating the need for a valuation allowance?

Response: Negative evidence stemming from cumulative losses in recent years is one of the most difficult pieces of negative evidence to overcome. By their nature, such losses are among the most objectively verifiable types of negative or positive evidence and therefore carry more weight than evidence that embodies some degree of subjectivity. We believe that, for a company suffering recent losses, realization of deferred tax assets is difficult to support if it is primarily dependent on a forecasted, but not yet demonstrated, turnaround to operating profitability. Because of the weight given to recent cumulative losses, forecasts of future income, absent qualifying tax-planning strategies or the types of positive evidence listed in paragraph 24, which includes a strong earnings history absent a loss caused by an unusual or infrequent event, will generally not overcome the need for a valuation allowance.

23-3. Other Examples of Negative Evidence

Question: In addition to recent cumulative losses, there are several other examples of negative evidence listed in paragraph 23 (items a through d). What other conditions or events should be considered when evaluating the need for a valuation allowance?

Response: Paragraph 6 of AICPA Statement on Auditing Standards (SAS) No. 59, *The Auditor's Consideration of an Entity's Ability to Continue as a Going Concern,* lists four broad categories of conditions and events that should be considered when evaluating an enterprise's ability to continue as a going concern. Those conditions and events may also be good examples of negative evidence that should be considered when evaluating the need for a valuation allowance:

- Negative trends (e.g., recurring operating losses, working capital deficiencies, negative cash flows from operating activities, or adverse key financial ratios);
- Other indications of possible financial difficulties (e.g., default on loan or similar agreements, arrearages in dividends, denial of usual trade credit from suppliers, restructuring of debt,

noncompliance with statutory capital requirements, or need to seek new sources or methods of financing or to dispose of substantial assets);

- Internal matters (e.g., work stoppages or other labor difficulties, substantial dependence on the success of a particular project, uneconomic long-term commitments, or need to significantly revise operations); and
- External matters (e.g., legal proceedings, legislation, or similar matters that might jeopardize an entity's ability to operate; loss of a key franchise, license, or patent; loss of a principal customer or supplier; or uninsured or underinsured catastrophe, such as a drought, earthquake, or flood).

As with other pieces of negative evidence, the presence of the previous conditions or events may or may not lead to the establishment of a valuation allowance. The need for a valuation allowance will depend on the relative amounts and weight of positive and negative evidence the enterprise has about the realization of its deferred tax assets.

23-4. Going-Concern Report as Negative Evidence

Question: AICPA Statement on Auditing Standards (SAS) No. 59, *The Auditor's Consideration of an Entity's Ability to Continue as a Going Concern,* requires an explanatory fourth paragraph in the auditor's report when the auditor concludes "that substantial doubt about the enterprise's ability to continue as a going concern for a reasonable period of time remains." Acknowledging that such a report represents negative evidence, what effect would this have on the evaluation of the realizability of deferred tax assets?

Response: In every circumstances we can envision in which the auditor's report will include an explanatory paragraph identifying a going-concern problem, a valuation allowance would be required for all deferred tax assets not assured of realization by either offsetting existing taxable temporary differences or carryback to open tax years.

On the other hand, the absence of a going-concern explanatory paragraph is not, in and of itself, positive evidence about the realization of deferred tax assets. Similarly, a conclusion that a valuation allowance is required for all or part of an enterprise's deferred tax assets is not necessarily indicative of a going-concern problem. For example, an enterprise that is experiencing financial reporting losses (i.e., recent cumulative losses), but generating positive cash flow that is sufficient to service its debt would have negative evidence about the realization of deferred tax assets. The enterprise may not have sufficient positive evidence to overcome that negative evidence and therefore would provide a valuation allowance for all or part of its deferred tax assets. However, due to the existence of positive cash flow combined with other factors, the auditor may conclude that a going-concern reference in the auditor's report is not required.

EXCERPT FROM OFFICIAL TEXT

24. Examples (not prerequisites) of positive evidence that might support a conclusion that a valuation allowance is not needed when there is negative evidence include (but are not limited to) the following:

    a. Existing contracts or firm sales backlog that will produce more than enough taxable income to realize the deferred tax asset based on existing sales prices and cost structures

    b. An excess of appreciated asset value over the tax basis of the entity's net assets in an amount sufficient to realize the deferred tax asset

    c. A strong earnings history exclusive of the loss that created the future deductible amount (tax loss carryforward or deductible temporary difference) coupled with evidence indicating that the loss (for example, an unusual, infrequent, or extraordinary item) is an aberration rather than a continuing condition.

INTERPRETATION

24-1. Appreciation in Market Value of an Asset as Positive Evidence

Question: One example of positive evidence that might offset negative evidence related to the realization of deferred tax assets is an excess of appreciated asset value over tax basis. What weight can be given to this type of evidence in the process of evaluating the need for a deferred tax asset?

Response: The weight given to this type of evidence in the process of evaluating the need for a deferred tax asset will vary with the type of asset (operating vs. nonoperating) and the type of support that exists to demonstrate market value. Similar to the discussion in Interpretation 22-5, the existence of appreciated operating assets may not represent a significant piece of positive evidence either because the sale of the asset may not be within management's control or because the sale of the asset may not be prudent.

The sale of appreciated nonoperating assets may not be subject to the same concerns. The ability to objectively verify the market value of the nonoperating assets can be enhanced by the existence of an independent appraisal.

Finally, paragraph 24(b) of Statement 109 prohibits "cherry picking" of appreciated assets. That is, the enterprise cannot consider appreciation of a specific asset in an amount greater than the excess of the appreciated asset value over the financial reporting basis of the enterprise's net assets.

24-2. Forecast of Future Income as Positive Evidence

Question: When there are roughly equal amounts of positive and negative evidence prior to considering future taxable income from future operations, the entity's budgets and forecasts become critical to assessing the need for a valuation allowance. Statement 109 explicitly states (footnote 16 to paragraph 225) that the need to consider future taxable income does not require either a financial forecast or financial projection as those terms are defined in the Statements on Standards of Accountants' Services on Prospective Financial Information. How formal should the entity's budget or forecast be for purposes of providing positive evidence within the framework of Statement 109?

Response: Factors or elements that could permit greater weight to be given to expected future income in the entity's budget or forecast include the following:

- Formal analysis of future income;
- History of accurately forecasting future results;
- Substantial history of operations on which to base a forecast;
- Conformity with independent assessments of future trends for the industry; or
- Conformity with reports on the enterprise prepared by external analysts.

Factors or elements that could minimize the weight to be given to expected future income in the entity's budget or forecast include the following:

- High sensitivity to a key assumption (e.g., an assumption of Food and Drug Administration approval of a key new product);
- Long-time horizon (e.g., a forecast of income 10 years out carries less weight than a forecast of income for the following year);
- History of inaccurate forecasts of future results;
- Short product life cycles (e.g., high technology products); or
- Volatile industry.

EXCERPT FROM OFFICIAL TEXT

25. An enterprise must use judgment in considering the relative impact of negative and positive evidence. The weight given to the potential effect of negative and positive evidence should be commensurate with the extent to which it can be objectively verified. The more negative evidence that exists (a) the more positive evidence is necessary and (b) the more difficult it is to support a conclusion that a valuation allowance is not needed for some portion or all of the deferred tax asset.

A Change in the Valuation Allowance

EXCERPT FROM OFFICIAL TEXT

A Change in the Valuation Allowance

26. The effect of a change in the beginning-of-the-year balance of a valuation allowance that results from a change in circumstances that causes a change in judgment about the realizability of the related deferred tax asset in future years ordinarily shall be included in income from continuing operations. The only exceptions are the initial recognition (that is, by elimination of the valuation allowance) of certain tax benefits that are allocated as required by paragraph 30 and paragraph 36 (items (c) and (e)–(g)). The effect of other changes in the balance of a valuation allowance are allocated among continuing operations and items other than continuing operations as required by paragraph 35.

AN ENACTED CHANGE IN TAX LAWS OR RATES

EXCERPT FROM OFFICIAL TEXT

An Enacted Change in Tax Laws or Rates

27. Deferred tax liabilities and assets shall be adjusted for the effect of a change in tax laws or rates. The effect shall be included in income from continuing operations for the period that includes the enactment date.

INTERPRETATION

27-1. Changes in Tax Law

Question: If corporate tax law changes (e.g., tax rates) include retroactive provisions, in what period should the change in tax law be reflected?

Response: Statement 109 requires that the effect of changes in tax law, including the effect of any retroactive changes, be reflected in income from continuing operations for the *period that includes the enactment date*. (In the United States, the enactment date is the day the president signs the legislation.) The FASB staff reiterated this position with respect to the Omnibus Budget Reconciliation Act of 1993 (see *EITF Abstracts*, Topic D-30, "Adjustment Due to Effect of a Change in Tax Laws or Rates").

Question: Do the provisions of paragraph 27 of Statement 109 apply only to changes in law or are new IRS regulations also covered?

Response: Paragraph 27 clearly covers all changes in tax laws or rates. However, IRS regulations are somewhat different. Generally, changes in IRS regulations or issuances of new regulations are interpretive or are clarifications of the existing law. However, sometimes Congress will authorize the IRS to determine and issue final regulations related to certain issues. As such, these new regulations are considered legislative regulations vs. interpretative regulations. Legislative regulations should be considered similar to a change in tax law and therefore the effect of the change should be recognized in the period in which the new regulations are finalized and issued.

FASB Interpretation (FIN) No. 48, *Accounting for Uncertainty in Income Taxes,* provides that enterprises should consider all of the facts, circumstances, and information available *at the balance-sheet date* when assessing recognition of a tax benefit from an uncertain tax position. Unlike the guidance in FASB Statement No. 5, *Accounting for Contingencies,* the facts, circumstances, and information that only becomes available after the date of the balance sheet should not be considered in making this more-likely-than-not assessment under FIN 48. Accordingly, once FIN 48 is adopted, changes in judgment caused by the issuance of interpretive regulations after the balance-sheet date but before issuance of the financial statements should be recognized in the period of the issuance of the interpretive regulations and not "pushed back" to the prior period financial statements.

Other forms of tax clarification are private letter rulings and case law. The IRS typically issues private letter rulings to a specific company covering a specific transaction or situation. Both private letter rulings and case law should be considered interpretive and therefore treated similar to the interpretive regulations discussed previously.

27-2. Effect of Tax Law Change on Current Tax Provision

Question: Paragraph 27 of Statement 109 addresses the recognition of the effect of a tax law change on deferred tax liabilities and assets, but is silent as to the appropriate period in which to report the effect of a change on the current provision. For example, the Omnibus Budget Reconciliation Act of 1993 (1993 Tax Act), enacted on August 10, 1993, increases the top corporate tax rate to 35% effective January 1, 1993. Thus, for a company with a July 31, 1993, year end, the top corporate tax rate for its 1993 tax return was approximately 34.6%. Should the effect of the higher tax rate on taxes currently payable and the current tax provision have been reported in fiscal year 1993 or in the first quarter of fiscal year 1994?

Response: The effects of all tax law changes—whether on deferred taxes or current taxes—should be reported in the period that the tax law is enacted, even when the change is effective retroactively and thus will alter the amount of taxes paid (payable) in a prior period. In the previous example, the company with a fiscal year end of July 31, 1993, should have reported all the effects of the 1993 Tax Act, including the additional tax charge related to the fiscal year 1993 tax return, in its first fiscal quarter of 1994. Disclosure of the aggregate effect of the tax law change should have been made in the fiscal year 1993 annual financial statements (and management's discussion and analysis of financial condition and results of operations, if the company is publicly held).

Although paragraph 27 of Statement 109 refers only to deferred tax liabilities and assets, paragraph 288(h) of Statement 109 amends APB Opinion No. 28, *Interim Financial Reporting,* and adds the following sentence to the end of paragraph 20 of Opinion 28, "The tax effect of a change in tax laws or rates on taxes payable or refundable for a prior year shall be recognized as of the enactment date of the change as tax expense (benefit) for the current year."

27-3. Calculation of the Effect of the Increase in Corporate Tax Rates

Question: It has been over 10 years since there has been a change in the U.S. federal corporate income tax rate. This interpretation has been retained to provide guidance should the corporate tax rate change in the future.

The Omnibus Budget Reconciliation Act of 1993 (1993 Tax Act), signed into law on August 10, 1993, increases the top corporate tax rate to 35%. The 35% rate applies to corporate taxable income in excess of $10 million, effective for tax years beginning on or after January 1, 1993. A top rate of 34% applies to corporate taxable income between $75,000 and $10 million and then phases-out the benefit of this 34% rate when the corporation's taxable income exceeds $15 million. As a result, a flat rate of 35% applies to corporations with taxable incomes over $18.3 million. For a fiscal-year taxpayer, the tax for its year that includes January 1, 1993, is computed using a "blended ratio" (i.e., a weighted average of old and new tax rates).

Statement 109 requires that the effect of the tax rate change be included in income from continuing operations in the period of enactment. How should the effect of the tax rate change be computed?

Response: Because of the retroactive nature of the tax rate change in the 1993 Tax Act, the income statement effect of the rate change in the *interim period* that includes August 10, 1993 (third quarter for calendar-year companies) has three components:

1. The effect of the higher rate on temporary differences that existed as of the first day of the year;
2. The effect of "adjusting" the annual effective tax rate used to record prior interim provisions for income tax expense related to *continuing operations* (this component affects the interim period that includes the enactment date, but is not included in the computation of the effect of the change in tax rates for the annual period); and
3. The effect of the tax rate change on all gains and losses recognized in the current year prior to the enactment date for items *not included in income from continuing operations*. Examples of this third component would be amounts recorded by a

calendar-year company between January 1, 1993, and August 9, 1993, for extraordinary items, discontinued operations, translation adjustments under FASB Statement No. 52, *Foreign Currency Translation*, and fair value adjustments for available-for-sale securities under FASB Statement No. 115, *Accounting for Certain Investments in Debt and Equity Securities*. (See Interpretation 27-4.)

We believe that the first component represents the effect of the tax rate increase on deferred tax liabilities and assets that is required to be disclosed in accordance with paragraph 45(g) of Statement 109 (see Interpretation 45-3). For companies with no gains or losses in the third component, the effect of the tax law change as disclosed under paragraph 45(g) for the annual period will equal the effect that is included as part of the reconciliation of the effective tax rate under paragraph 47. We believe that the second component represents an interim "catch-up" adjustment that results from the way in which interim tax provisions are recorded and is not part of the effect of the tax rate change for the *annual* period (i.e., calendar-year corporations with taxable income in excess of $18.3 million will reconcile to a 35% federal statutory tax rate in 1993 and therefore the interim catch-up adjustment will not affect the corporation's effective tax rate for the year 1993).

Statement 109 requires that all effects of a tax law change be included in income from continuing operations, even if the original tax effect was charged or credited directly to shareholders' equity (see paragraph 36 of Statement 109). Because the effective tax rate reconciliation required by Statement 109 reconciles to the tax provision for income from continuing operations, the computation of the effect of the tax law change to be included in the effective tax rate reconciliation will need to include the effects of the tax rate increase on those items not included in income from continuing operations that have been recognized in the interim periods prior to the enactment date (the third component listed previously).

Question: What tax rate should be used to measure deferred tax assets and liabilities for a company that currently reports less than $10 million in taxable income, but expects to be in the 35% tax bracket in the future?

Response: Statement 109 requires that deferred taxes be measured using the enacted tax rate that is expected to apply to taxable income in the years that the liability is expected to be settled or the asset recovered. Thus, the company in this example should measure its deferred tax assets and liabilities at 35% if all of the temporary differences are expected to reverse in periods when taxable income is expected to be in excess of $18.3 million.

27-4. Effect of Tax Law Changes on Items Other Than Income From Continuing Operations in the Year of the Change

Question: Paragraph 27 of Statement 109 is clear about how to treat a change in tax laws or rates. It states, "The effect shall be included in income from continuing operations for the period that includes the enactment date." This results in the total effect of the tax rate change, regardless of the original source of the deferred tax asset or liability (i.e., extraordinary items, discontinued operations, capital accounts, and so forth) being reflected in income from continuing operations. Does this rule also apply to prior interim periods of the year of enactment when the change in tax laws or rates is retroactive to the beginning of the year? Using the Omnibus Budget Reconciliation Act of 1993 (1993 Tax Act) as an example, what if a calendar-year company had an extraordinary gain in the first quarter of 1993 and recorded that gain net of federal tax of 34% and the federal rate increased to 35% in the third quarter of 1993?

Response: In the previous example, the incremental tax effect would be reflected as part of the third-quarter tax provision for income from continuing operations. The EITF concluded in EITF Issue No. 93-13, "Effect of a Retroactive Change in Enacted Tax Rates That Is Included in Income from Continuing Operations," that Statement 109's rule on tax law or tax rate changes applies to prior interim periods of the year of the change as well as prior years. The EITF reached a consensus that the effect of tax law changes on items other than income from continuing operations that occurred prior to the enactment date should be included in income from continuing operations in the interim period that includes the enactment date.

The same provisions apply to private companies. The tax effects of any items other than income from continuing operations that occur prior to the enactment date (August 10, 1993, for the change in the U.S. federal tax laws pursuant to the 1993 Tax Act) should have been recognized at the rate (and under the laws) in existence at the date the transaction or event occurred, regardless of whether the subsequent change in laws or rates was retroactive to a date prior to the transaction. Any effects of the change in laws or rates on these other items should have been reflected in the provision for income taxes for income from continuing operations.

27-5. Computing the Effect of the Tax Law Change on Certain Business Combinations

Question: An example of tax legislation that retroactively affected certain business combinations was the Omnibus Budget Reconciliation Act of 1993 (1993 Tax Act) that was enacted in August 1993. The 1993 Tax Act provided for a tax deduction for the amortization of most purchased intangible assets, including goodwill, over a 15-year period (this includes goodwill acquired in a stock purchase that, under Section 338 of the Internal Revenue Code, is treated as an asset purchase). The 1993 Tax Act's transitional rules allowed taxpayers to elect to apply the new tax rules on the amortization of purchased intangible assets to all property acquired after July 25, 1991. Under this election, the 15-year amortization period applied on a retroactive basis (prior year tax returns were amended). How was the effect of the change in this portion of the tax law computed for corporate taxpayers electing to apply the new tax rules to a prior business combination and in what period was that effect recognized?

Response: Assuming a valuation allowance was not required, the effect of the change in that portion of the tax law was the tax benefit of the tax goodwill amortization, including the effect of any goodwill related temporary differences that now exist, from the date of the prior business combination to the date the 1993 Tax Act was enacted (August 10, 1993). That benefit was recognized in income in the period that includes the enactment date (i.e., the interim period that includes August 10, 1993). Consider Example 27-5A.

Example 27-5A

Assume that: (*a*) Company A acquired Company B in an asset purchase exactly one year before the enactment of the 1993 Tax Act, (*b*) $150 of goodwill was created by that acquisition for financial reporting and tax purposes, (*c*) Company A was amortizing this goodwill for financial reporting purposes over 20 years, and (*d*) Company A was not affected by the change in tax rates (i.e., Company A's taxable income was less than $10 million). The benefit from the change in that portion of the tax law that was included in the income tax provision for income from continuing operations in the period that includes the enactment date was $2.55. That benefit was the net of a current tax benefit of $3.40 ($10 of tax goodwill amortization × 34%) and a deferred tax expense of $0.85 (financial reporting basis of goodwill of $142.50 – tax basis of goodwill of $140 × the 34%). (It should be noted that FASB Statement No. 142, *Goodwill and Other Intangible Assets,* requires that goodwill be evaluated for impairment rather than being amortized as this example demonstrates.)

If the tax basis of goodwill exceeds the financial reporting basis of goodwill at the date of acquisition, a question arises as to whether that future deduction (the excess of the tax basis of goodwill over the financial reporting basis of goodwill) should be recognized as a deferred tax asset in the period that includes the enactment date of the change in tax law. The EITF addressed this question in EITF Issue No. 93-12, "Recognition and Measurement of the Tax Benefit of Excess Tax-Deductible Goodwill Resulting from a Retroactive Change in Tax Law." The EITF reached a consensus that the tax benefit related to the excess of goodwill for tax purposes over goodwill for financial reporting purposes was a deductible temporary difference that should be recognized as a deferred tax asset at the enactment date of the change in tax law. Assuming a valuation allowance was not required, the benefit from recognizing that deferred tax asset was included in income from continuing operations. That conclusion is different than the accounting for an excess of goodwill for tax purposes over goodwill for financial reporting purposes for a business combination that occurs after the enactment date of the change in tax law. (See Interpretation 30-19 for an explanation of the accounting for a business combination that occurs after the enactment date of the change in tax law.)

27-6. Accounting for the Effect of a Tax Rate Change on an Acquired Deferred Tax Asset for Which a Full or Partial Valuation Allowance Has Been Provided

Question: Assume Company A acquires Company B in a business combination during 20X2 and that Company A concludes that a full valuation allowance ($100) is required for the $100 of deferred tax assets (an operating loss carryforward of $250 at a 40% tax rate) recognized in the purchase price allocation of Company B's assets and liabilities. Also assume that more than $100 of goodwill was created in the purchase price allocation. In accordance with paragraph 30 of Statement 109, if that valuation allowance is reduced in the future, goodwill recognized as part of the acquisition will be reduced. If the tax rate changes subsequent to the acquisition, but prior to any reduction in the valuation allowance, how should the effect of the tax rate change on the acquired (and fully reserved) deferred tax asset be recognized?

Response: How the effect of the tax rate change on the acquired (and fully reserved) deferred tax asset should be recognized depends on whether the subsequent change in tax rate is an increase or a decrease. Assume that during 20X3 the tax rate decreases from 40% to 35%. That change in tax rates reduces the gross amount of the acquired deferred tax asset from $100 to $87.50 ($250 × 35%). In this case, the gross deferred tax asset and the valuation allowance should both be adjusted to $87.50 (no effect on the net deferred tax asset or goodwill) and goodwill would be reduced in the future by up to $87.50 if and when the valuation allowance is reduced.

Now assume that the tax rate increases in 20X3 from 40% to 45%. That change in tax rate increases the gross amount of the acquired deferred tax asset from $100 to $112.50 ($250 × 45%). In this case, the gross deferred tax asset and the valuation allowance should both be adjusted to $112.50 (no effect on the net deferred tax asset or goodwill) and, consistent with the treatment of a decrease in tax rates, we believe the preferable approach would be to reduce goodwill in the future by up to $112.50 if and when the valuation allowance is reduced.

However, the FASB staff has indicated that two other approaches are acceptable when the subsequent change in tax rates is an increase. Under one approach, the enterprise would first reduce goodwill in the future by the original purchased benefit (i.e., $100) and once the valuation allowance has been reduced by $100, the next $12.50 of benefit would be reflected in the income statement. Under the second approach, the reduction in the valuation allowance would be prorated between goodwill and the income statement. We believe any of the previous approaches, consistently applied, are acceptable.

27-7. Presentation of Effect of Tax Law Change in the Income Statement

Question: How should the effects of a tax law change be presented in the income statement? For example, on August 10, 1993, a new U.S. federal tax law was enacted which, among other things, increased the top corporate income tax rate to 35% retroactive to January 1, 1993. How was the effect of that tax law change presented in income statements?

Response: Statement 109 requires that the effects of a tax law change be included as a component of income tax expense related to income from continuing operations. The statement also requires that adjustments of deferred taxes for enacted changes in tax laws be disclosed. These requirements apply to both publicly and privately held companies. (See Interpretations 27-3 and 27-4 for guidance on how to compute the effect of the tax law change and Interpretation 45-3 for guidance on the disclosure of the effect of changes in tax law on deferred tax assets and liabilities. The effect of the change in the tax law is different for the *interim* period that includes the enactment date than for the *annual* period that includes the enactment date.)

A company could present the effects of a tax law change and still meet the requirements of Statement 109 by the following methods:

- The effect of the change is included in income tax expense on the face of the income statement and is disclosed in the tax footnote either as part of the effective tax rate reconciliation or separately.

- The effect of the change is presented as a component of income tax expense on the face of the income statement, as shown in Table 1.
- The effect of the change is included in income tax expense on the face of the income statement with a parenthetical reference to the effect of the tax law change, as shown in Table 2.

Tables 1 and 2 clarify this presentation.

Table 1: Income Statement Presentation, Alternative A

Income before taxes		$1,350,000
Income tax expense:		
Effect of change in tax law	125,000	
Other current and deferred taxes	475,000	
Total		600,000
Net income		$750,000

Table 2: Income Statement Presentation, Alternative B

Income before taxes	$1,350,000
Income tax expense (includes $125,000 in 1993 related to the change in tax law)	600,000
Net income	$750,000

Note that the effective tax rate reconciliation for publicly held companies (and the qualitative discussion of reconciling items for privately held companies) will include the effects of the tax law change. Also note that for publicly held companies, Regulation S-K, Item 303, "Management's Discussion and Analysis of Financial Condition and Results of Operations," (MD&A) calls for the discussion of any known trends or events that a registrant reasonably expects will have a material effect on liquidity or income from continuing operations. Although the financial statements and related notes will adequately quantify the effect of the change on current year income, a registrant that expects the new law to affect its future liquidity or operating results should discuss that fact in its MD&A.

27-8. Accounting for Rate Regulation Implication of a Tax Rate Change

Question: Statement 109 requires deferred tax liabilities and assets to be adjusted for the effect of a change in tax law or rates with the offsetting effect included in income from continuing operations. However, paragraph 29(c) of Statement 109 states that if, as a result of an action by a regulator, it is probable that the increase or decrease in deferred tax liabilities or assets caused by a change in enacted tax rates will be recovered from, or returned to, customers through future rates, a regulatory asset or liability is recognized pursuant to FASB Statement No. 71, *Accounting for the Effects of Certain Types of Regulation*. What about increases in current tax expense (taxes currently payable)? Should enterprises that meet the criteria to apply Statement 71 defer that consequence of the change in tax rates?

Response: Generally, enterprises that meet the criteria to apply Statement 71 should not defer the consequence of the change in tax rates. Statement 71 requires that, in order to recognize a regulatory asset, "[T]he future revenue will be provided to permit recovery of the previously incurred cost rather than to provide for expected levels of similar future costs." Therefore, absent action by a regulator, there is no basis to defer that additional tax expense.

The same notion applies to increases in deferred tax liabilities caused by an increase in tax rates. Absent action by a regulator to provide specific recovery through future rates of the increase in current tax expense that results from an increase in tax rates, the increase in deferred tax liabilities caused by the increase in tax rates related to taxable temporary differences *that are expected to reverse (i.e., affect taxes currently payable) prior to a change in rates being charged to customers* will not result in an increase in future revenue from customers. That portion of the effect of the change in tax rates therefore fails the criteria for recognition as a regulatory asset and should be expensed in the period of the tax rate change.

27-9. Determining the Enactment Date in Tax Jurisdictions Outside of the United States

Question: Statement 109 states that deferred tax assets and liabilities should be adjusted for the effects of a change in tax law or rates in the period that includes the enactment date. In the United States, the enactment date for a change in federal tax law is the date the President signs the legislation and it becomes law. How should the enactment date be determined for other tax jurisdictions?

Response: The enactment date for a change in tax law or rates occurs when all of the steps in the process for legislation in that jurisdiction to become law have been completed.

For example, in Australia the final step in enacting legislation is the "Royal Assent" from the Queen's representative, the Governor-General. Because the Governor-General, in practice, has only withheld the Royal Assent in the unusual circumstance of a request from the Prime Minister, some have argued that the Royal Assent is a perfunctory step that lacks sufficient substance to be the determining factor in establishing the enactment date for purposes of accounting for income taxes. On December 21, 1995, the AICPA's International Practice Task Force considered this question and concluded that the enactment date in Australia for purposes of Statement 109 is the date the Royal Assent is signed.

A Change in the Tax Status of an Enterprise

EXCERPT FROM OFFICIAL TEXT

A Change in the Tax Status of an Enterprise

28. An enterprise's tax status may change from nontaxable to taxable or from taxable to nontaxable. An example is a change from a partnership to a corporation and vice versa. A deferred tax liability or asset shall be recognized for temporary differences in accordance with the requirements of this Statement at the date that a nontaxable enterprise becomes a taxable enterprise. A deferred tax liability or asset shall be eliminated at the date an enterprise ceases to be a taxable enterprise. In either case, the effect of (a) an election for a voluntary change in tax status is recognized on the approval date or on the filing date if approval is not necessary and (b) a change in tax status that results from a change in tax law is recognized on the enactment date. The effect of recognizing or eliminating the deferred tax liability or asset shall be included in income from continuing operations.

INTERPRETATION

28-1. Disclosures Required for a Post-Balance Sheet Date Change in Tax Status

Question (from FASB Staff Implementation Guide, Question 11):

What disclosure is required if a change in an enterprise's tax status becomes effective after year-end but before the financial statements for the year are issued?

Response (from FASB Staff Implementation Guide, Question 11):

If an election to change an enterprise's tax status is approved by the tax authority (or filed, if approval is not necessary) early in year 2 and prior to issuing financial statements for year 1, the effect of that change in tax status should not be recognized in the financial statements for year 1. However, the enterprise's financial statements for year 1 should disclose (a) the change in the enterprise's tax status for year 2 and (b) the effects of that change, if material.

28-2. Deferred Tax Liability for Built-In Gains of an S Corporation

Question (from FASB Staff Implementation Guide, Question 12):

Should an enterprise that changes from taxable C corporation status to nontaxable S corporation status eliminate its entire U.S. federal deferred tax liability?

Response (from FASB Staff Implementation Guide, Question 12):

An enterprise that makes that status change should continue to recognize a deferred tax liability to the extent that the enterprise would be subject to a corporate-level tax on net unrecognized "built-in gains."

A C corporation that has temporary differences as of the date of change to S corporation status should determine its deferred tax liability in accordance with the tax law. Since the timing of realization of a built-in gain can determine whether it is taxable, and therefore significantly affect the deferred tax liability to be recognized, actions and elections that are expected to be implemented should be considered. For purposes of determining that deferred tax liability, the lesser of an unrecognized built-in gain (as defined by the tax law) or an existing temporary difference is used in the computations described in the tax law to determine the amount of the tax on built-in gains.

For example, assume that an enterprise's S corporation election is effective for calendar-year 1990 and that at the conversion date its assets comprise marketable securities, finished goods inventory, and depreciable assets as follows:

	Fair Market Value	Tax Basis	Reported Amount	Temporary Difference	Statement 109 Built-in Gain (Loss)
Marketable Securities	$90	100	80	$(20)	$(10)
Inventory (FIFO)	100	50	100	50	50
Depreciable assets	95	80	90	10	10
	$285	$230	$270	$40	$50

Assuming that (a) the enterprise has no tax loss or credit carryforwards available to offset the built-in gains, (b) the depreciable assets will be recovered by use in operations (and, therefore, will not result in a taxable amount pursuant to the tax law applied to built-in gains), and (c) the marketable securities will be sold in the same year that the inventory is sold, the $50 built-in gain on the inventory is reduced by the $10 built-in loss on the marketable securities, and $40 would be taxed in the year that the inventory turns over and the securities are sold. Accordingly, the enterprise should continue to display in its balance sheet a deferred tax liability for that $40 net taxable amount.

At subsequent financial statement dates until the end of the 10 years following the conversion date, the enterprise should remeasure the deferred tax liability for net built-in gains based on the provisions of the tax law. Deferred tax expense or benefit should be recognized for any change in that deferred tax liability.

28-3. Change in Tax Status Is Not a Qualifying Tax-Planning Strategy

Question (from FASB Staff Implementation Guide, Question 28):

Under current U.S. federal tax law, approval of an enterprise's change from taxable C corporation status to nontaxable S corporation status is automatic if the criteria for S corporation status are met. If an enterprise meets those criteria but has not changed to S corporation status, would a strategy to change to nontaxable S corporation status be a qualifying tax-planning strategy that would permit an enterprise to not recognize deferred taxes?

Response (from FASB Staff Implementation Guide, Question 28):

No. A change in tax status is a discrete event. Paragraph 28 requires that the effect of a change in tax status be recognized at the date that the change in tax status occurs, that is, at the date that the change is approved by the tax authority (or on the date of filing the change if approval is not necessary).

Regulated Enterprises

EXCERPT FROM OFFICIAL TEXT

Regulated Enterprises

29. Regulated enterprises that meet the criteria for application of FASB Statement No. 71, *Accounting for the Effects of Certain Types of Regulation*, are not exempt from the requirements of this Statement. Specifically, this Statement:

    a. Prohibits net-of-tax accounting and reporting

    b. Requires recognition of a deferred tax liability (1) for tax benefits that are flowed through to customers when temporary differences originate and (2) for the equity component of the allowance for funds used during construction

    c. Requires adjustment of a deferred tax liability or asset for an enacted change in tax laws or rates.

    If, as a result of an action by a regulator, it is probable that the future increase or decrease in taxes payable for items (b) and (c) above will be recovered from or returned to customers through future rates, an asset or liability is recognized for that probable future revenue or reduction in future revenue pursuant to paragraphs 9–11 of Statement 71. That asset or liability also is a temporary difference for which a deferred tax liability or asset shall be recognized.

INTERPRETATION

29-1. Accounting for Income Tax Related Regulatory Assets

Question: Regulatory commissions sometimes ignore the deferred tax consequences of some current events when establishing rates to be charged to a regulated enterprise's customers with the implicit or explicit understanding that the future payment of those tax consequences will be included in the establishment of rates to be charged to the regulated enterprise's customers in that future period. Paragraph 29 of Statement 109 provides that enterprises meeting the criteria to apply FASB Statement No. 71, *Accounting for the Effects of Certain Types of Regulation,* and that will be recovering past deferred tax expense from customers through future rates should recognize a regulatory asset for that incurred cost (the deferred tax expense), assuming the criteria for recognition of a regulatory asset contained in Statement 71 are met. Paragraph 29 further states that the regulatory asset itself is a temporary difference. What is the "other side of the entry" when establishing a regulatory asset related to deferred income taxes and when subsequently collecting (and writing off) that regulatory asset?

Response: The other side of the entry is a credit to both deferred tax liabilities and deferred tax expense at the time a deferred tax related regulatory asset is created. The reverse entry is then reflected at the time the deferred income tax expense is included in rates charged to customers. Consider Example 29-1A.

Example 29-1A

Assume that: (*a*) Enterprise incurs a $100 cost that is deductible currently for income tax purposes, (*b*) the $100 cost is capitalizable and amortizable for financial reporting purposes (and rate purposes) over a 10-year life, (*c*) the current tax benefit will be used to reduce rates charged to current customers (by ignoring the current period deferred tax expense for purposes of establishing rates), (*d*) the related tax expense will be included in costs used to compute rates to be charged to customers in future periods as the temporary difference affects each future period's current tax expense, (*e*) the regulatory asset meets the criteria for recognition contained in Statement 71, and (*f*) the tax rate in effect during all periods is 40%.

The first entry is a debit to deferred tax provision and a credit to deferred tax liabilities for $40 (required under Statement 109 regardless of rate regulation). The entry to reflect the effects of rate regulation is a debit to a regulatory asset of $67, a credit to the deferred tax provision of $40, and a credit to deferred tax liabilities of $27. The regulatory asset is the sum of the $40 incurred cost (the deferred tax provision) that is being deferred in addition to the "tax-on-tax" effect of $27 that is due to the regulatory asset itself being a temporary difference (computed by multiplying the $40 by [tax rate/(1 − tax rate)] which, in this case = $27). The $67 is the amount by which current revenues are reduced as a result of excluding the $40 deferred tax expense from the computation of current period rates and is the amount of future revenues that will need to be collected to recover the carrying amount of the regulatory asset. The net effect of the previous entries is a $0 deferred tax provision, deferred tax liabilities of $67 (which can be proved by multiplying the taxable temporary differences at the report date of $100 and $67 by 40%), and a regulatory asset of $67.

The annual journal entries during the financial reporting amortization period would be as follows:

- The pretax asset amortization is recognized by debiting amortization expense and crediting accumulated amortization for $10.

Continued on page 118

Continued from page 117

- The deferred tax effect of that first entry is a debit to deferred tax liabilities and a credit to deferred tax provision for $4 (those first two entries are required regardless of rate regulation).
- The effect of rate regulation would be a debit to the deferred tax provision of $4, a debit to deferred tax liabilities of $2.70, and a credit to regulatory asset of $6.70.
- The net effect of the last two entries is a $0 deferred tax provision and a reduction in both the regulatory asset and the deferred tax liability of $6.70.

29-2. Accounting for the Tax Effects of the Equity Component of the Allowance for Funds Used During Construction

Question: Paragraph 253 of Statement 109 contains a numerical example of the computation of the regulatory asset required to be recognized (assuming the criteria in FASB Statement No. 71, *Accounting for the Effects of Certain Types of Regulation,* are met) for the future tax consequences of the equity component of allowance for funds used during construction (AFUDC). What is the appropriate financial statement presentation of the equity component of AFUDC and related regulatory assets once Statement 109 is adopted?

Response: For enterprises that continue to meet the criteria to apply Statement 71 (and meet the probability test for recognizing a regulatory asset for the tax effect of the equity component of AFUDC), we believe there should be no change in the income statement presentation of the equity component of AFUDC. However, we believe that enterprises that capitalize interest costs on a net-of-tax basis (i.e., if the debt component of AFUDC is computed on a net-of-tax basis) would be required to "gross up" the interest capitalized and related tax effect in the income statement and the balance sheet. This conclusion is based on the distinction made in Statement 109 between the treatment of the equity component of AFUDC and net-of-tax accounting in general.

Paragraph 253 contains the following example of the accounting for the equity component of AFUDC:

> The following example illustrates recognition of an asset for the probable future revenue to recover future income taxes related to the deferred tax liability for the equity

component of the allowance for funds used during construction (AFUDC). The assumptions are as follows:

a. During year 1, the first year of operations, total construction costs for financial reporting and tax purposes are $400,000 (exclusive of AFUDC).

b. The enacted tax rate is 34 percent for all future years.

c. AFUDC (consisting entirely of the equity component) is $26,000. The asset for probable future revenue to recover the related income taxes is calculated as follows:

   34 percent of ($26,000 + A) = A (where A equals the asset for probable future revenue)

   A = $13,394

At the end of year 1, the related accounts are as follows:

Construction in progress	$426,000
Probable future revenue	$ 13,394
Deferred tax liability [34 percent of ($26,000 + $13,394)]	$ 13,394

[Footnote reference omitted.]

The complete journal entry to record the equity component of AFUDC for Year 1 in the previous example is as follows:

Construction in progress	$26,000	
Regulatory asset	13,394	
AFUDC-equity (part of other income)		$26,000
Deferred tax liability		13,394

In contrast, changing the previous example to assume that the entire amount of AFUDC is a net-of-tax debt amount results in the following journal entry for Year 1:

Construction in progress	$39,394	
Regulatory asset	13,394	
AFUDC-debt (reduction of interest expense)		$39,394
Deferred tax liability		13,394

Business Combinations

EXCERPT FROM OFFICIAL TEXT

Business Combinations

30. A deferred tax liability or asset shall be recognized in accordance with the requirements of this Statement for differences between the assigned values and the tax bases of the assets and liabilities (except the portion of goodwill for which amortization is not deductible for tax purposes, unallocated excess over cost (also referred to as negative goodwill), leveraged leases, and acquired Opinion 23 differences[8]) recognized in a purchase business combination (refer to paragraphs 259–272 for additional guidance). If a valuation allowance is recognized for the deferred tax asset for an acquired entity's deductible temporary differences or operating loss or tax credit carryforwards at the acquisition date, the tax benefits for those items that are first recognized (that is, by elimination of that valuation allowance) in financial statements after the acquisition date shall be applied (a) first to reduce to zero any goodwill related to the acquisition, (b) second to reduce to zero other noncurrent intangible assets related to the acquisition, and (c) third to reduce income tax expense.

[8] Acquired Opinion 23 differences are accounted for in accordance with the requirements of Opinion 23, as amended by this Statement.

INTERPRETATION

30-1. Adjustment of Negative Goodwill

Question (from FASB Staff Implementation Guide, Question 13):

Paragraph 30 of Statement 109 requires that the tax benefit of acquired deductible temporary differences and carryforwards that are initially recognized in financial statements subsequent to the acquisition date (because a previously established valuation allowance is reduced or eliminated) shall be applied (a) first to reduce to zero any goodwill related to that acquisition, (b) second to reduce to zero other noncurrent intangible assets related to that acquisition, and (c) third to reduce income tax expense. Does the requirement to adjust goodwill for subsequently recognized deductible temporary differences and carryforwards relate to negative goodwill as well as positive goodwill?

Response (from FASB Staff Implementation Guide, Question 13):

> No. The requirement to reduce goodwill for those tax benefits relates to positive goodwill; unallocated negative goodwill should not be increased by such tax benefits.
>
> Upon adoption of FASB Statement No. 141, *Business Combinations,* negative goodwill is recognized as an extraordinary item.

30-2. Reduction of Acquiring Enterprise's Valuation Allowance as a Result of a Business Combination

Question: If the *acquiring* enterprise in a business combination has a valuation allowance and that valuation allowance is reduced as a result of the business combination (e.g., the purchase is nontaxable and the acquired entity has significant taxable temporary differences that, under existing tax law, can be used to offset deductible temporary differences and carryforwards of the acquiring enterprise in the future years in which the temporary differences will reverse), is that reduction in valuation allowance accounted for as part of the business combination or as a reduction in the current period's tax expense?

Response: Paragraph 266 of Statement 109 requires that the reduction in the valuation allowance of the acquiring company be accounted for as part of the business combination. That is, the reduction in the acquiring enterprise's valuation allowance reduces goodwill or noncurrent assets (except long-term investments in marketable securities) of the acquired entity or creates or increases negative goodwill.

30-3. Subsequent Recognition of Acquiring Enterprise Tax Benefits

Question (from FASB Staff Implementation Guide, Question 14):

> The tax law may permit an *acquiring enterprise's* deductible temporary differences and carryforwards to reduce future taxable income attributable to the acquired enterprise if consolidated tax returns are filed subsequent to the acquisition. In those circumstances, accounting for the business combination should recognize reductions in the acquiring enterprise's existing valuation allowances for deferred tax assets as a result of an assessment of realization (paragraph 21) by the *combined enterprise.*

If there is a valuation allowance for the acquiring enterprise's deferred tax assets at the acquisition date, how should tax benefits for the related deductible temporary differences and carryforwards be reported if and when recognized in the financial statements for subsequent years?

Response (from FASB Staff Implementation Guide, Question 14):

Because the tax benefit recognized does not result from utilizing the deductible temporary differences or carryforwards of the acquired enterprise, the tax benefit should be reported as a reduction of income tax expense when recognized in financial statements for subsequent years.

30-4. Subsequent Adjustment of the Acquiring Enterprise's Tax Benefits Recognized in a Business Combination

Question: Assume an acquiring enterprise has recognized a reduction in its valuation allowance as a result of a business combination (see Interpretation 30-2). Subsequently, the enterprise loses the tax benefits so recognized. Should the adjustment of deferred tax assets be charged to income or to the purchase price of the entity previously acquired?

Response: Determining whether the adjustment of deferred tax assets should be charged to income or to the purchase price of the entity previously acquired depends on how the tax benefits were "lost." If, on settlement with the taxing authority of periods *preceding* the business combination, there is a reduction of tax benefits (deductible temporary differences or carryforwards) that were thought to exist at the date of the business combination, we believe it is appropriate to adjust the business combination in the manner described in EITF Issue No. 93-7, "Uncertainties Related to Income Taxes in a Purchase Business Combination" (Interpretation 30-9). In all other situations, the adjustment of the deferred tax asset should be charged to income. For example, assume the tax benefits of the acquiring enterprise's carryforwards so recognized subsequently expire unused. In such situations, the loss of those tax benefits is the result of events and transactions occurring after the date of the acquisition (i.e., losses incurred or profits anticipated that did not occur after the date of the acquisition) and therefore should be reflected in the results of operations for those periods.

30-5. Step Acquisitions

Question: Assume Company A has owned 30% of Company B for some period of time and has provided for deferred taxes related to the excess of its financial reporting basis over its tax basis in that investment (e.g., such a temporary difference could be caused by undistributed earnings of Company B). Company A now acquires an additional 50% of Company B (Company A now owns 80% of Company B). Should Company A eliminate its deferred taxes related to its investment in Company B? If so, where does the credit go?

Response: The determination of whether Company A should eliminate its deferred taxes related to its investment in Company B depends on whether Company B is a foreign or domestic subsidiary of Company A. If Company B is a foreign subsidiary, the deferred tax liability should continue to be recognized regardless of whether the investment now meets the "indefinite reversal criterion" (refer to paragraph 288(f) of Statement 109 that amends paragraph 13 of Opinion 23). If Company B is a domestic subsidiary and, under paragraph 33 of Statement 109, the outside basis difference is not a taxable temporary difference, the deferred tax liability would be eliminated and the reduction in deferred taxes should be treated as a reduction in the purchase price of the 50% of Company B being acquired. That is, no immediate gain is recognized as a result of the acquisition of a majority interest in Company B. This is similar to a situation specifically covered by Statement 109 in which an enterprise has a valuation allowance that is reduced as a result of it acquiring another enterprise in a transaction accounted for as a business combination (see Interpretation 30-2). In that situation, the reduction in the acquiring company's valuation allowance is treated as an additional asset acquired (the same effect as a reduction in the purchase price of the acquired enterprise).

30-6. Deferred Taxes in a "Bargain" Business Combination

Question (from FASB Staff Implementation Guide, Question 15):

> How should a deferred tax liability or asset be determined for a purchase business combination that results in allocated negative goodwill?

Response (from FASB Staff Implementation Guide, Question 15):

> Allocation of negative goodwill reduces the values otherwise assignable to the noncurrent assets acquired

(except long-term investments in marketable securities). However, that reduction in assigned values changes the amounts of temporary differences related to those assets, which changes the amount of deferred tax asset or liability, which changes negative goodwill, and so on. The amount of negative goodwill and any deferred tax asset or liability arising from a purchase business combination are mutually dependent, and the determination of values assigned to noncurrent assets (that is, net of allocated negative goodwill) requires the simultaneous computation of the assigned value of those acquired assets and the related deferred tax asset or liability. (An iterative process could also be followed but that would be more time-consuming.) For example, assume the following:

a. An enterprise is acquired for $20,000 in a nontaxable business combination.
b. That enterprise's only assets are depreciable assets with a pretax fair value of $30,000 and a tax basis of $15,000. The only liability is the deferred tax liability for the temporary difference related to those depreciable assets.
c. The enacted tax rate is 40 percent for all years.

The amounts recorded to account for the purchase transaction are determined as follows:

a. First, the assigned value (net of allocated negative goodwill) of the depreciable assets (DA) is determined as follows:

$$DA - (\text{tax rate} \times \text{basis difference}) = \text{purchase price}$$

$$DA - .4\ (DA - \$15{,}000) = \$20{,}000$$

$$DA = \$23{,}333$$

b. The deferred tax liability is then determined as follows:

Assigned value of depreciable assets	$23,333
Tax basis of depreciable assets	15,000
Temporary difference	$8,333
Deferred tax liability (40 percent)	$3,333

c. The $23,333 assigned to all depreciable assets is then allocated to the individual depreciable assets.

The amounts recorded to account for the purchase transaction are as follows:

Depreciable assets	$23,333
Deferred tax liability	(3,333)
Purchase price of the acquired enterprise	$20,000

The formula used in the illustration is not applicable to every business combination involving negative goodwill. A different equation than that illustrated would be necessary if, for example, (a) the computation of deferred taxes involves more than one tax rate, (b) an acquiring enterprise's valuation allowance for deductible temporary differences and carryforwards is eliminated or reduced because of the availability of future taxable amounts from the acquired enterprise, or (c) the deferred tax asset for deductible temporary differences related to acquired long-term assets will require a valuation allowance. The equations used should reflect the interdependence of negative goodwill and deferred tax assets or liabilities considering the particular facts about the deferred tax computation related to the business combination.

30-7. Tax-on-Tax Effect of Subsequent Recognition of Tax Benefits That Reduces an Intangible Asset Other Than Goodwill

Question: Statement 109 requires that subsequent reductions in valuation allowances that relate to acquired tax benefits be credited first to goodwill, second to other intangible assets acquired as part of that business combination, and third to income. If the reduction in valuation allowance is used to reduce an intangible asset other than goodwill (or goodwill that is amortizable for tax purposes and therefore treated as a temporary difference), that reduction also has a tax effect (i.e., the temporary difference related to the intangible asset has been changed). How should that "tax-on-tax" effect of the reduction in a valuation allowance related to acquired tax benefits be treated?

Response: Paragraph 263 of Statement 109 contains a numerical example of how to compute and account for the tax-on-tax effect related to reductions of goodwill that is amortizable for tax purposes and therefore treated as a temporary difference. The additional benefit (from the change in the temporary difference related to the goodwill) is also used to reduce the financial reporting carrying amount of the goodwill. The total "charge in lieu of taxes" can be determined by doing iterations of the above or by multiplying the resultant of the following equation (1 + [tax rate/(1 – tax rate)]) by the reduction in valuation allowance. Therefore, the debit to tax expense (charge in lieu of taxes) and credit to intangible assets would be $152 if the reduction in the valuation allowance related to acquired tax benefits is $100 and the appropriate tax rate is 34%.

The entire journal entry to reflect the $100 reduction in the valuation allowance is as follows.

Deferred tax asset valuation allowance	$100	
Deferred tax liability	52	
Charge in lieu of taxes	152	
Intangible asset		$152
Deferred tax benefit		152

The reduction in deferred tax liability is caused by the reduction in the financial reporting basis of the intangible asset ($152 × 34% = $52). The deferred tax benefit is the sum of the reduction in the valuation allowance ($100) and the reduction in the deferred tax liability ($52).

The example in paragraph 263 and the previous equation also apply to reductions of other intangible assets acquired as part of the business combination. Note that the above does not apply to a reduction of goodwill that is not amortizable for tax purposes because that goodwill is not treated as a temporary difference.

30-8. Accounting for Tax Contingencies in a Taxable Business Combination

Question (from FASB Staff Implementation Guide, Question 17):

> In a taxable purchase business combination, an enterprise allocates for tax purposes the purchase price to the assets acquired and liabilities assumed so as to maximize the potential income tax benefits from the combination. Although the enterprise has a basis under the tax law for the allocations claimed in initial filings with the tax authority, that enterprise believes that portions of the allocation will be denied by the tax authority and the amount assigned to goodwill will be increased. How should deferred income taxes at the date of the business combination be accounted for? What is the appropriate accounting in periods subsequent to the business combination for changes in the purchase price allocation for tax purposes?

Response (from FASB Staff Implementation Guide, Question 17):

> The tax basis of an asset or liability is a question of fact under the tax law. The tax basis of most assets and liabilities is not subject to dispute and can be determined from initial filings with the tax authority. However, the tax

basis of some assets and liabilities is unclear and will be determined by tax regulations, negotiations with the tax authority, appeals procedures, or, in some cases, litigation. The tax basis of those assets and liabilities may not be appropriately determined from initial filings with the tax authority because those filings are only the first step in the process to establish the tax basis. The tax bases used in the calculation of deferred tax assets and liabilities as well as amounts due to or receivable from taxing authorities related to prior tax returns at the date of a business combination shall be calculated pursuant to FASB Interpretation No. 48, *Accounting for Uncertainty in Income Taxes*.

At or before settlement with the tax authority, management may change its assessment of the amount that will be realized upon ultimate settlement with the taxing authority. At the date of that change in judgment and at the date that the tax basis of the acquired assets and liabilities is settled, the enterprise should adjust its deferred tax asset or liability to reflect the revised tax basis and the amount of any settlement with the tax authority for prior year income taxes. The effect of that adjustment should be applied to increase or decrease the remaining balance of goodwill attributable to that acquisition. (If goodwill is reduced to zero, the remaining portion of that adjustment should be applied initially to reduce to zero other noncurrent intangible assets related to that acquisition. Any remaining benefits should be recognized in income.)

30-9. Accounting for Preacquisition Income Tax Contingencies (and Contingencies Arising From the Acquisition)

Question: Are preacquisition income tax related contingencies covered by paragraphs 40 and 41 of FASB Statement No. 141, *Business Combinations*?

Response: Paragraphs 40 and 41 of Statement 141 carried forward the guidance previously contained in FASB Statement No. 38, *Accounting for Preacquisition Contingencies of Purchased Enterprises*. The EITF addressed this question in EITF Issue No. 93-7, "Uncertainties Related to Income Taxes in a Purchase Business Combination," and concluded that Statement 38 does not apply to income tax related preacquisition contingencies. The same conclusion applies to paragraphs 40 and 41 of Statement 141. The EITF also concluded that all income tax related contingencies related to a business combination (both preacquisition and contingencies arising from the acquisition) should be accounted for pursuant to Question and Answer (Q&A) 17 of the FASB Staff Implementation Guide, *A Guide to Implementation of Statement 109 on Accounting for Income*

Taxes (see Interpretation 30-8). Under Q&A 17, goodwill is adjusted (up or down) for all changes in estimates about contingencies regardless of the time elapsed since the date of acquisition. (If goodwill has been reduced to zero, the remaining portion of any favorable adjustment should be applied initially to reduce to zero other noncurrent intangible assets related to that acquisition. Any remaining benefits should be recognized in income.)

FASB Interpretation (FIN) No. 48, *Accounting for Uncertainty in Income Taxes,* amends Issue 93-7 (and Q&A 17) and requires that uncertainties related to income taxes in a business combination be recognized and measured using the FIN 48 model (i.e., a more-likely-than-not criterion for recognition of uncertain tax positions). Prior to FIN 48, enterprises recognized uncertainties related to income taxes in a business combination based on management's best estimate of the ultimate resolution of the uncertainty. (See Interpretation 10-1 and Appendix I for a further discussion of FIN 48.)

However, Issue 93-7 does not affect the accounting for changes in valuation allowances. Initial recognition of acquired tax benefits is governed by paragraph 30 of Statement 109. All other changes in valuation allowances (i.e., all increases or decreases in the valuation allowance other than the *initial* recognition of acquired tax benefits) should be included in income.

In certain circumstances, a favorable settlement with the IRS, while reducing goodwill, could also result in a charge to the income statement if a valuation allowance is now needed for a deferred tax asset. Consider Example 30-9A.

Example 30-9A

Assume that Company A acquired Company B in a taxable business combination. In performing the purchase price allocation for financial reporting and tax purposes, Company A assigned value to an identifiable intangible asset. However, Company A believed that upon audit the IRS would likely reallocate that amount to nonamortizable goodwill. Accordingly, for purposes of quantifying temporary differences, Company A treated that portion of the purchase price as nonamortizable goodwill for tax purposes and not as an identifiable intangible asset (and reflected a deferred tax liability for the difference between the book value assigned to the intangible asset and the expected tax basis of zero). Subsequent to the acquisition, Company A incurred operating losses that resulted in operating loss carryforwards for tax purposes. Absent that deferred tax liability, a valuation allowance would have been required for the operating loss carryforward deferred tax asset.

In the current year, the IRS examined the year of the acquisition and did not question Company A's purchase price allocation. As a

Continued on page 129

Continued from page 128

> result, Company A eliminates the deferred tax liability related to the intangible asset and reduces goodwill in accordance with Issue 93-7. However, once that deferred tax liability is eliminated, Company A now requires a valuation allowance for its postacquisition operating loss carryforward since it is more-likely-than-not-that the deferred tax asset will not be realized. This increase in valuation allowance should be reflected in the income statement. The net effect of the favorable resolution of a tax related uncertainty in this situation is to reduce goodwill and charge the income statement.

The EITF minutes include a comment by the SEC Observer that the SEC staff will not accept analogies to this consensus for other business combination related contingencies.

30-10. Acquired Opinion 23 Differences

Question: Assume that, in 20X1, Company A acquires Company B in a nontaxable business combination (i.e., Company B's tax basis in its assets is not affected by the acquisition) and that, among other assets, Company B has two subsidiaries, Foreign Company and Domestic Company. At the time of the purchase, Company B had outside basis differences caused by undistributed earnings in both subsidiaries. In allocating the purchase price to the assets acquired, Company A increases the financial reporting carrying amounts of the investment in both subsidiaries of Company B, thereby increasing the outside basis difference. Should Company A recognize a deferred tax liability for the outside basis differences for either of Company B's subsidiaries as part of reflecting the business combination?

Response: Footnote 8 to paragraph 30 of Statement 109 states that "[a]cquired Opinion 23 differences are accounted for in accordance with the requirements of Opinion 23, as amended by this Statement." For the foreign subsidiary, the answer depends on whether all or a portion of the outside basis difference meets the indefinite reversal criterion of Opinion 23. To the extent it does, no deferred taxes should be provided. Note that Opinion 23, as amended by Statement 109, applies to the entire outside basis difference related to an investment in a foreign subsidiary, not just the portion of the outside basis difference caused by undistributed earnings.

For the domestic subsidiary, the answer depends on whether "the tax law provides a means by which the reported amount of that investment can be recovered tax-free and the enterprise expects that it will ultimately use that means." (See Interpretation 33-1.) Finally, the "grandfather" provision in Statement 109 for undistributed earnings of domestic subsidiaries that arose in years beginning on or before December 15, 1992, does not apply to this example. Company A did not own Domestic Company for any period prior to December 15, 1992; therefore, there are no undistributed earnings in the Company A consolidated financial statements from Domestic Company that are eligible for the paragraph 31(b) grandfather provision.

30-11. Acquisitions Involving Oil and Gas Properties

Question: In nontaxable business combinations involving the acquisition of oil and gas properties, deferred taxes will need to be provided for the basis difference related to the oil and gas properties. When goodwill is not recognized in business combinations involving oil and gas properties, recognition of the deferred tax liability will increase the financial reporting basis of the oil and gas properties and thereby increase the temporary difference. Should additional deferred taxes be recognized for that increase in the temporary difference?

Response: Statement 109 has no "special rules" for oil and gas properties and its general rule is quite clear—deferred taxes must be provided for all temporary differences. Assuming goodwill is not recorded in these circumstances, the solution to this problem is solved using the following equation:

$$[(P - TB) / (1 - R)]R = DTL$$

For example, assuming the following:

Purchase price (P) = \$100
Tax basis of net assets (TB) = \$0
Tax rate (R) = 40%

The computation of the deferred tax liability (DTL) would be:

$$[(\$100 - \$0) / (1 - .4)].4 = \$67$$

Entry to record the purchase:

Oil and gas assets	$167	
Deferred tax liability		$67
Cash		$100

Proof:

$$(\text{Assets} - \text{Tax basis})\ (R) = \text{DTL}$$
$$(\$167 - \$0).40 = \$67$$

In practice under Statement 109, some oil and gas enterprises recognized a deferred tax liability of $40 and oil and gas assets of $140 (deferred taxes being equal to 40% of the difference between the acquisition price of $100 and the tax basis of $0). Under EITF Issue No. 98-11, "Accounting for Acquired Temporary Differences in Certain Purchase Transactions That Are Not Accounted for as Business Combinations," this practice is no longer acceptable. Instead, an entity must use the simultaneous equation calculation discussed previously. Although the scope in Issue 98-11 is specifically limited to asset acquisitions that are not business combinations, this approach is consistent with the view expressed by the SEC staff in a SEC Observer comment to the consensus. In that previous SEC Observer comment, the SEC staff stated that it would apply the consensus to business combinations of oil and gas companies where goodwill is not normally recognized. Subsequent to that comment, the SEC staff changed its long stated view that acquisitions of oil and gas entities should not result in the creation of goodwill. As a result, the SEC staff removed the comment from Issue 98-11 in order to eliminate the implication that it is not appropriate to record goodwill resulting from the acquisition of an oil and gas company. Nonetheless, companies should follow the guidance in Issue 98-11 for business combinations involving oil and gas companies when goodwill is not recognized.

If on the other hand goodwill is recognized, the accounting is the same as for any other enterprise where positive goodwill exists. Assume the same facts above except that the fair value of the properties is $90. The following equation is used:

X	=	$R(NA - TB) + P - NA$
where R	=	Tax rate
NA	=	Fair value of the net assets purchased, excluding deferred taxes
TB	=	Tax basis of the net assets purchased
P	=	Purchase price

If X is positive, the amount of goodwill to be recorded equals X. Furthermore, although goodwill technically is a temporary difference requiring deferred taxes, Statement 109 specifically exempts goodwill for which amortization is not deductible for tax purposes from deferred tax accounting. As a result, no deferred taxes are recorded as a result of recording nonamortizable goodwill. The following examples assume amounts assigned to goodwill are not amortizable for tax purposes.

To illustrate, assume:

Purchase price (P) = \$100
Fair market value (FMV) of net assets (NA) before deferred tax liability (DTL) = \$90
Tax rate (R) = 40%
Tax basis of net assets (TB) = \$0

Using the equation described previously:

$X = R(NA - TB) + P - NA$
or
$\$46 = .4(\$90 - \$0) + \$100 - \$90$

Thus, goodwill exists and equals \$46.
The computation of deferred income taxes is:*

$DTL = R(NA - TB)$
or
$\$36 = .4(\$90 - \$0)$

Entry to record purchase:

Oil and gas assets	\$940	
Goodwill	\$46	
Deferred tax liability		\$ 36
Cash		\$100

Proof:

[(Assets – Liabilities) – Tax basis] × R should equal \$36
[(\$90 – \$0) – \$0].4 = \$36

Question: If a valuation allowance is established as part of a nontaxable business combination in which goodwill is not recognized, should the subsequent reduction in that valuation allowance be credited to the oil and gas properties or to income tax expense (assuming there are no identified intangible assets acquired as part of the purchase)?

Response: Consistent with Issue 98-11, if a valuation allowance is established as part of a nontaxable business combination in which goodwill is not recognized, the reduction in the valuation allowance should be reflected as a reduction in income tax expense. Statement 109 provides that after all intangible assets acquired as part of the purchase have been eliminated, any further benefit from the reduction of a valuation allowance should be reflected in income. Oil and gas properties are tangible assets and should not be reduced for the subsequent recognition of acquired tax benefits. If goodwill is recognized, any reduction in the valuation allowance should first reduce goodwill, then noncurrent intangible assets, then income tax expense.

---

* Because it is not amortizable for tax purposes, goodwill is not included in net assets for purposes of computing deferred taxes.

30-12. Change in the Tax Bases of Assets and Liabilities as a Result of an LBO

Question: Leveraged buyout (LBO) transactions accounted for pursuant to EITF Issue No. 88-16, "Basis in Leveraged Buyout Transactions," frequently result in "NEWCO's" financial reporting carrying amount of its investment in OLDCO being partially based on continuing stockholders' predecessor basis and partially based on fair value (e.g., assume that NEWCO's investment in OLDCO determined under Issue 88-16 is to be reported 30% at predecessor basis and 70% at fair value). Issue 88-16 is based on an analogy to a step acquisition and only to the extent of new stockholders' interests in NEWCO (70% in this example) is there considered to be a purchase transaction. When the tax bases of OLDCO's assets and liabilities are unaffected by the LBO, temporary differences are created by the change to fair value for the percentage of all assets and liabilities that are treated as purchased by Issue 88-16 (70% in this example). The deferred tax effects of those temporary differences are treated as a liability assumed (or asset acquired) in the allocation of purchase price.

In other situations, the tax bases of *all* of OLDCO's assets and liabilities are affected by the LBO (i.e., the transaction is a taxable business combination). In that situation, temporary differences are created by the change in tax basis of the portion of the carrying amount of assets and liabilities that is unchanged for financial reporting purposes (30% in the previous example—the portion that Issue 88-16 concludes should not be adjusted to fair value). Should the tax effect of those temporary differences (the temporary differences related to the 30% for which the financial reporting bases did not change) be included in the allocation of purchase price to the portion treated as purchased (70% in this example—the effect being an adjustment of goodwill) or should the tax effect of those temporary differences be charged or credited directly to equity?

Response: Statement 109 does not address such a situation. We believe that reasonable arguments can be made for either approach and therefore that either approach is acceptable. Example 30-12A illustrates the effect of a change in tax basis on the accounting for a leveraged buyout.

Example 30-12A

Assumptions for the Base Case (Case 1)

NEWCO borrows $19,000 and uses the proceeds and $700 cash from management (the new investors) plus 30 shares of NEWCO stock to purchase all OLDCO stock. OLDCO was previously wholly owned by Parent Company.

Continued on page 134

Continued from page 133

The transaction is a nontaxable business combination (i.e., OLDCO's tax basis in the individual assets and liabilities carries over).

Parent Company's predecessor basis equals OLDCO book value.

The tax rate is 50%.

Change in Assumptions for Comparative Case (Case 2)

The transaction is a taxable business combination.

The purchase price (and amount borrowed) increase by the amount of the deferred taxes eliminated ($11,000).

Ownership Interests Before and After the Transaction

	OLDCO			NEWCO	
	Shares	Book Value	Fair Value	Shares	Fair Value
Parent Company	100	$10,000	$20,000	30	$ 300
Management	0	0	0	70	700
	100	$10,000	$20,000	100	$1,000

Balance Sheets at Date of Acquisition

	OLDCO			
			Fair Value	
	Books	Tax	Case 1	Case 2
Assets (no goodwill)	$12,000	$10,000	$ 32,000	$32,000
Liabilities, except deferred taxes	(1,000)	(1,000)	(1,000)	(1,000)
Deferred tax liability	(1,000)	0	(11,000)	0
Equity	$10,000	$ 9,000	$ 20,000	$31,000

Method of Acquisition of OLDCO Interest

	Case 1	Case 2
Sources of cash:		
Debt	$19,000	$30,000
Common equity (70 shares × $10)	700	700
	19,700	30,700
NEWCO stock issued to Parent Company	300	300
OLDCO fair value	$20,000	$31,000

Continued on page 135

Continued from page 134

Summary of Accounting

		Case 1	Case 2
Valuation:			
Retained interest (based on predecessor basis)	30%	$3,000	$3,000
New interest (based on fair value)	70%	14,000	21,700
Basis of NEWCO investment in OLDCO		17,000	24,700
Less NEWCO debt		(19,000)	(30,000)
NEWCO common equity		($2,000)	($5,300)

Analysis of NEWCO Equity Account

	Case 1	Case 2
Stock issued to Parent Company valued at predecessor basis	$3,000	$3,000
Less deemed dividend to Parent Company (30% × new debt)	(5,700)	(9,000)
Stock issued to management (new investor) valued at fair value	700	700
	($2,000)	($5,300)

Reconciliation of Equity Amounts

The difference in NEWCO equity between Case 1 and Case 2 (and the carrying amounts of NEWCO's investment in OLDCO) is due to the step-up in tax basis of the 30% of OLDCO assets that are valued at carryover basis for financial reporting purposes:

New tax basis of assets	$32,000
Old tax basis of assets	10,000
Step-up in basis of assets	22,000
Percentage of NEWCO valued at carryover basis	30%
	6,600
Tax rate	50%
Tax effect of the step-up in basis that could be credited to equity in Case 2	$ 3,300

If the $3,300 tax effect of the step-up in tax basis of the assets valued at carryover basis for financial reporting is credited to NEWCO equity, NEWCO's equity will be the same ($2,000) in both a carryover tax basis situation and taxable transaction. Therefore, we believe it is preferable to credit the $3,300 in this example to equity, but there is no requirement to do so. Alternatively, the entire tax effect of the step-up in tax basis of assets could be accounted for as part of the allocation of purchase price (the net effect being a reduction in the carrying amount of NEWCO's investment in OLDCO) on

Continued on page 136

Continued from page 135

the theory that the "extra" tax basis is a direct result of the acquisition of OLDCO by NEWCO and that acquisition is accounted for as a business combination.

If deferred taxes related to the change in tax basis of the portion of the carrying amount of assets and liabilities that are unchanged for financial reporting purposes (the 30% in this example) are charged or credited directly to equity as part of the deemed dividend to the carryover shareholders, one further issue may need to be considered. What should be done with a reduction in an existing valuation allowance (related to the 30% in this example)? In an actual step acquisition, if the transaction would allow the acquiring enterprise to reduce its existing valuation allowance, the reduction in the valuation allowance would be accounted for as part of the purchase. We believe reductions in existing valuation allowances caused by a LBO should likewise be treated as part of the purchase. That is, the reduction in the valuation allowance would reduce the recorded amount of any goodwill related to the portion purchased (70% in this example). This approach is also consistent with comments made by the SEC Observer on EITF Issue No. 90-12, "Allocating Basis to Individual Assets and Liabilities for Transactions within the Scope of Issue No. 88-16." The SEC Observer stated, "[T]he entire NOL carryforward (that existed at the date of the LBO) should be viewed as an acquired carryforward." (See Interpretation 30-13 for the subsequent accounting when a valuation allowance is established as part of the opening balance sheet of a LBO company.)

30-13. Subsequent Accounting for Effects of Changes in a Valuation Allowance Recognized as Part of the Opening Balance Sheet of an LBO Company

Question: Assume a valuation allowance is recognized as part of the opening balance sheet of an enterprise accounting for a leveraged buyout (LBO) pursuant to EITF Issue No. 88-16, "Basis in Leveraged Buyout Transactions." Should subsequent reductions in that valuation allowance be credited to income, goodwill, or directly to equity?

Response: We believe the best analogy is to the guidance in Statement 109 for acquired tax benefits. Statement 109 requires that subsequent reductions of a valuation allowance related to acquired tax benefits first reduce goodwill, second reduce other identified intangibles, and third reduce income tax expense. This guidance is consistent with the view expressed by the SEC Observer in EITF Issue No. 90-12, "Allocating Basis to Individual Assets and Liabilities for Transactions within the Scope of Issue No. 88-16."

30-14. Reduction in a Valuation Allowance Initially Established When Emerging From Bankruptcy (or a Quasi Reorganization) as the Result of a Business Combination

Question: Assume that an enterprise emerges from bankruptcy, qualifies for fresh-start accounting, and provides a valuation allowance for its net deferred tax asset. Subsequently, the enterprise acquires another enterprise and reduces its valuation allowance as the result of that business combination. Should the reduction in the valuation allowance be accounted for as part of the purchase (as indicated in paragraph 266 of Statement 109) or accounted for as required by AICPA Statement of Position (SOP) 90-7, *Financial Reporting by Entities in Reorganization Under the Bankruptcy Code*?

Response: Neither Statement 109 nor SOP 90-7 contemplated such an interaction between the provisions of the two documents. Although arguments can be made for either approach, we believe the arguments for treating the reduction in valuation allowance as prescribed by SOP 90-7 (see Interpretation 37-3 for guidance on how enterprises emerging from bankruptcy should account for the subsequent recognition of tax benefits) are more persuasive.

Further, we understand the SEC staff has addressed the same question with a registrant that had a valuation allowance that related to pre-quasi reorganization deferred tax assets and required that the benefit from the reduction in the valuation allowance be recognized directly to equity.

30-15. Tax Effects of Expensing Acquired Research and Development Costs in Business Combinations

Question: FASB Statement No. 2, *Accounting for Research and Development Costs*, as interpreted in FASB Interpretation (FIN) No. 4, *Applicability of FASB Statement No. 2 to Business Combinations Accounted for by the Purchase Method*, requires that amounts allocated to research and development costs in a business combination be charged to expense at the date of consummation of the business combination. In a nontaxable business combination (i.e., a business combination in which the acquired entity's tax bases in its assets and liabilities are carried forward), the amount allocated to research and development costs for financial reporting will generally have no tax basis because the amounts expended for research and development in prior periods were expensed as incurred for tax purposes by the acquired enterprise prior to acquisition. Should deferred taxes be provided on the initial basis difference related to the research and development costs (and then immediately credited to income when the research and development costs are expensed)?

Response: For nontaxable business combinations, EITF Issue No. 96-7, "Accounting for Deferred Taxes on In-Process Research and Development Activities Acquired in a Purchase Business Combination," addresses whether a deferred tax liability should be recognized at the consummation date of a purchase combination for the initial difference (prior to the expensing of the amount allocated to in-process research and development activities) between the amounts assigned for financial reporting purposes and the underlying tax basis.

The EITF reached a consensus in Issue 96-7 that for nontaxable business combinations, the amount allocated to the acquired in-process research and development activities should be charged to expense on a gross basis and no tax benefit should be reflected when the in-process research and development activities have no tax basis (as would normally be the case in a nontaxable business combination).

Absent the need for a valuation allowance, to the extent the in-process research and development activities have a tax basis, there should be a tax benefit reflected in the income statement for the in-process research and development activities charged to expense.

For taxable business combinations (i.e., a business combination treated as the acquisition of assets for tax purposes), the acquired in-process research and development activities should be considered as an identifiable intangible asset for financial reporting and tax purposes. Most intangible assets acquired in a taxable business combination are amortizable for tax purposes over 15 years without any need to specifically identify and value the individual intangible assets. Those intangible assets are often referred to as "Section 197" intangible assets. Due to the valuation process that is required to be performed in order to determine the value of the acquired in-process research and development activities for financial reporting purposes, the tax balance sheet should generally reflect the same amount for tax purposes. Absent the need for a valuation allowance, there should be a tax benefit reflected in the income statement for the in-process research and development activities charged to expense for the transactions described in this paragraph.

To summarize, the following statement is true whether the business combination is the acquisition of stock (nontaxable) or the acquisition of assets (taxable). Any book/tax basis difference related to in-process research and development activities that: (*a*) exists prior to expensing the amount allocated to in-process research and development activities is *not* a temporary difference and (*b*) is created by the immediate expensing of such costs is a temporary difference.

30-16. [Not Used]

30-17. [Not Used]

30-18. [Not Used]

30-19. Accounting for Differences Between the Financial Reporting and Tax Bases of Goodwill When Goodwill Is Amortizable for Tax Purposes

Question: Paragraph 9(d) of Statement 109 "[p]rohibits recognition of a deferred tax liability or asset related to goodwill (or the portion thereof) for which amortization is not deductible for tax purposes." How should differences between the financial reporting and tax bases of goodwill be accounted for in a jurisdiction, such as the U.S. federal jurisdiction, which provides for deductions for the amortization of goodwill?

Response: Paragraphs 262 and 263 of Statement 109 provide the relevant guidance.

As indicated in paragraph 262 of Statement 109:

> . . . the reported amount of goodwill and the tax basis of goodwill are each separated into two components as of the combination date for purposes of deferred tax calculations. The first component of each equals the lesser of (a) goodwill for financial reporting or (b) tax-deductible goodwill. The second component of each equals the remainder of each, that is, (1) the remainder, if any, of goodwill for financial reporting or (2) the remainder, if any, of tax-deductible goodwill. Any difference that arises between the book and tax basis of that first component of goodwill in future years is a temporary difference for which a deferred tax liability or asset is recognized based on the requirements of this Statement. No deferred taxes are recognized for the second component of goodwill. If that second component is an excess of tax-deductible goodwill over the reported amount of goodwill, the tax benefit for that excess is recognized when realized on the tax return, and that tax benefit is applied first to reduce to zero the goodwill related to that acquisition, second to reduce to zero other noncurrent intangible assets related to that acquisition, and third to reduce income tax expense.

The above is fairly self-explanatory when goodwill for financial reporting is greater than goodwill for tax purposes. Any differences related to the first component of goodwill at future reporting dates (e.g., differences caused by using different lives for the amortization of goodwill for financial reporting and tax purposes) should be treated as temporary differences and deferred taxes should be recognized. The second component (the excess of financial reporting goodwill over tax goodwill) is not treated as a temporary difference. That is, no deferred taxes are recognized related to that amount of goodwill and the tax effect of the related amortization will be a reconciling item between a corporation's reported tax expense for a period and its "expected" tax expense.

The accounting for goodwill subsequent to the business combination is not as straightforward when goodwill for tax purposes is greater than goodwill for financial reporting purposes. Paragraph 262 prohibits immediately recognizing a tax asset for that excess of tax goodwill over book goodwill and requires that when the benefit for that excess is recognized (when realized on a tax return), it is recognized consistent with the initial recognition of an acquired tax benefit. That is, the benefit is applied first to reduce goodwill. The complication arises because, in this fact situation, any goodwill for financial reporting is being treated as a temporary difference and therefore any reduction in financial reporting goodwill as a result of recognizing a tax benefit for the excess tax goodwill has a deferred tax consequence. A simultaneous equation is required to determine the "tax-on-tax-effect" and thereby the appropriate reduction in financial reporting goodwill. Paragraph 263 of Statement 109 has a numerical example of the subsequent accounting. The simultaneous equation to determine the reduction in financial reporting goodwill works as follows: multiply the resultant of the following equation $(1 + [\text{tax rate}/(1 - \text{tax rate})])$ by the tax benefit realized from the amortization of the excess tax goodwill. Therefore, if the tax deduction from the amortization of "excess" tax goodwill is $100 and the appropriate tax rate is 35%, the tax benefit realized (assuming no valuation allowance is required) is $35. The reduction in goodwill and the "charge in lieu of tax" as a result of the $35 tax benefit would be $53.85. The proof is as follows: the charge in lieu of tax ($53.85) should equal the current tax benefit ($35) plus the deferred tax benefit of the total reduction in the goodwill related temporary difference (.35 × $53.85 = $18.85).

30-20. Accounting for the Tax Benefits of Nonqualified Options Issued in a Business Combination

Question: An enterprise will receive tax deductions from an employee's exercise of nonqualified employee options that were issued or granted in connection with a business combination. How should the enterprise account for such tax benefits?

Response: How the enterprise should account for such tax benefits depends on the accounting standard used by the enterprise to account for its share-based compensation arrangements (i.e., APB Opinion No. 25, *Accounting for Stock Issued to Employees*, FASB Statement No. 123, *Accounting for Stock-Based Compensation*, or FASB Statement No. 123 (Revised 2004), *Share-Based Payment*) and whether or not the options were vested at the date of the business combination.

Opinion 25

Vested. Question 17 of FASB Interpretation (FIN) No. 44, *Accounting for Certain Transactions involving Stock Compensation*, provides that vested stock options issued by an acquirer in exchange for outstanding stock options held by employees of the acquiree should be measured at fair value and considered part of the purchase price paid for the acquired business. In Issue 29(a) of EITF Issue No. 00-23, "Issues Related to the Accounting for Stock Compensation under APB Opinion No. 25 and FASB Interpretation No. 44," the EITF concluded that: (*a*) a deferred tax asset should not be recognized at the date of the business combination for the expected tax benefits related to vested nonqualified options, (*b*) any future deduction realized up to the fair value of the nonqualified stock options recognized as part of the purchase price should be recognized as an adjustment to the purchase price of the acquired business, and (*c*) any future deductions realized in excess of the fair value of the nonqualified stock options recognized as part of the purchase price should be recognized in additional paid-in capital.

Unvested. Question 17 of FIN 44 provides that a portion of the fair value of unvested stock options issued by an acquirer in exchange for outstanding stock options held by employees of the acquiree should be considered part of the purchase price paid for the acquired business and a portion should be allocated to unearned compensation and recognized as compensation cost over the remaining future vesting period. In Issue 29(b) of Issue 00-23, the EITF concluded that: (*a*) the proportion of unvested employee stock options granted as consideration in a business combination equal to the proportion of the vesting period that has expired as of the consummation date should be accounted for in the same manner as vested stock options and (*b*) the proportion of unvested nonqualified stock options granted in a business combination related to the future vesting period (compensatory period) should be the same as for nonqualified stock options granted to employees absent a business combination. The accounting for the tax consequences of the unvested options should follow the pretax accounting. That is, the tax effects of the portion of the unvested options accounted for in the same manner as vested stock options should be accounted for as described previously for vested stock options and the tax effect of the remaining portion should be accounted for in the same manner as for nonqualified stock options granted to employees absent a business combination.

Statement 123 and Statement 123R

Acquiring enterprises that follow the guidance in Statement 123 or Statement 123R should account for the exchange of stock options in a business combination in a manner similar to an exchange of stock options under Opinion 25 and FIN 44, except that the amount, if any, allocated to unearned compensation should be based on fair value not intrinsic value. In addition, in the event that the fair value of the stock options given is greater than the fair value of the stock options surrendered, the excess fair value is compensation cost. That compensation cost should be accrued over the vesting period of the new award, if any, or immediately, if the award is fully vested.

We believe that any future excess tax benefits under Statement 123 or Statement 123R should be accounted for in the same manner as described previously for future excess tax benefits under Opinion 25.

Commentary: For additional guidance on this issue, including examples, refer to Interpretation 141.38-6, "Income Tax Benefits From Nonqualified Stock Options Issued in a Nontaxable Business Combination," in the publication, *CCH Accounting for Business Combinations, Goodwill, and Other Intangible Assets.*

30-21. Subsequent Recognition of Acquired Tax Benefits

Question: If a valuation allowance is recognized for some or all of an acquired enterprise's deferred tax asset at the acquisition date, how is any subsequent reduction in that valuation allowance recognized in the financial statements?

Response: That valuation allowance will be reduced when the associated deferred tax asset either: (*a*) expires unused or (*b*) meets the criteria in Statement 109 for recognition. When a fully reserved deferred tax asset expires unused, the gross deferred tax asset and the valuation allowance are reduced by the same amount with no effect on the net deferred tax asset that is recognized. Absent a contingent consideration agreement that might result in the recognition of an additional cost of the acquired entity, when the associated deferred tax asset meets the criteria in Statement 109 for recognition, the valuation allowance is reduced and the tax benefit is recognized as follows:

- First, to reduce to zero any goodwill related to the acquisition;
- Second, to reduce to zero, on a pro rata basis, other noncurrent intangible assets related to the acquisition; and
- Third, to reduce income tax expense.

If a contingent consideration agreement exists that might result in the recognition of an additional cost of the acquired entity, we believe the enterprise should, by analogy, follow the guidance in paragraph 46 of FASB Statement No. 141, *Business Combinations,* and defer reducing noncurrent intangible assets other than goodwill and income tax expense until the contingency is resolved.

Question: Assume that subsequent to the acquisition date the enterprise's valuation allowance increases due to losses incurred in those subsequent periods. Assume it is now appropriate to eliminate a portion of the valuation allowance. What portion of the valuation allowance is reduced first—the portion related to the tax benefits acquired in the business combination or the portion subsequently recognized for losses incurred after the acquisition date?

Response: Paragraph 268 of Statement 109 addresses this issue. If determinable by provisions in the tax law, the ordering should be based on specific identification. That is, if the tax benefit recognized through the reduction in the valuation allowance can be attributed to acquired tax benefits or subsequently created tax benefits by looking to the provisions of the tax law, the ordering for financial statement recognition should follow that same attribution. If it is not possible to determine by provisions in the tax law whether the tax benefit recognized is attributable to acquired or subsequently created tax benefits, the reduction in the valuation allowance should be prorated between a reduction of: (*a*) goodwill and other noncurrent intangible assets and (*b*) income tax expense.

30-22. Accounting for a Decrease in a Valuation Allowance Associated With Acquired Deferred Tax Assets Due to a Change in Tax Law

Question: Should a decrease in valuation allowance for deferred tax assets acquired as part of a business combination that is caused by a change in tax law be treated as the effect of a change in tax law and recognized as part of the income tax provision related to income from continuing operations (pursuant to paragraph 27 of Statement 109) or be treated as the initial recognition of an acquired tax benefit (pursuant to paragraph 30 of Statement 109)?

Response: The EITF concluded in EITF Issue No. 99-15, "Accounting for Decreases in Deferred Tax Asset Valuation Allowances Established in a Purchase Business Combination As a Result of a Change in Tax Regulations," that such a decrease in valuation allowance for deferred tax assets acquired in a business combination should be treated as the effect of a change in tax law and accounted for pursuant to paragraph 27 of Statement 109 as a part of the income tax provision related to income from continuing operations. The consensus states that it "applies to any reduction in the valuation allowance that otherwise would not have been recognized except for the change in tax law or regulation, regardless of whether the valuation allowance is reduced in the period of the tax law change or a subsequent period."

30-23. Present Value of Future Profits Is an Intangible Asset

Question: As discussed in Interpretation 30-21, subsequent reductions in valuation allowances related to tax benefits acquired in business combinations reduce goodwill, then other noncurrent intangible assets, and finally any remaining amount is recognized as a reduction of income tax expense. The EITF observed in EITF Issue No. 92-9, "Accounting for the Present Value of Future Profits Resulting from the Acquisition of a Life Insurance Company," that industry practice is to amortize the present value of future profits (PVP) using an interest method with accrual of interest added to the unamortized balance. In the Status section of Issue 92-9, the FASB staff concludes that PVP is not within the scope of FASB Statement No. 144, *Accounting for the Impairment or Disposal of Long-Lived Assets*. Is PVP an intangible asset that should be reduced before acquired tax benefits are recognized as a reduction of income tax expense?

Response: Yes. PVP represents the present value of estimated net cash flows embedded in the contracts acquired as part of the acquisition of a life insurance company. The accounting model applied to PVP is fairly unique for an intangible asset and is based on an analogy to the accounting for deferred policy acquisition costs. Nevertheless, PVP is an intangible asset and should be treated as such when recognizing subsequent reductions in valuation allowances related to tax benefits acquired in a business combination.

Opinion 23 and U.S. Steamship Enterprise Temporary Differences

EXCERPT FROM OFFICIAL TEXT

Opinion 23 and U.S. Steamship Enterprise Temporary Differences

31. A deferred tax liability is not recognized for the following types of temporary differences unless it becomes apparent that those temporary differences will reverse in the foreseeable future:

    a. An excess of the amount for financial reporting over the tax basis of an investment in a foreign subsidiary or a foreign corporate joint venture as defined in APB Opinion No. 18, *The Equity Method of Accounting for Investments in Common Stock*, that is essentially permanent in duration

    b. Undistributed earnings of a domestic subsidiary or a domestic corporate joint venture that is essentially permanent in duration that arose in fiscal years beginning on or before December 15, 1992[9]

    c. "Bad debt reserves" for tax purposes of U.S. savings and loan associations (and other "qualified" thrift lenders) that arose in tax years beginning before December 31, 1987 (that is, the base-year amount)

    d. "Policyholders' surplus" of stock life insurance companies that arose in fiscal years beginning on or before December 15, 1992.

    The indefinite reversal criterion in Opinion 23 shall not be applied to analogous types of temporary differences.

---

[9] A last-in, first-out (LIFO) pattern determines whether reversals pertain to differences that arose in fiscal years beginning on or before December 15, 1992.

INTERPRETATION

31-1. Distinguishing Foreign From Domestic Subsidiaries

Question: Prior to Statement 109, the criteria for recognition of deferred taxes related to outside basis differences (i.e., an excess of the amount for financial reporting over the tax basis of an investment in a subsidiary) were the same for foreign and domestic subsidiaries. However, Statement 109 has different criteria for the recognition of potential tax liabilities related to outside basis differences of foreign and domestic subsidiaries. When is a subsidiary a foreign subsidiary? For example, is a Puerto Rican subsidiary of a U.S. company a foreign or domestic subsidiary?

Response: We believe enterprises should look to the Internal Revenue Code (IRC) in determining whether a subsidiary is foreign or domestic. If a subsidiary of a U.S. company is a domestic subsidiary under the IRC, it is a domestic subsidiary under Statement 109. It is our understanding that Puerto Rican subsidiaries are domestic subsidiaries (in some cases with special tax credits, but nevertheless domestic subsidiaries) under the IRC and therefore we believe they should be treated as domestic subsidiaries under Statement 109.

Statement 109 requires deferred taxes be provided for an outside basis difference in a domestic subsidiary, including basis differences caused by undistributed earnings, unless "the tax law provides a means by which the reported amount of that investment can be recovered tax-free and the enterprise expects that it will ultimately use that means."

Accordingly, any tax consequences of an outside basis difference related to an investment in a Puerto Rican subsidiary should be considered a temporary difference unless, as stated in paragraph 33 of Statement 109, "the tax law provides a means by which the reported amount of that investment can be recovered tax-free and the enterprise expects that it will ultimately use that means." If there is not a "prudent and feasible" method of recovering an investment in a Puerto Rican subsidiary without incurring the Puerto Rican withholding (tollgate) taxes, that tax should be accrued as the temporary difference arises (i.e., as the income of the Puerto Rican subsidiary is included in financial reporting income).

A similar question arises when a U.S. company elects to treat its Canadian subsidiary as a domestic subsidiary for purposes of its U.S. federal tax return (such an election is allowed under IRC Section 1504(d)). In that situation, the U.S. tax law views the Canadian subsidiary as a domestic subsidiary and therefore we believe the subsidiary should be treated as a domestic subsidiary under Statement 109 when computing U.S. federal deferred taxes.

Outside basis differences in other tax jurisdictions will need to be evaluated using the criteria in paragraph 33 to determine if the outside basis difference is a temporary difference. For example, assume a French first tier subsidiary of a U.S. company has a French subsidiary and a German subsidiary. In preparing the French first tier subsidiary's consolidated financial statements for inclusion in the U.S. consolidated financial statements, any outside basis difference related to the French first tier subsidiary's investment in its French subsidiary is an outside basis difference related to a *domestic* subsidiary that needs to be evaluated under paragraph 33 of Statement 109 using the provision of the French tax law. Any outside basis difference related to the French first tier subsidiary's investment in its German subsidiary is an outside basis difference in a foreign subsidiary.

31-2. Temporary Differences Related to CTA

Question: Are deferred taxes required to be provided for temporary differences related to cumulative translation adjustments (CTA)? If so, is the effect recorded in the income statement or through the CTA?

Response: Under FASB Statement No. 52, *Foreign Currency Translation,* the assets and liabilities of a foreign investee whose functional currency is the local currency are translated from that foreign currency into the reporting currency using current exchange rates. Translation adjustments that result from this process are not recognized in income, but are reported as a separate component of equity (CTA). The translation process, after a change in exchange rates, gives rise to a temporary difference in an amount equal to the translation adjustment because it changes the investor's financial reporting carrying amount of its investment in the foreign investee, but the investor's tax basis in its investment in the foreign investee does not change. This is true regardless of whether the investor consolidates the investee or accounts for its investment under the equity method.

Whether the investor is required to recognize deferred taxes on this temporary difference depends on whether the recognition would result in a deferred tax asset or deferred tax liability, the ownership of the investee, and whether the indefinite reversal criterion of Opinion 23 applies.

Potential deferred tax asset (investee is a subsidiary or corporate joint venture). Paragraph 34 of Statement 109 precludes recognition of a deferred tax asset for an excess of tax basis over financial reporting basis in an investment in a subsidiary or corporate joint venture unless "it is apparent that the temporary difference will reverse in the foreseeable future" (see Interpretation 34-1). Accordingly, deferred taxes generally should not be recognized on translation adjustments that would result in a net deferred tax asset.

Potential deferred tax asset (investee accounted for under the equity method). A deferred tax asset should be recorded for the excess of tax basis over financial reporting basis of an equity method investment that is not a subsidiary or corporate joint venture.

Potential deferred tax liability (investee is a subsidiary or corporate joint venture). Whether the investor is required to recognize a deferred tax liability depends on whether the indefinite reversal criterion of Opinion 23 applies to the outside basis difference of that investee. If deferred taxes are not provided as is allowed by Opinion 23, deferred taxes would not be provided on temporary differences resulting from a translation adjustment relating to the investment in that investee. If the indefinite reversal criterion of Opinion 23 does not apply, deferred taxes would be provided.

Potential deferred tax liability (investee accounted for under the equity method). A deferred tax liability should be recorded for the excess of financial reporting basis over tax basis of an equity method investment that is not a subsidiary or corporate joint venture.

Opinion 23 only applies to investments in foreign subsidiaries and foreign joint ventures that are essentially permanent in duration. Investors cannot apply the indefinite reversal criterion of Opinion 23 to other investments in foreign investees and therefore are required to provide deferred taxes on any difference between its financial reporting and tax basis of its investment in such other foreign investees.

The incremental tax effect of the translation adjustments (see Interpretation 35-1) should be charged or credited to other comprehensive income related to CTA with one exception described in the following paragraph.

Paragraph 51 of Statement 109 states that the effect of initially applying Statement 109 should be recorded as a cumulative effect of a change in accounting principle, except for tax benefits related to items that are *excluded* from comprehensive income. Paragraph 36 indicates that a translation adjustment under Statement 52 is an example of an item that is *included* in comprehensive income. Therefore, any tax effects of translation adjustments at adoption of Statement 109 should be charged or credited to income as part of the cumulative effect of adoption. This transition approach is a practical one, as it eliminates the need to allocate the transition adjustment between equity and income for gains and losses included in comprehensive income but excluded from net income.

Question: Enterprises sometimes enter into transactions to hedge their net investment in a foreign subsidiary (e.g., through the use of a forward contract). Gains and losses on such hedging transactions are credited or charged directly to the CTA. If such a hedging transaction creates a temporary difference, but the parent does not provide for deferred taxes related to translation adjustments, should deferred taxes be recognized for the temporary difference created by the hedging transaction?

Response: Yes. The future tax consequences of the hedging transaction undertaken by the parent are not indefinitely deferred and therefore deferred taxes should be recognized for temporary differences created by such hedging transactions. The current and deferred tax effects of hedging transactions for which the pretax effects are credited or charged to CTA should also be charged or credited directly to the CTA.

31-3. Deferred Tax Accounting for "Outside Basis Differences" When a Change From Consolidation to Equity or Cost Method of Accounting Occurs

Question: Assume an enterprise has an unfavorable outside basis difference related to its investment in a subsidiary (i.e., an excess of the amount for financial reporting over the tax basis of its investment in a subsidiary) and that no deferred tax liability has been previously recognized. The enterprise sells or otherwise disposes of a part of its investment in that subsidiary (e.g., exchanges a portion of its investment in the subsidiary for an investment in another enterprise) such that the enterprise's remaining investment is accounted for following the equity or cost method of accounting. What deferred tax accounting is required, if any, for the basis difference in the enterprise's remaining investment in its former subsidiary?

Response: Whether deferred tax accounting is required depends on whether the former subsidiary was a foreign or domestic subsidiary. For a remaining investment in a foreign subsidiary, enterprises should continue to follow APB Opinion No. Opinion 23, *Accounting for Income Taxes—Special Areas,* for the remaining "outside basis difference." (See paragraph 13 of Opinion 23, as amended by Statement 109.) Consider Example 31-3A.

Example 31-3A

Parent Company sells 60% of its previously wholly owned foreign subsidiary, Company B. Immediately prior to the sale, Parent Company had a $100 outside basis difference related to its investment in Company B and, immediately after the sale, has a basis difference related to its remaining 40% investment in Company B of $55. (Assume Parent Company had purchased its interest in Company B over time. By using specific identification of shares sold for tax purposes, Parent Company was able to reduce the gain reported on the sale of its 60% interest [thereby reducing current taxable income] by $15. This in turn increases the basis difference in the

Continued on page 150

Continued from page 149

remaining investment by $15.) In this example, Parent Company should continue to follow Opinion 23 for $40 of the $55 basis difference (Opinion 23 only exempts basis differences arising during the period the investee was a subsidiary—the $15 basis difference did not arise while the investee was a subsidiary). The $15 increase in the remaining basis difference caused by the use of specific identification of securities sold for tax purposes and all future basis differences (e.g., subsequent periods' undistributed earnings) should be treated as temporary differences.

Parent Company could also cease consolidation of its previously wholly owned foreign subsidiary, Company B, as a result of Company B issuing new shares and diluting Parent Company's investment from 100% to 40% of the outstanding common stock of Company B. For example, assume Parent Company's investment in Company B is $200 for financial reporting and $100 for tax purposes immediately preceding Company B's stock offering. After the stock offering, Parent Company's now 40% investment in Company B is $250 for financial reporting (Company B issued its stock for an amount in excess of its net book value and Parent Company recognized a "SAB 51" gain of $50—see Interpretation 33-1 for a definition of a SAB 51 gain), but its tax basis in its investment in Company B is still $100. In that fact situation, Parent Company should treat the $50 increase in the basis difference as a temporary difference and should continue to follow Opinion 23 for the $100 basis difference that existed prior to Company B's stock offering.

Unfavorable basis differences related to remaining investments in former domestic subsidiaries are now taxable temporary differences and deferred taxes should be provided no later than when it becomes apparent that the reversal of that basis difference will have a future tax consequence (which could not be later than the time the parent reflects the sale of the controlling interest in its former subsidiary). However, to the extent the basis difference relates to undistributed earnings for periods beginning on or prior to December 15, 1992, that portion of the basis difference is "grandfathered" by Statement 109 and the Opinion 23 criteria for recognition applies (i.e., a deferred tax liability is not recognized unless it becomes apparent that the temporary difference will reverse in the foreseeable future).

The parent's sale or disposal of its controlling interest in the subsidiary should be classified as a discontinued operation if the presentation requirements are met as described in FASB Statement No. 144, *Accounting for the Impairment or Disposal of Long-Lived Assets,* (one requirement being that the parent cannot retain an ownership interest in its former subsidiary that is accounted for under the equity method). (See Interpretation 34-2.)

31-4. Future Percentage-of-Taxable-Income Bad-Debt Deductions of a Savings and Loan Association

Question (from FASB Staff Implementation Guide, Question 8):

The temporary difference under current U.S. federal tax law for the "base-year tax reserve"[5] of a savings and loan association is one of the exceptions to comprehensive recognition of deferred taxes under Statement 109. If a deferred tax liability is not recognized for that temporary difference, should a savings and loan association anticipate future percentage-of-taxable-income (PTI) bad-debt deductions in determining the deferred tax liability for other types of temporary differences?

---

5 The "base-year tax reserve" is the income tax bad-debt reserve that arose in tax years beginning before December 31, 1987 as provided by the income tax law changes enacted in 1986. The excess of a tax bad-debt reserve over the base-year reserve is a temporary difference for which deferred taxes must be provided.

Response (from FASB Staff Implementation Guide, Question 8):

No. Under Statement 109, deferred tax assets and liabilities for temporary differences are measured by applying the enacted tax rate expected to apply to taxable income in the periods in which the deferred tax asset or liability is expected to be realized or settled. Currently this would be the 35 percent rate for associations for which graduated rates are not a significant factor. It is not permissible to reduce a deferred tax liability so determined by anticipated future PTI bad-debt deductions for the same reasons that other special deductions may not be anticipated as set forth in paragraphs 231 and 232. However, for associations for which graduated tax rates are a factor, the existence of the PTI bad-debt deductions may result in a lower average graduated tax rate being applied in measuring deferred taxes if it results in taxable income falling into a lower tax rate bracket.

31-5. Opinion 23 Exception Related to the Tax Bad Debt Reserve of a Savings and Loan Association

Question: Statement 109 states that a deferred tax liability is not recognized for the temporary difference related to "bad debt reserves" for tax purposes of U.S. savings and loan associations (and other "qualified" thrift lenders) that arose in tax years beginning before December 31, 1987 (i.e., the base-year amount) unless it becomes apparent that those temporary differences will reverse in the foreseeable future.

How is the book reserve for bad debts treated? Is there any limitation on recognizing a deferred tax asset related to the book reserve for bad debts?

Response: The *entire* amount of the book bad debt reserve is a deductible temporary difference. In contrast, the "indefinite reversal" notion in Opinion 23 is applied to the entire amount of the base-year bad debt reserve for tax purposes. However, the excess, if any, of the total tax reserve over the base-year amount is a taxable temporary difference. An excess would be caused, for example, by percentage-of-taxable-income bad debt deductions in excess of experience method bad debt deductions since 1988. Consider Example 31-5A.

Example 31-5A

Assume a savings and loan association has adopted Statement 109 as of January 1, 1993. As of that date, Association's total bad debt reserve for tax purposes is $10, its base-year tax bad debt reserve is $8, and its book bad debt reserve is $5. Association should recognize a deferred tax liability related to a $2 taxable temporary difference ($10 – $8) and a deferred tax asset related to a $5 deductible temporary difference (the entire book reserve). The deferred tax asset should be assessed for realizability the same as any other deferred tax asset. Association would disclose in its notes to the financial statements that it has a base-year bad debt reserve for tax purposes of $8 for which deferred taxes have not been provided.

Question: Certain events would cause the entire tax bad debt reserve to be included in gross taxable income (e.g., changing the charter of the institution to a bank charter) and other events would force a reduction in the base-year reserve for tax purposes. For example, if the association's qualifying loans are reduced below a certain level, the base-year bad debt reserve for tax purposes is also reduced (technically this reduction is accomplished by a limitation on tax deductions for charge-offs, not by a direct increase in gross taxable income, but the effect is the same). How is a reduction in the base-year bad debt reserve for tax purposes accounted for?

Response: A reduction in the base-year bad debt reserve for tax purposes will increase taxes currently payable (by limiting the tax deduction for bad debt charge-offs) and, all other things being equal, result in a higher than normal effective tax rate (there is no offset from deferred taxes because a deferred tax liability has not previously been established). Further, if circumstances indicate that the association is likely to pay income taxes in future years because of a known or expected reduction in the base-year bad debt reserve, income taxes attributable to that reduction should be accrued as tax expense of the current period as that portion of the reserve would no longer meet the indefinite reversal criterion of Opinion 23. For example, if the association makes a decision to shrink its qualifying loans over the next several years, the reduction in the base-year bad debt reserve for tax purposes that is expected to occur as a result of that reduction in qualifying loans should be treated as a taxable temporary difference and a deferred tax liability should be recognized in the period that decision is made. Future increases in the base-year bad debt reserve for tax purposes should not be anticipated.

A related but different question arises when the association currently has the ability under the tax law to obtain a tax deduction to "refill" the base-year tax bad debt reserve, but has elected to defer taking that deduction until a future year. In this situation, the deferred deduction may be recognized as a deferred tax asset (and assessed as any other deferred tax asset for realizability) because it is currently within the association's control to obtain that tax deduction (i.e., no future events are required to occur, such as a future increase in qualifying loans). The timing of taking that deduction on the tax return should not change the association's financial reporting.

Question: Assume: (*a*) an association's base-year bad debt reserve for tax purposes decreased in prior years due to a reduction in qualifying loans, (*b*) the decrease in the bad debt reserve increased tax expense in those prior years as described in the first part of the previous question and answer (above), and (*c*) the association's qualifying loans increase in the current year and thereby increase the base-year bad debt reserve for tax purposes. Is the current year increase in the base-year bad debt reserve for tax purposes treated as a temporary difference that requires recognition of a deferred tax liability?

Response: Statement 109 is not clear on this question. We believe it is acceptable to conclude that the increase in the base-year bad debt reserve for tax purposes in this example should *not* be treated as a temporary difference unless it is apparent that the temporary difference will reverse in the foreseeable future. Therefore, current tax expense is reduced (by the deduction allowed to restore the base-year bad debt reserve) without an offsetting increase in deferred tax expense.

Question: In August 1996, legislation was passed that repealed the section of the Internal Revenue Code that has historically afforded saving and loan associations favorable treatment when calculating their tax bad debt deduction. What are the financial reporting implications of that legislation?

Response: The legislation results in savings and loan associations effectively being treated as banks for federal income tax purposes. Pursuant to the legislation, all savings and loan associations are required to recapture their tax bad debt reserve in an amount equal to the difference between their allowable beginning reserve (the greater of the amount determined as if the savings and loan association were always a bank or the savings and loan association's base-year reserve) and their actual tax basis reserve for bad debts for the first tax year beginning after 1995.

As discussed previously, savings and loan associations have provided deferred taxes for all temporary differences related to their bad debt reserves except for temporary differences related to the bad debt reserve for tax purposes that arose in tax years beginning before December 31, 1987 (the base year). Accordingly, thrifts have previously established deferred tax liabilities related to the portion of their bad debt reserve for tax purposes that will now be recaptured.

The base-year reserve is not permanently forgiven and is subject to recapture on the occurrence of certain events. Therefore, consistent with prior years, saving and loan associations will need to continue to disclose in their notes to the financial statements the amount of deferred tax liability not recognized in their financial statements related to the base-year reserve for tax purposes temporary difference and the types of events that would cause the temporary difference to become taxable.

31-6. [Not Used]

31-7. Scope of Opinion 23 Exception Related to Investments in Foreign Subsidiaries

Question: Opinion 23, as amended by Statement 109, provides that a deferred tax liability is not recognized for the temporary difference created by an excess of the amount for financial reporting over the tax basis of an investment in a foreign subsidiary (an "outside" basis difference) as long as that excess (usually caused by undistributed earnings) is indefinitely invested in the foreign subsidiary. Does that exception to providing deferred taxes also apply to inside basis differences of the foreign subsidiary that meet the indefinite reversal criterion?

Response: No. We believe that the previous exception only applies to the *investor's* (i.e., the parent's) tax consequences of the reversal of the outside basis difference. Further, Statement 109 specifically precludes the application of the indefinite reversal criterion to temporary differences other than those listed in paragraph 31 of Statement 109. In addition, if the previous exception were applied to a foreign subsidiary's inside basis differences, a foreign corporation's results of operations under U.S. generally accepted accounting principles would differ depending on whether it was a subsidiary of a U.S. corporation—a result that we believe is not credible. The application of this principle to a specific fact situation was addressed by the EITF in EITF Issue No. 93-16, "Application of FASB Statement No. 109 to Basis Differences within Foreign Subsidiaries That Meet the Indefinite Reversal Criterion of APB Opinion No. 23." (See Interpretation 31-8.)

31-8. Monetary Restatement of Fixed Assets in Italy

Question: In Italy, fixed assets have occasionally been restated for tax purposes to compensate for the effects of inflation. The "other side" of the journal entry to increase the tax basis of fixed assets is a credit to "revaluation surplus." The revaluation surplus becomes taxable only in the event of a liquidation of the enterprise or in the case of distribution of the earnings associated with the revaluation surplus. The sale of the related fixed asset does not trigger the revaluation surplus into taxable income. Therefore, it is possible to defer the tax related to the revaluation surplus indefinitely. However, it is our understanding that there is no feasible strategy that would allow the shareholders of the enterprise to ultimately realize their investment in the enterprise without the enterprise incurring a tax liability for the revaluation surplus. Neither the increase in carrying amount of the fixed assets or the revaluation surplus is recognized for U.S. generally accepted accounting principles reporting.

Do the increases in the carrying amounts of the fixed assets for tax purposes and the revaluation surplus create temporary differences under Statement 109?

Response: Yes. The increase in the carrying amount of the fixed assets for tax purposes creates a deductible temporary difference (or reduces a taxable temporary difference) and the revaluation surplus creates a taxable temporary difference. (We believe the revaluation surplus represents deferred income on the tax basis balance sheet). In EITF Issue No. 93-16, "Application of FASB Statement No. 109 to Basis Differences within Foreign Subsidiaries That Meet the Indefinite Reversal Criterion of APB Opinion No. 23," the EITF addressed this issue and concluded that the indefinite reversal criterion of Opinion 23 should not be applied to the taxable temporary difference related to the revaluation surplus. Therefore, at the time of a monetary restatement of fixed assets, an Italian enterprise's gross deferred tax assets and gross deferred tax liabilities will both increase (and offset) such that no net deferred tax expense or benefit would be expected to be recognized at the date of a monetary restatement. Similarly, as the restated fixed assets are depreciated for tax purposes in the future, there is no net effect on income tax expense since the deferred tax expense (resulting from the reduction in the deductible temporary difference related to the fixed assets) will be offset by the current tax benefit (resulting from the additional depreciation for tax purposes).

However, there is an exception to that conclusion when the local currency is not the functional currency as documented in paragraph 9(f) of Statement 109:

> Prohibits recognition of a deferred tax liability or asset for differences related to assets and liabilities that, under FASB Statement No. 52, *Foreign Currency Translation,* are remeasured from the local currency into the functional currency using historical exchange rates and that result from (1) changes in exchange rates or (2) indexing for tax purposes.

This exception therefore will apply to U.S. multinationals that use the U.S. dollar as the functional currency for their Italian subsidiaries. In such situations, no deferred tax asset or liability would be recognized at the date of the monetary revaluation—the increase in the fixed assets and revaluation surplus for tax purposes is the result of "indexing" and therefore paragraph 9(f) would apply. As the fixed assets are depreciated or sold, the additional tax deductions received as a result of the monetary revaluation would be treated as permanent items in the current period's financial statements (current tax expense would be reduced as a result of the additional tax deductions). Similarly, the tax effect of the revaluation surplus would be charged to income when triggered into taxable income (or when inclusion in taxable income becomes probable).

31-9. Recognition of a Deferred Tax Liability for a Portion of an Outside Basis Difference

Question: Paragraph 31(a) of Statement 109 states that a deferred tax liability is not required for an excess of the amount for financial reporting purposes over the tax basis of an investment in a foreign corporate joint venture that is essentially permanent in duration or in a foreign subsidiary. Is it possible to provide deferred taxes for a portion, but not all, of the future tax consequences of the outside basis difference? For example, the parent company intends to remit only a portion of the previously unremitted earnings.

Response: Yes. Paragraph 31(a) of Statement 109 is not an all-or-nothing proposition. With respect to foreign subsidiaries or foreign corporate joint ventures, Statement 109 expanded the Opinion 23 exception from only basis differences caused by unremitted earnings to the entire outside basis difference. However, paragraph 12 of Opinion 23 has not been changed and that paragraph allows for recognition of a tax liability for a portion of unremitted earnings when some but not all earnings will be remitted in the foreseeable future. Under Statement 109, this concept now applies to the portion of the outside basis difference that does not relate to unremitted earnings as well. However, the enterprise must respect the actual workings of the applicable tax law. That is, if the tax law provides that the portion of the outside basis difference caused by "A" will be reported as taxable income before the portion of the outside basis difference caused by "B," it would not be appropriate to provide deferred taxes for the future tax consequence of the portion of the outside basis difference caused by "B," but not provide for the future tax consequence of the portion of the outside basis difference caused by "A."

31-10. Dividends Received Deduction on the Repatriation of Certain Foreign Earnings Allowed by the 2004 Tax Act

Question: The American Jobs Creation Act of 2004 (2004 Tax Act) provides for a tax deduction of 85% of certain foreign earnings that are repatriated in either an enterprise's last tax year that began before the enactment date of the 2004 Tax Act (October 22, 2004) or the first tax year that begins during the one-year period beginning on the date of enactment. We understand that a number of enterprises are requesting that Congress or the Treasury Department provide additional clarifying guidance on certain key elements of the repatriation provision.

APB Opinion No. 23, *Accounting for Income Taxes—Special Areas,* contains a presumption that a deferred tax liability should be recognized for taxable temporary differences related to investments in foreign subsidiaries or corporate joint ventures that are essentially permanent in duration. However, Opinion 23 provides that this presumption can be overcome "if sufficient evidence shows that the subsidiary has invested or will invest the undistributed earnings indefinitely." When an enterprise no longer has such sufficient evidence, the enterprise is required to immediately recognize a deferred tax liability for any tax temporary differences related to investments in foreign subsidiaries or corporate joint ventures that are essentially permanent in duration.

The limited time dividends received deduction contained in the 2004 Tax Act may cause enterprises to consider repatriating foreign earnings that the enterprises had previously concluded were indefinitely reinvested in foreign operations. If an enterprise in this situation has not yet finished its evaluation of the dividends received deduction contained in the 2004 Tax Act as of its first reporting date after the enactment of the 2004 Tax Act, should that enterprise provide deferred taxes on all of its taxable temporary differences related to investments in foreign subsidiaries or corporate joint ventures that are essentially permanent in duration?

Response: The FASB staff addressed this situation in FASB Staff Position (FSP) 109-2, "Accounting and Disclosure Guidance for the Foreign Earnings Repatriation Provision within the American Jobs Creation Act of 2004." The FASB staff concludes in this FSP that "the lack of clarification of certain provisions within the Act and the timing of the enactment necessitate a practical exception to the Statement 109 requirement to reflect in the period of enactment the effect of a new tax law." In this situation, FSP FAS 109-2 allows an enterprise to apply the provisions of Statement 109 as it decides on a plan for reinvestment or repatriation of its unremitted earnings.

FSP FAS 109-2 also contains specific disclosure requirements for periods during which an enterprise has not completed its evaluation of the repatriation provision of the 2004 Tax Act and a disclosure requirement for the period in which the enterprise completes its evaluation of the repatriation provision of the 2004 Tax Act. The following disclosure requirements are listed in Paragraphs 9 and 10 of FSP FAS 109-2:

> The following information shall be disclosed for an enterprise that has not yet completed its evaluation of the repatriation provision for purposes of applying Statement 109 for each period for which financial statements covering periods affected by the Act are presented:
>
> a. A summary of the repatriation provision as it applies to the enterprise, including the status of the enterprise's evaluation of the effects of the repatriation provision as well as the evaluation's expected completion date.
>
> b. If the entity makes decisions in stages, the effect on income tax expense (or benefit) for any amounts that have been recognized under the repatriation provision. For annual financial statements, any effect should be shown separately in the same place (either on the face of the income statement or in the footnotes) that the amounts of current and deferred taxes are disclosed for the period.

> c. The range of reasonably possible amounts of unremitted earnings that is still being considered for repatriation as a result of the repatriation provision and the related potential range of income tax effects of such repatriation.[2] If the related range of income tax effects of such repatriation cannot be reasonably estimated at the time of issuance of its financial statements, an enterprise shall provide a statement to that effect.
>
> d. Pro forma financial data for any effect of the repatriation provision (at a minimum, the effect on income tax expense (or benefit)) if the enterprise decides on a plan for reinvestment or repatriation of foreign earnings (as a result of the repatriation provision) subsequent to the date of its financial statements but prior to the issuance of those financial statements.
>
> The following information shall be provided in an enterprise's financial statements for the period in which it completes its evaluation of the repatriation provision:
>
> a. The total effect on income tax expense (or benefit) for amounts that have been recognized under the repatriation provision. For annual financial statements, any effect should be shown separately in the same place (either on the face of the income statement or in the footnotes) that the amounts of current and deferred taxes are disclosed for the period.
>
> ---
>
> [2] The ranges disclosed shall exclude amounts that have been recognized in the financial statements.

Finally, the FASB staff states that analogies should not be made to FSP FAS 109-2.

EXCERPT FROM OFFICIAL TEXT

32. A deferred tax liability shall be recognized for the following types of taxable temporary differences:

    a. An excess of the amount for financial reporting over the tax basis of an investment in a domestic subsidiary that arises in fiscal years beginning after December 15, 1992
    b. An excess of the amount for financial reporting over the tax basis of an investment in a 50-percent-or-less-owned investee except as provided in paragraphs 31(a) and (b) for a corporate joint venture that is essentially permanent in duration
    c. "Bad debt reserves" for tax purposes of U.S. savings and loan associations (and other "qualified" thrift lenders) that arise in tax years beginning after December 31, 1987 (that is, amounts in excess of the base-year amount).

    The tax effects of temporary differences related to deposits in statutory reserve funds by U.S. steamship enterprises that arose in fiscal years beginning on or before December 15, 1992 and that were not previously recognized shall be recognized when those temporary differences reverse or in their entirety at the beginning of the fiscal year for which this Statement is first applied.

INTERPRETATION

32-1. Tax Effects of Investments in Partnerships

Question: A partnership is not subject to federal income tax; rather, it is an entity through which income or loss "flows through" to partners that are taxable in their individual capacities on their distributive shares of partnership taxable income. How should a partner compute the deferred tax consequences of its investment in a partnership?

Response: The objective of the computation is to recognize the partner's future tax consequences of recovering the financial reporting carrying amount of its investment in the partnership.

Some partnership agreements provide for disproportionate allocations of certain expenses, such as depreciation, or vary the percentage of taxable income allocated to the individual partners over time. Accounting for the tax effects of investments in those partnerships is complex, but the objective is still the same—recognize the partner's future tax consequences of recovering the financial reporting carrying amount of its investment in the partnership.

32-2. Measurement of Deferred Tax Liabilities and Assets Related to Investments in Equity Method Investees

Question: In the United States, the future tax consequences of an excess of the amount for financial reporting over the tax basis of an investment in an equity method investee is dependent on the means of recovering the investment in the investee (i.e., the investor could recover its investment through a sale of the stock of the investee or through dividends). How should an investor measure the future tax consequences of a temporary difference related to its investment in an equity method investee?

Response: Paragraph 237 of Statement 109 states that such temporary differences should be "measured using currently enacted tax rates applicable to capital gains, ordinary income, and so forth, based on the expected type of taxable or deductible amounts in future years." Paragraph 237 also specifically states that the "computation of a deferred tax liability for undistributed earnings based on dividends should also reflect any related dividends received, deductions or foreign tax credits, and taxes that would be withheld from the dividend." However, it is important to analyze what needs to occur for a temporary difference related to an investment in an investee to reverse as a dividend. That is, in some future period, the investee must dividend an amount in excess of its earnings in that future period—an unusual occurrence. We believe it will be relatively unusual that a conclusion will be reached that an investor expects its investee to dividend amounts in some future periods that are greater than it earns in those future periods.

EXCERPT FROM OFFICIAL TEXT

33. Whether an excess of the amount for financial reporting over the tax basis of an investment in a more-than-50-percent-owned domestic subsidiary is a taxable temporary difference must be assessed. It is not a taxable temporary difference if the tax law provides a means by which the reported amount of that investment can be recovered tax-free and the enterprise expects that it will ultimately use that means. For example, under current U.S. federal tax law:

    a. An enterprise may elect to determine taxable gain or loss on the liquidation of an 80-percent-or-more-owned subsidiary by reference to the tax basis of the subsidiary's net assets rather than by reference to the parent company's tax basis for the stock of that subsidiary.

    b. An enterprise may execute a statutory merger whereby a subsidiary is merged into the parent company, the minority shareholders receive stock of the parent, the subsidiary's stock is cancelled and no taxable gain or loss results if the continuity of ownership, continuity of business enterprise, and certain other requirements of the tax law are met.

    Some elections for tax purposes are available only if the parent company owns a specified percentage of the subsidiary's stock. The parent company sometimes may own less than that specified percentage, and the price per share to acquire a minority interest may significantly exceed the per share equivalent of the amount reported as minority interest in the consolidated financial statements. In those circumstances, the excess of the amount for financial reporting over the tax basis of the parent's investment in the subsidiary is not a taxable temporary difference if settlement of the minority interest is expected to occur at the point in time when settlement would not result in a significant cost. That could occur, for example, toward the end of the life of the subsidiary, after it has recovered and settled most of its assets and liabilities, respectively. The fair value of the minority interest ordinarily will approximately equal its percentage of the subsidiary's net assets if those net assets consist primarily of cash.

INTERPRETATION

33-1. Excess of Financial Reporting Basis Over Tax Basis (or Vice Versa) of Investments in Subsidiaries ("Outside" Basis Differences)

Question: A parent company's basis in its investment in a subsidiary is shown as a one line item in the parent's "corporate" (unconsolidated) balance sheet and is eliminated when the subsidiary is consolidated in preparing the group's consolidated financial statements. Differences between a parent's financial reporting and tax bases of an investment in a subsidiary (outside basis differences) could be caused by undistributed earnings, SAB 51 gains (i.e., an increase in the financial reporting basis of a parent's investment in a subsidiary caused by the subsidiary issuing stock for value in excess of book basis—so named because of the SEC staff accounting bulletin that allows such gain, in certain circumstances, to be included in income), or certain other transactions. What deferred tax accounting, if any, is required for outside basis differences?

Response: The type of deferred tax accounting depends on whether the outside basis difference is a potential deferred tax asset (an excess of tax basis over financial reporting basis) or potential deferred tax liability (an excess of financial reporting basis over tax basis) and, if a potential deferred tax liability, whether it relates to a foreign or domestic subsidiary.

Potential deferred tax asset. Paragraph 34 of Statement 109 precludes recognition of a deferred tax asset for an excess of tax basis over financial reporting basis in an investment in a subsidiary (foreign or domestic) unless "it is apparent that the temporary difference will reverse in the foreseeable future." We believe a reasonable approach is to link the foreseeable future to the time period used in FASB Statement No. 144, *Accounting for the Impairment or Disposal of Long-Lived Assets*, as part of the criteria for classifying an asset as held for sale—that is, generally a one-year time horizon. At the point in time it is apparent that the temporary difference will reverse in the foreseeable future, an excess of tax basis over financial reporting basis in an investment in a subsidiary should be recognized as an asset and an assessment made of the need for a valuation allowance. (See Interpretations 34-1 and 34-2.)

Potential deferred tax liability-investment in foreign subsidiary. The indefinite reversal criterion of Opinion 23, as amended by Statement 109, applies to the entire outside basis difference. (See Interpretations 31-1 to 31-3 and 31-7 to 31-8 for related interpretations.)

Potential deferred tax liability-investment in domestic subsidiary. Undistributed earnings of a domestic subsidiary that arose in tax years beginning on or before December 15, 1992, are "grandfathered" by Statement 109 and the indefinite reversal criterion of Opinion 23 continues to apply. Opinion 23, as amended by Statement 109, does not apply to any other outside basis differences related to domestic subsidiaries (regardless of when it arose). Therefore, deferred tax liabilities must be recognized for those outside basis differences unless there is "no future tax consequence" associated with the reversal of the outside basis difference. (Please note that a temporary difference is a basis difference for which the future reversal of the difference will have a future tax consequence).

Paragraph 33 of Statement 109 addresses this issue and states that an outside basis difference "is not a taxable temporary difference if the tax law provides a means by which the reported amount of that investment can be recovered tax-free and the enterprise expects that it will ultimately use that means." Paragraph 33 goes on to indicate that if a significant cost would be incurred to execute the recovery of the investment in a tax-free manner, the basis difference would be considered a temporary difference and recognition of deferred taxes would be required. The thrust of paragraph 33 is that, because of elections permitted under current U.S. federal income tax law, deferred tax liabilities will generally not be required for outside basis differences in the U.S. federal tax jurisdiction. Exceptions to this general rule will occur when: (*a*) the parent owns less than 80% of the subsidiary and acquiring the additional interest in the subsidiary necessary to execute a statutory merger (or liquidation by reference to inside tax basis) and thereby eliminate the outside basis difference with no tax consequence is not substantially within the parent's control, (*b*) it is not reasonable to expect that the parent will ultimately effect a tax-free recovery of its investment in the subsidiary, or (*c*) the parent expects to incur a significant cost to accomplish the statutory merger (see Interpretation 33-4 for more guidance related to significant cost and the acquisition of minority interests; see also Interpretation 31-1 for another situation in which an outside basis difference related to a "domestic" subsidiary requires deferred taxes).

Situations that would not meet the control requirement of paragraph 33 include situations in which: (*a*) the parent needs a regulator's approval to increase its ownership interest in the subsidiary (or the regulator's approval to merge with the subsidiary or liquidate the subsidiary) and the regulatory approval is other than perfunctory or (*b*) the parent has agreed with the other shareholders of the subsidiary not to increase its ownership interest in the subsidiary.

Another issue relates to how the enterprise "expects" to recover the investment in the subsidiary. Possible ways to recover the investment in the subsidiary include: (*a*) the sale of the investment in the subsidiary; (*b*) dividends from the subsidiary; (*c*) holding the investment in the subsidiary until virtually all of the assets in the subsidiary have been converted to cash and all liabilities settled, acquiring sufficient additional stock in the subsidiary to allow for a statutory merger (at this point, book value and fair value should be approximately the same), and then merging the parent and subsidiary in such a manner that the outside basis difference is eliminated without any tax consequence; or (*d*) a combination of (*a*), (*b*), or (*c*).

If the enterprise expects to recover its investment, in whole or in part, through (*a*) or (*b*), a temporary difference exists and deferred taxes should be provided. Consider Example 33-1A.

> **Example 33-1A**
>
> Assume the outside basis difference relates to undistributed earnings of a 60% owned Subsidiary and Parent expects those undistributed earnings to be distributed in the form of a dividend at some future date. That outside basis difference should be treated as a temporary difference and a deferred tax liability (net of the benefit for the dividends received deduction) should be accrued.

33-2. Accounting for Outside Basis Differences Caused by a Subsidiary's Inside Basis Differences

Question: Interpretation 33-1 addresses when deferred tax accounting is required for outside basis differences and indicates that the answer depends on whether the outside basis difference is a potential deferred tax asset (an excess of tax basis over financial reporting basis) or potential deferred tax liability (an excess of financial reporting basis over tax basis) and, if a potential deferred tax liability, whether it relates to a foreign or domestic subsidiary.

Deferred tax liabilities are not recognized under Statement 109 for outside basis differences related to: (*a*) investments in foreign subsidiaries for which the indefinite reversal criterion of Opinion 23 is met, (*b*) investments in domestic subsidiaries for which there is a means that is substantially within the parent's control by which the reported amount of that investment can be recovered tax-free and the parent expects it will ultimately use that means, and (*c*) undistributed earnings of a domestic subsidiary that arose in fiscal years beginning on or before December 15, 1992, and for which the indefinite reversal criterion of Opinion 23 is met.

Assume a parent company has a wholly owned domestic subsidiary that is included in the consolidated tax return, but it is not substantially within the parent company's control to effect a statutory merger of the subsidiary into the parent or to liquidate the subsidiary (e.g., the parent company would be required to ask for regulatory approval for a merger or liquidation of the subsidiary and such approval is not perfunctory). How should a parent company's *outside* basis difference caused by a subsidiary's *inside* basis differences be treated? That is, do such outside basis differences fall into one of the exceptions to providing deferred taxes listed in the previous paragraph or should deferred taxes be provided for such outside basis differences?

Response: Because enterprises usually have the ability to recover their investments in subsidiaries that are part of a consolidated tax return group without triggering any additional tax related to outside basis differences caused by a subsidiary's inside basis differences, typically no deferred taxes need to be provided. Example 33-2A illustrates how an outside basis difference is created by a subsidiary's inside basis differences and how the outside basis difference reverses without any additional tax consequences to the parent.

Example 33-2A

Example assumptions:

ParentCo establishes SubCo with a $100 cash investment.

SubCo uses that cash to purchase a single depreciable asset for $100.

SubCo's depreciation expense in Year 1 is $20 for financial reporting and $40 for tax purposes.

SubCo's pretax book income for Year 1 is $50 (net income of $30) and taxable income is $30 (SubCo has no temporary differences other than the temporary difference related to its single depreciable asset and there are no permanent items in Year 1).

ParentCo has no income or loss in Year 1 other than its equity pickup of SubCo's income.

The tax rate in Year 1 is 40% (state taxes and the U.S. federal alternative minimum tax are ignored for purposes of this example). SubCo has paid its currently payable taxes for Year 1 of $12 prior to the end of the year.

SubCo's balance sheet is as follows at the end of Year 1:

	Book	Tax		Book	Tax
Cash	$ 58	$ 58	Deferred tax liability	$ 8	$ 0
Asset	80	60	Equity	130	118
	$138	$118		$138	$118

ParentCo's balance sheet is as follows at the end of Year 1:

Investment in SubCo	$130	$118	Equity	$130	$118

In this example, ParentCo has a $12 outside basis difference ($130 – $118) related to its investment in SubCo that is caused by a SubCo inside basis difference (a property basis difference caused by the use of an accelerated depreciation method for tax purposes).

Continued on page 167

Continued from page 166

If ParentCo would sell its investment in SubCo at the end of Year 1 for its book carrying amount ($130), ParentCo would have no pretax accounting income and $4.80 ([$130 – $118] × 40%) of tax expense. Should ParentCo accrue and charge to expense $4.80 of deferred tax at the end of Year 1?

Not necessarily. ParentCo can recover its investment in SubCo without incurring the $4.80 of tax by either: (*a*) operating SubCo until the asset is completely depreciated for book and tax (at which time ParentCo would no longer have an outside basis difference related to its investment in SubCo and the sale of SubCo at book value would not trigger any additional tax) or (*b*) causing SubCo to sell its asset for its book carrying amount, which would trigger the payment of SubCo's deferred tax liability and thereby eliminate ParentCo's outside basis difference related to its investment in SubCo. Because there is a means that is substantially within the parent's control by which the reported amount of that investment can be recovered tax-free and the parent expects it will ultimately use that means, the outside basis difference is not a taxable temporary difference.

The same issue arises (i.e., a ParentCo outside basis difference caused by a SubCo inside basis difference) if SubCo has an Opinion 23 temporary difference for which it does not provide deferred taxes (e.g., SubCo is a savings and loan association and does not provide deferred taxes related to its base-year bad debt reserve for tax purposes). However, the approach of the preceding paragraph (i.e., assuming sale or liquidation of the subsidiary) is inconsistent with the logic for not providing deferred taxes on the Opinion 23 temporary difference at the SubCo level (Opinion 23 is based on an "indefinite reversal" notion) and therefore would not appear to work for an outside basis difference caused by a subsidiary's Opinion 23 inside basis difference.

However, we understand that the FASB staff has concluded that the Opinion 23 exception at the subsidiary level carries through to the parent's outside basis difference related to its investment in the subsidiary. Therefore, ParentCo would not be required to provide deferred taxes on the portion of its outside basis difference related to its investment in SubCo that is caused by a SubCo Opinion 23 temporary difference.

33-3. Deferred Tax Accounting on Inside Basis Differences of a Subsidiary in the Consolidated Financial Statements of the Parent

Question: Assume that an enterprise (Parent) acquires another enterprise (Sub) in a nontaxable business combination (i.e., Parent purchased the stock of Sub and Sub's tax basis in its individual assets and liabilities was unaffected by the purchase) and that Sub has significant taxable temporary differences as a result of allocating the purchase price for financial reporting purposes to assets acquired and liabilities assumed in the business combination. Further assume that the most significant taxable temporary difference relates to a temporary difference that will not reverse in the foreseeable future (e.g., a temporary difference related to last-in, first-out [LIFO] inventory).

If Parent expects to realize its investment in Sub by selling the stock of Sub (in the same manner as it purchased Sub—in a nontaxable transaction) prior to the expected reversal of the LIFO-related temporary difference, should Parent's consolidated financial statements reflect a deferred tax liability related to the LIFO temporary difference?

Response: Yes. If Parent sells Sub in a nontaxable transaction, the purchaser of Sub would assume the deferred tax liability. The fact that a liability of a subsidiary is expected to be assumed by an eventual purchaser before the liability is otherwise settled does not make the liability any less of a liability in the consolidated financial statements. This is true whether the liability in question is a deferred tax liability, long-term debt, or any other liability of the subsidiary. At a 1993 EITF meeting, the FASB staff announced that it believes that Statement 109 requires deferred taxes to be recognized related to LIFO inventory basis differences whether the LIFO inventory is held at the parent or in a subsidiary (see *EITF Abstracts*, Topic D-31, "Temporary Differences Related to LIFO Inventory and Tax-to-Tax Differences").

33-4. Acquisition of Minority Interest of a Subsidiary at an Amount in Excess of Book Value

Question: An excess of the amount for financial reporting over the tax basis of an investment in a domestic subsidiary (an outside basis difference) is not a taxable temporary difference if: (*a*) the tax law provides a means by which the reported amount of that investment can be recovered tax-free, (*b*) the enterprise expects that it will ultimately use that tax-free means to recover its investment in the subsidiary, and (*c*) the enterprise does not expect to incur a significant cost to recover its investment in such a tax-free manner. Paragraph 33 of Statement 109 discusses two examples of how a U.S. enterprise may recover its investment in a domestic subsidiary tax-free. In some situations, the enterprise does not currently own enough stock of the subsidiary to be able to effect such a tax-free liquidation or merger. In such cases, Statement 109 allows enterprises to assess the likelihood that it will settle the minority interest toward the end of the life of the subsidiary, after the subsidiary has recovered and settled most of its assets and liabilities, respectively. At that time, the fair value of the minority interest ordinarily will approximately equal its percentage of the subsidiary's net assets (if those net assets consist primarily of cash) and settlement of the minority interest would not result in a significant cost. If such an "end of time" scenario is expected to occur, any outside basis difference in the stock of the subsidiary would not be considered a taxable temporary difference and a deferred tax liability would not be required. How is this end of time scenario affected by an acquisition of the minority interest in an amount in excess of the current book value of the minority interest?

Response: It is our understanding that the FASB staff has taken the position that at the time a decision is made that indicates a significant cost will be incurred to settle the minority interest (e.g., a decision to acquire some or all of the minority interest for an amount in excess of the current book value of the minority interest), the outside basis difference becomes a taxable temporary difference and a deferred tax liability (with a charge to income) should be recognized. When the tax-free merger or liquidation is effected, the deferred tax liability that is no longer required should be reversed and reflected as a reduction of the purchase price of the minority interest.

We believe the answer depends on the reason for the acquisition of the minority interest. If the minority interest is acquired for substantive business reasons *other* than to effect the tax-free merger or liquidation, we do not believe deferred taxes need to be provided because there is no *incremental* significant cost to the enterprise to ultimately eliminate the outside basis difference with no tax consequence to the enterprise. Such substantive business reasons could be that the enterprise believes the subsidiary's stock is undervalued and therefore acquisition of the minority interest at the current market value makes economic sense, the enterprise wants to more fully integrate the parent and the subsidiary operations, and so forth.

However, if the enterprise acquires the minority interest at an amount in excess of the current book value of the minority interest in order to effect a tax-free merger or liquidation, the enterprise's expectations about incurring a significant cost to effect the tax-free merger or liquidation must have changed. That is, at the time the enterprise decides to acquire the minority interest at an amount in excess of the current book value of the minority interest, the enterprise no longer expects the outside basis difference to reverse in a manner that does not involve a significant cost and therefore the outside basis difference becomes a temporary difference and a deferred tax liability (with a charge to income from continuing operations) should be recognized for all of the outside basis difference not "grandfathered" by paragraph 31 of Statement 109. We believe that the acquisition of a minority interest followed shortly by the actual liquidation or merger would result in a rebuttable presumption that the acquisition of the minority interest was done in order to effect the liquidation or merger. When the tax-free merger or liquidation is effected, the deferred tax liability that is no longer required should be reversed and reflected as a reduction of the purchase price of the minority interest.

33-5. Deferred Tax Accounting for Investments in Entities Consolidated Pursuant to FIN 46R

Question: Enterprises may be required, pursuant to FASB Interpretation (FIN) No. 46 (Revised December 2003), *Consolidation of Variable Interest Entities,* to consolidate variable interest entities (VIEs) in which they have little or no equity ownership or voting rights. Do the principles in Statement 109 that apply to investments in subsidiaries consolidated pursuant to Accounting Research Bulletin (ARB) No. 51, *Consolidated Financial Statements,* also apply to investments in consolidated VIEs?

Response: Generally, yes. Just as with an investment in a subsidiary consolidated pursuant to ARB 51, it is important when evaluating the deferred tax consequences of an investment in a consolidated VIE to understand: (*a*) whether the consolidated VIE is a tax pass-through entity or a taxpaying (corporate) entity, (*b*) whether, if a corporate entity, the VIE will be a member of a consolidated tax return or a separate taxpayer, and (*c*) what temporary differences exist related to the parent's investment in the VIE.

However, because FIN 46R requires consolidation in situations in which the parent (primary beneficiary) may not have voting control of the VIE (a situation that does not occur with subsidiaries consolidated pursuant to ARB 51), the application of the principles in Statement 109 to a difference between a parent's financial reporting and tax bases of an investment in a consolidated VIE (an "outside basis difference") may differ from the application of those principles to an outside basis difference in a subsidiary consolidated pursuant to ARB 51. (See Interpretation 33-1 for guidance on applying Statement 109 to outside basis differences related to investments in subsidiaries consolidated pursuant to ARB 51.)

Potential deferred tax liability—outside basis difference related to an investment in a foreign consolidated VIE. Paragraph 12 of APB Opinion No. 23, *Accounting for Income Taxes—Special Areas,* as amended by Statement 109, provides:

> The presumption that all undistributed earnings will be transferred to the parent company may be overcome, and no income taxes should be accrued by the parent

> company, if sufficient evidence shows that the subsidiary has invested or will invest the undistributed earnings indefinitely ....

Paragraph 31(a) of Statement 109 extends that exception to the entire outside basis difference related to an investment in a foreign subsidiary. However, as stated in paragraph 170 of Statement 109:

> The underlying rationale for Opinion 23 is based on an enterprise's ability and intent to control the timing of the events that cause temporary differences to reverse and result in taxable amounts in future years.

We believe that enterprises with investments in foreign consolidated VIEs should carefully consider the facts and circumstances of each such investment to determine whether they possess the "ability and intent" to control the timing of the reversal of the temporary difference related to any outside basis difference related to the investment in the foreign VIE. If the enterprise does not possess the ability and intent to control the timing of the reversal of the temporary difference related to any outside basis difference in the foreign VIE, we believe the enterprise does not meet the conditions necessary to use the Opinion 23 exception and therefore should recognize a deferred tax liability related to any outside basis difference.

Potential deferred tax liability—outside basis difference related to an investment in a domestic consolidated VIE. Paragraph 33 of Statement 109 provides guidance on how to determine whether an outside basis difference related to an investment in a domestic subsidiary meets the definition of a temporary difference. Because that guidance was written in the context of outside basis differences of domestic subsidiaries consolidated pursuant to ARB 51 (i.e., consolidated due to the parent's voting control over the subsidiary), questions have arisen about how to apply that guidance to domestic VIE subsidiaries. Unlike Opinion 23, the guidance in paragraph 33 of Statement 109 is an application of the principles in Statement 109 (i.e., guidance on how to determine if a specific type of basis difference meets the definition of a temporary difference), not an exception to the principles of Statement 109. To determine whether deferred taxes should be provided for outside basis differences related to investments in consolidated domestic VIEs for which the parent does not have voting control, we believe enterprises should look to Statement 109's definition of a temporary difference. (See Interpretation 14-2 for guidance on how to determine whether book/tax basis differences are temporary differences.)

EXCERPT FROM OFFICIAL TEXT

34. A deferred tax asset shall be recognized for an excess of the tax basis over the amount for financial reporting of an investment in a subsidiary or corporate joint venture that is essentially permanent in duration only if it is apparent that the temporary difference will reverse in the foreseeable future. The need for a valuation allowance for that deferred tax asset and other deferred tax assets related to Opinion 23 temporary differences (for example, a deferred tax asset for foreign tax credit carryforwards or for a savings and loan association's bad-debt reserve for financial reporting) shall be assessed. Paragraph 21 identifies four sources of taxable income to be considered in determining the need for and amount of a valuation allowance for those and other deferred tax assets. One source is future reversals of temporary differences. Future reversals of taxable differences for which a deferred tax liability has not been recognized based on the exceptions cited in paragraph 31, however, shall not be considered. Another source is future taxable income exclusive of reversing temporary differences and carryforwards. Future distributions of future earnings of a subsidiary or corporate joint venture, however, shall not be considered except to the extent that a deferred tax liability has been recognized for existing undistributed earnings or earnings have been remitted in the past.

INTERPRETATION

34-1. Foreseeable Future

Question: Why does Statement 109 limit the recognition of a deferred tax asset for an excess of the tax basis over the amount for financial reporting of an investment in a corporate joint venture that is essentially permanent in duration or a subsidiary? Is the term "foreseeable future" defined?

Response: Because deferred tax liabilities for *taxable* outside basis differences (an excess of the amount for financial reporting over the tax basis of an investment in a corporate joint venture that is essentially permanent in duration or a subsidiary) will generally be recognized only if those temporary differences are expected to reverse in the foreseeable future, the FASB believes the same criterion should be applied to the recognition of deferred tax assets for *deductible* outside basis differences.

Statement 109 does not define the term "foreseeable future." We believe a reasonable approach is to link that term to the time period used in FASB Statement No. 144, *Accounting for the Impairment or Disposal of Long-Lived Assets*, as part of the criteria for classifying an asset as held for sale—that is, generally a one-year time horizon. At the point in time it is apparent that the temporary difference will reverse in the foreseeable future, the deductible outside basis difference should be recognized as an asset (and an assessment made of the need for a valuation allowance). This approach is also supported by the observation of the EITF in EITF Issue No. 93-17, "Recognition of Deferred Tax Assets for a Parent Company's Excess Tax Basis in the Stock of a Subsidiary That Is Accounted for as a Discontinued Operation," that "the criterion of paragraph 34 of Statement 109 is met at the Opinion 30 measurement date." (See Interpretation 34-2 for a discussion of that EITF issue and an illustration of the interaction of this provision of Statement 109 and Statement 144.)

34-2. Recognition of Deferred Tax Assets for a Parent Company's Excess Tax Basis in the Stock of a Subsidiary That Is Accounted for as a Discontinued Operation

Question: Assume an enterprise decides to sell a subsidiary that meets the requirements of FASB Statement No. 144, *Accounting for the Impairment or Disposal of Long-Lived Assets*, to be displayed as a discontinued operation. The parent company's tax basis in the stock of the subsidiary (outside tax basis) exceeds the financial reporting amount of its investment and the decision to sell the subsidiary makes it apparent that the basis difference in the stock of the subsidiary will reverse in the foreseeable future. Should the parent company now recognize the deferred tax asset for the temporary difference as called for by paragraph 34 of Statement 109 or is the recognition of the tax benefit precluded by Statement 144, which precludes recognizing gains on disposals of assets until realized?

Response: The EITF concluded in EITF Issue No. 93-17, "Recognition of Deferred Tax Assets for a Parent Company's Excess Tax Basis in the Stock of a Subsidiary That Is Accounted for as a Discontinued Operation," that Opinion 30 did not limit the recognition of deferred tax assets under paragraph 34 of Statement 109. Similarly, Statement 144 does not limit the recognition of deferred tax assets under paragraph 34 of Statement 109. In the previous fact pattern, the parent company should recognize a deferred tax asset for the excess of tax basis over the financial reporting basis of its investment in the subsidiary in its consolidated financial statements at the date it meets the criteria to display the assets as an asset held for sale. If a valuation allowance is not required for that deferred tax asset, we believe the deferred tax benefit should be shown as part of discontinued operations.

The EITF also noted that the same criterion should apply for the recognition of a deferred tax liability related to an excess of financial reporting basis over outside tax basis of an investment in a subsidiary. That is, the deferred tax consequences of temporary differences related to investments in foreign subsidiaries that were not previously recognized due to the provisions of Opinion 23 should be recognized (accrued with a charge to tax expense) no later than when it becomes apparent that the temporary difference will reverse in the foreseeable future. Similarly, the potential tax consequences of basis differences related to investments in domestic subsidiaries that were not previously recognized due to the provisions of paragraph 33 of Statement 109 should be recognized (accrued with a charge to tax expense) no later than when it becomes apparent that the reversal of that basis difference will have a future tax consequence.

In effect, the EITF concluded that Opinion 30 (now Statement 144) governs the pretax accounting for discontinued operations and Statement 109 governs the tax accounting. Therefore, an enterprise that anticipates a pretax gain on the disposition of a business would be precluded from recognizing that gain until realized but would be required to recognize (and expense) any previously unrecognized deferred tax liability, as described in the preceding paragraph, at the date it meets the criteria to display the business as an asset held for sale.

34-3. Foreseeable Future and the Realization of Tax Benefits in One of Two Jurisdictions

Question: Assume U.S. Corporation establishes a subsidiary in a foreign country (Foreign Sub) and that subsidiary incurs a loss in its first year of operations. Due to uncertainty about Foreign Sub's future prospects, a valuation allowance is established for its entire deferred tax asset. Because Foreign Sub's loss is recognized by U.S. Corporation for financial reporting purposes but the loss is not recognized for U.S. federal tax purposes, U.S. Corporation has a deductible outside basis difference related to its investment in its subsidiary (an excess of tax basis over the amount for financial reporting of its investment in its subsidiary) in the U.S. federal tax jurisdiction. U.S. Corporation's strategy will be to continually assess the subsidiary's performance/prospects over the next three to five years. If Foreign Sub does not meet targeted performance goals by the end of that period, the foreign operation will be disposed of and U.S. Corporation will be entitled to a deduction in its U.S. federal tax return for its investment in Foreign Sub. U.S. Corporation believes that, within five years, it will realize a tax benefit for Foreign Sub's first year loss—either through future profitable operations of Foreign Sub or through a deduction on its U.S. federal tax return (on an assumed disposition). In this fact situation, could U.S. Corporation tax affect Foreign Sub's loss in U.S. Corporation's consolidated financial statements by recognizing a U.S. deferred tax asset at the end of Year 1 for its deductible outside basis difference in Foreign Sub?

Response: The previous fact situation presents a reasonable economic argument for the recognition of a deferred tax asset; however, we believe U.S. Corporation should not recognize a deferred tax asset in the above situation. Although U.S. Corporation expects to receive a benefit in one tax jurisdiction or the other within approximately five years for the loss incurred by Foreign Sub, it does not know whether the deductible outside basis difference it has in the U.S. federal tax jurisdiction will provide U.S. Corporation with a tax deduction within the foreseeable future.

From a practical standpoint, the previous arguments made to recognize a deferred tax asset could be made about most foreign business operations that are currently incurring losses—either the operation will become profitable within a certain time period or the parent will dispose of the foreign operation and thereby trigger a tax deduction in the U.S. federal tax jurisdiction for any outside basis difference. For multinational companies that are profitable on a consolidated basis but have a loss operation in a particular tax jurisdiction, we believe the better approach to recognizing a tax benefit for the loss in the foreign jurisdiction is to focus on the loss in the foreign jurisdiction itself. For example, would it be feasible for the parent to shift income to that tax jurisdiction (and something the parent corporation would do if needed to prevent that foreign loss carryforward from expiring unused)? If so, a valuation allowance may not be needed for the foreign operating loss carryforward.

PARAGRAPHS 35–39: INTRAPERIOD TAX ALLOCATION

EXCERPT FROM OFFICIAL TEXT

Intraperiod Tax Allocation

35. Income tax expense or benefit for the year shall be allocated among continuing operations, discontinued operations, extraordinary items, other comprehensive income, and items charged or credited directly to shareholders' equity (paragraph 36). The amount allocated to continuing operations is the tax effect of the pretax income or loss from continuing operations that occurred during the year, plus or minus income tax effects of (a) changes in circumstances that cause a change in judgment about the realization of deferred tax assets in future years (paragraph 26), (b) changes in tax laws or rates (paragraph 27), (c) changes in tax status (paragraph 28), and (d) tax-deductible dividends paid to shareholders (except as set forth in paragraph 36 for dividends paid on unallocated shares held by an employee stock ownership plan [ESOP] or any other stock compensation arrangement). The remainder is allocated to items other than continuing operations in accordance with the provisions of paragraph 38.

INTERPRETATION

35-1. Computation of the Incremental Effect of an Item Other Than Income From Continuing Operations

Question: Statement 109 generally requires that the tax effect of pretax income from continuing operations be determined by a computation that does not consider the tax effects of items that are not included in continuing operations (i.e., the tax effect allocated to items that are not part of continuing operations is generally their incremental tax effect). Should the computation of the incremental tax effect of items other than continuing operations consider the effect a change in valuation allowance would have had on income tax expense if the items other than income from continuing operations did not exist (i.e., should the incremental "with-and-without" computation include changes in the valuation allowance)?

Response: Yes, the general rule for intraperiod tax allocation under Statement 109 is a strict incremental computation (see Interpretation 35-2 for exceptions to that general rule). First, *total* tax expense or benefit for the period is computed by adding the deferred tax expense or benefit for the period (determined by computing the change in deferred tax liabilities [assets] during the period) to the current tax expense or benefit for the period. The computation of total tax expense includes: (*a*) the effects of all taxable income or loss items regardless of the source of the taxable income or loss and (*b*) the effect of all changes in the valuation allowance except those changes required by paragraphs 37 or 39 of Statement 109 to be credited directly to intangible assets or equity.

Second, tax expense or benefit related to income from continuing operations is computed as the tax effect of the pretax income or loss from continuing operations for the period added to or subtracted from the tax effects of the four items specifically identified in paragraph 35. The treatment of one of those items, "changes in circumstances that cause a change in judgment about the realization of deferred tax assets in future years," requires further elaboration. An example of such a change in valuation allowance is a change produced by additional facts or new circumstances that causes the estimate of future taxable income considered in the determination of the valuation allowance to change. The practical effect of that requirement is that almost all changes in valuation allowances will be included in income from continuing operations. The only changes in valuation allowances that would not be included in income from continuing operations are: (*a*) those changes required by paragraphs 37 or 39 of Statement 109 to be credited directly to intangible assets or equity (see Interpretation 35-3) and (*b*) any increases or decreases in the valuation allowance recognized *due solely to income or loss recognized in the current year* in a category other than income from continuing operations.

The difference between total income tax expense or benefit and income tax expense or benefit allocated to income from continuing operations is the incremental effect of item(s) other than income from continuing operations. That incremental effect is allocated among those items as indicated in paragraph 38 of Statement 109.

EITF Abstracts, Topic D-32, "Intraperiod Tax Allocation of the Tax Effect of Pretax Income from Continuing Operations," includes the following example prepared by the FASB staff that illustrates the effect of a valuation allowance on intraperiod tax allocation:

> To illustrate, assume that in the current year an enterprise has $1,000 of income from continuing operations and a $1,000 loss from discontinued operations. At the beginning of the year, the enterprise has a $2,000 net operating loss carryforward for which the deferred tax asset, net of its valuation allowance, is zero, and the

> enterprise did not reduce that valuation allowance during the year. The staff believes that no tax expense should be allocated to income from continuing operations because the $2,000 loss carryforward is sufficient to offset that income. Thus, no tax benefit is allocated to the loss from discontinued operations.

In that example, after considering the valuation allowance, total tax expense for the year is zero and tax expense related to continuing operations for the year is zero. Therefore, there is no incremental tax benefit to the loss from discontinued operations and no tax benefit is allocated to the loss from discontinued operations.

Example 35-1A is another example that illustrates the general "incremental" intraperiod tax allocation rule.

Example 35-1A

Assume that Company A began business on the first day of Year 1. Company A then loses $50 from operations in each of Years 1, 2, and 3. Company A had no temporary differences in any period and fully reserved for its deferred tax asset related to its operating loss carryforward at the end of each year. The tax rate in all periods is 40%. Prior to releasing its financial statements for Year 3, Company A decides to discontinue its operations in business segment X. After reclassifying its statements of operations for Years 1, 2, and 3 in accordance with FASB Statement No. 144, *Accounting for the Impairment or Disposal of Long-Lived Assets,* pretax income from continuing operations is $100 in each year and the pretax loss from discontinued operations is $150 in each year. Total tax expense is zero in each year and therefore the key to the intraperiod tax allocation question is the computation of income tax allocated to continuing operations in each year. Table 1 shows Company A's reclassified statement of operations:

Table 1: Statement of Operations, as Reclassified

	Year-Ended December 31,		
	20X1	**20X2**	**20X3**
Income from continuing operations before tax	$100	$100	$100
Tax (expense) benefit	(40)	(20)	–
Income from continuing operations	60	80	100
Income (loss) from discontinued operations	(150)	(150)	(150)
Tax (expense) benefit	40	20	–
Income (loss) from discontinued operations	(110)	(130)	(150)
Net income (loss)	$(50)	$(50)	$(50)

Continued on page 180

Continued from page 179

Absent the loss from discontinued operations, tax expense would have been $40 in Year 1 and therefore, in Year 1, a $40 tax expense is allocated to continuing operations and a $40 tax benefit is allocated to the loss from discontinued operations. Absent the Year 2 loss from discontinued operations, tax expense would have been $20 in Year 2 ($40 of tax expense from Year 2's income from continuing operations less the beginning of Year 2 valuation allowance of $20 that would have been reversed if the loss from discontinued operations had not occurred in Year 2) and therefore, in Year 2, a $20 tax expense is allocated to continuing operations and a $20 tax benefit is allocated to the loss from discontinued operations. Absent the Year 3 loss from discontinued operations, tax expense would have been $0 in Year 3 ($40 of tax expense from Year 3's income from continuing operations less the beginning of Year 3 valuation allowance of $40 that would have been reversed if the loss from discontinued operations had not occurred in Year 3) and therefore, in Year 3, no tax expense is allocated to continuing operations or discontinued operations.

35-2. Exceptions to the General Rule That the Tax Effect of an Item Other Than Income From Continuing Operations Is Computed as the Incremental Tax Effect of That Item

Question: Interpretation 35-1 states that, in general, the tax effects of items other than income from continuing operations are computed as the incremental tax effects of those items. What are the exceptions to that general rule?

Response: One exception to the general rule relates to a situation in which an enterprise has a loss from continuing operations and income related to other items, such as an extraordinary item or discontinued operations. In that situation, paragraph 140 of Statement 109 requires that all items (including extraordinary items, discontinued operations, and so forth) be considered for purposes of determining the amount of tax benefit that results from a loss from continuing operations and that should be allocated to continuing operations. Assume that the facts in the FASB staff example in Interpretation 35-1 were changed such that the enterprise has a $1,000 loss from continuing operations and income of $1,000 from discontinued operations. In that situation, even though there is no incremental tax effect of the income from discontinued operations, Statement 109 requires that a tax benefit be reflected in continuing operations and tax expense be reflected as part of discontinued operations. The FASB staff also addressed this question at the July 22, 1993, EITF meeting (see *EITF Abstracts*, Topic D-32, "Intraperiod Tax Allocation of the Tax Effect of Pretax Income from Continuing Operations,") and stated that the previous exception to the incremental approach was made to be consistent with the approach in Statement 109 to consider the tax consequences of taxable income expected in future years in assessing the realizability of deferred tax assets.

A second exception relates to the classification in the income statement of changes in estimates of amounts recognized for income tax uncertainties directly related to discontinued operations. As explained in Interpretation 35-10, enterprises may elect an accounting policy to classify changes in estimates for income tax uncertainties directly related to discontinued operations as part of discontinued operations rather than apply the general intraperiod tax allocation provisions of Statement 109.

35-3. Intraperiod Tax Allocation of Changes in Valuation Allowances

Question: Statement 109 indicates that the effect of changes in valuation allowances should ordinarily be included in income from continuing operations. Changes in valuation allowances could be caused by the following four circumstances:

1. The expiration of a reserved carryforward, which reduces the valuation allowance similar to the way that writing off a reserved account receivable reduces the reserve for bad debts;
2. Business combinations and fresh-start accounting;
3. Changes in judgment about the realizability of deferred tax assets; and
4. The generation of deductible temporary differences and carryforwards in the current year.

Items included in 1. above would not affect tax expense and therefore would not affect intraperiod tax allocation. Items included in 2. above also generally would not affect tax expense or intraperiod tax allocation. Decreases in an acquiring enterprise's valuation allowance as a result of a business combination, the recording of a "date of acquisition" valuation allowance of an acquired enterprise, and the recording of a "date of fresh-start" valuation allowance are accounted for as part of the business combination or fresh-start accounting. However, an increase in an acquiring enterprise's valuation allowance as a result of a business combination is not accounted for as part of the business combination and would therefore affect tax expense and intraperiod tax allocation.

In what situations would changes in valuation allowances related to 2. (only to the extent of an increase, if any, in an acquiring enterprise's valuation allowance caused by the business combination), 3., and 4. above *not* be allocated to income from continuing operations?

Response: Changes in valuation allowances related to 2. (only to the extent of an increase, if any, in an acquiring enterprise's valuation allowance caused by the business combination), 3., and 4. above would not be allocated to income from continuing operations in the following situations:

- Initial recognition of acquired tax benefits (through reductions in the valuation allowance established at the acquisition date) that, as required by paragraph 30 of Statement 109, are used to first reduce goodwill and second to reduce other intangible assets acquired as part of that business combination.
- Initial recognition of tax benefits (through reductions in the valuation allowance established at the time the deductible temporary difference or carryforward was generated) related to the following:
  - — A decrease in contributed capital (e.g., deductible expenditures reported as a reduction of the proceeds from issuing capital stock);
  - — Expenses for employee stock options recognized differently for financial reporting and tax purposes (refer to paragraphs 58 through 63 of FASB Statement No. 123 (Revised 2004), *Share-Based Payment*;
  - — Dividends that are paid on unallocated shares held by an employee stock ownership plan (ESOP) and that are charged to retained earnings; and
  - — Deductible temporary differences and carryforwards that existed at the date of: (*a*) a quasi reorganization (with certain exceptions—see Interpretation 39-1) and (*b*) the opening balance sheet of an enterprise qualifying for fresh-start accounting on emerging from bankruptcy (see Interpretation 37-3).
- Any increases or decreases in the valuation allowance (other than those listed previously) recognized *due solely to income or loss recognized in the current year* in a category other than income from continuing operations (in that case, the effect of the change in the valuation allowance is allocated to that other category, e.g., an extraordinary gain). The only exception to the rule in the previous sentence relates to a situation in which the enterprise has a loss from continuing operations and income related to other items, such as an extraordinary item or discontinued operations. (Refer to Interpretation 35-2.)

With respect to the last bullet point, in some situations it will be difficult to determine if a change in valuation allowance is due solely to one item. Because Statement 109 requires that income tax allocated to continuing operations be determined first and that the effects of all changes in valuation allowances (except for the items listed in the first two bullet points above) due to changes in judgments about future years (including changes in judgments about future years' income or loss related to income categories other than income from continuing operations) be allocated to income from continuing operations, we believe that, when in doubt, the effect of any change in the valuation allowance should be reflected in income tax allocated to continuing operations.

35-4. Valuation Allowance Required Due to Spinoff

Question: Company A has a deferred tax asset related to a FASB Statement No. 5, *Accounting for Contingencies,* loss contingency (i.e., the contingency has been accrued for financial reporting, but will be deductible in some future period for tax purposes) and its wholly owned subsidiary, Subsidiary B, has deferred tax liabilities (e.g., Subsidiary B's financial reporting basis in its property exceeds its tax basis in that property). Company A files a consolidated tax return with Subsidiary B and the taxable and deductible temporary differences mentioned above will reverse within the same approximate period and, under existing tax law, will offset in those future years. Company A does not have a valuation allowance for its deferred tax asset because of the future taxable income that it knows will occur as Subsidiary B's taxable temporary differences reverse (as allowed by paragraph 21 of Statement 109, the enterprise did not explicitly consider any other source of future taxable income because the reversal of existing taxable temporary differences provided sufficient future taxable income to realize its deferred tax asset). Company A spins off Subsidiary B to its shareholders and, in accordance with APB Opinion No. 29, *Accounting for Nonmonetary Transactions,* as amended, assuming Subsidiary B's fair value equals or exceeds its book value, records the spinoff as a distribution to shareholders at the historical cost of its investment in Subsidiary B (i.e., there is no gain recognized as a result of the spinoff). However, now that Subsidiary B's taxable temporary differences are gone, Company A concludes that it needs to recognize a valuation allowance for a part or all of its deferred tax asset. Is the charge for establishing that valuation allowance a charge to income or should it be charged directly to equity?

Response: That charge should be included in tax expense allocated to continuing operations. The EITF concluded in EITF Issue No. 94-10, "Accounting by a Company for the Income Tax Effects of Transactions among or with Its Shareholders under FASB Statement 109," that changes in valuation allowances caused by transactions among or with stockholders should be charged (or credited) to the income statement. Statement 109 provides that, in general, all changes in valuation allowances be reflected in income from continuing operations. Interpretation 35-3 lists the only exceptions to that rule. Further, although related to the spinoff, the increase in the valuation allowance represents the impairment of a *retained* asset and Opinion 29 does not allow the impairment of *retained* assets to be charged directly to equity. For example, if Company A had retained a manufacturing facility that was impaired by the spinoff of complementary facilities, that impairment write-down would not be charged directly to equity.

Question: Assume the opposite of the situation described in the previous question. Subsidiary B has the deferred tax asset that in consolidation did not require a valuation allowance but now, as a result of the spinoff, it will require a valuation allowance in the separate financial statements of Subsidiary B. How should this change in valuation allowance be reflected?

Response: For Subsidiary B, the answer depends on whether income taxes have been allocated to Subsidiary B using the separate return method or the pro rata method for the periods during which it was a member of Company A's consolidated tax return (see Interpretations 40-1 through 40-3). If income taxes have been allocated to Subsidiary B using the separate return method, the valuation allowance would already have been recognized in Subsidiary B's financial statements (i.e., the valuation allowance would have been reflected in the period in which the deferred tax asset was created that gave rise to the valuation allowance). As a result, there would be no additional accounting required in Subsidiary B's financial statements at the date of the spinoff. However, if income taxes have been allocated to Subsidiary B using the pro rata method and as a result Subsidiary B did not reflect a valuation allowance in its prior period financial statements because the consolidated group did not need a valuation allowance, Subsidiary B should recognize a valuation allowance (and a charge to the income statement) in the period of the spinoff as a result of no longer being included in the consolidated tax return of Company A.

A second issue relates to whether Company A needs to reflect a tax charge related to the change in valuation allowance in its consolidated financial statements. Spinoffs in which the fair value of the spun off entity equals or exceeds its book value are typically done at book value whereby the book value of the assets and liabilities spun off are charged to equity with no income statement recognition. However, paragraph 23 of Opinion 29 requires that any impairment of the assets to be spun off must be recognized in the consolidated financial statements prior to the spinoff. The issue is whether the deferred tax asset to be spun off is "impaired" when it is spun off and, if so, whether Company A must recognize that impairment in its consolidated financial statements prior to the spinoff. The FASB staff has indicated that Company A should recognize the impairment of the deferred tax asset in its consolidated financial statements as an income statement charge prior to the spinoff.

35-5. Change in Tax Basis of Assets and Liabilities as a Result of a Spinoff

Question: In some situations, the spinoff of a subsidiary is structured as a taxable transaction. That is, the carrying amounts of assets and liabilities of the subsidiary being spun off are unchanged for financial reporting, but are changed for tax purposes. As a result, deferred taxes need to be provided by the former subsidiary at the time of the spinoff. Should those deferred taxes be charged or credited to the former subsidiary's income statement or directly to its equity?

Response: The deferred taxes should be charged directly to the former subsidiary's equity. The EITF concluded in EITF Issue No. 94-10, "Accounting by a Company for the Income Tax Effects of Transactions among or with Its Shareholders under FASB Statement 109," that the tax effects of all changes in the tax bases of assets and liabilities caused by transactions among or with shareholders should be included in equity. The effect of valuation allowances initially required related to such an increase in tax basis should also be included in equity. Any subsequent reduction in such a valuation allowance should be reported as a reduction of income tax expense. However, we believe that *changes in tax bases* of the asset or liabilities (e.g., as the result of an Internal Revenue Service review) should be reflected as adjustments of the original accounting (i.e., directly to equity), similar to the accounting guidance in EITF Issue No. 93-7, "Uncertainties Related to Income Taxes in a Purchase Business Combination." (See Interpretation 30-9 and Interpretation 36-5 for guidance related to other similar transactions.)

Question: In the previous situation, the spinoff is a taxable event for the former parent company. Should any tax expense recognized by the former parent company be charged to income or to equity?

Response: The tax consequences to the former parent should be segregated into two parts: (1) the tax consequences related to recovering the financial reporting carrying amount of the investment in the subsidiary and (2) the tax consequences caused by the fair value of the subsidiary exceeding the financial reporting carrying amount of the investment in the subsidiary. Any previously unrecognized tax consequences related to recovering the financial reporting carrying amount of the investment in the subsidiary (whether related to a foreign subsidiary and not provided due to the provisions of Opinion 23, or related to a domestic subsidiary and not provided due to the provisions of paragraphs 31 or 33 of Statement 109) should be recognized no later than the measurement date of the spinoff. (See Interpretations 33-1 and 34-2.) That tax consequence is the result of a change in the former parent company's expectations about the timing (for foreign subsidiaries) or method (for domestic subsidiaries) of ultimately recovering its investment in the subsidiary and the effect of that change should be recognized as part of tax expense in the period that expectation changes.

The tax consequence caused by the fair value of the subsidiary exceeding the financial reporting carrying amount of the investment in the subsidiary should be recognized when the pretax effects of the transaction are recognized (i.e., at the time the spinoff is recognized) and the associated incremental tax effect should be charged to equity. However, consistent with the guidance in Issue 94-10 (see Interpretation 36-5), any increases in valuation allowances related to the parent's deferred tax assets should not be charged to equity.

Example 35-5A illustrates the distinction made in the preceding paragraphs.

Example 35-5A

Assume that Parent Company's investment in a domestic subsidiary, Sub, is $100 for financial reporting and $80 for tax purposes and that Parent Company has not previously provided a deferred tax liability for that basis difference because Parent Company expected to recover its investment in Sub without incurring a tax liability for that basis difference. Parent Company now decides to spinoff Sub to Parent Company's shareholders in a taxable transaction. Sub's current fair value is $150. Once that decision is made, Parent Company should accrue a liability (and charge tax expense) for the tax effect of the $20 basis difference that is now a temporary difference (previously that basis difference was not expected to have a future tax consequence to Parent Company and therefore was not a temporary difference). The *incremental* tax consequence of the excess of fair value ($150) over financial reporting carrying amount ($100) should be recognized as a charge directly to equity at the time of the spinoff.

35-6. Intraperiod Tax Allocation When the Enacted Tax Law Provides for Phased-In Changes in Tax Rates

Question (from FASB Staff Implementation Guide, Question 19):

How should income tax expense be allocated between pretax income from continuing operations and other items when the enterprise has temporary differences?

Response (from FASB Staff Implementation Guide, Question 19):

Paragraph 35 states that the amount of income tax expense or benefit allocated to continuing operations is the tax effect of pretax income or loss from continuing operations that occurred during the year (after certain adjustments).[7] The allocation of income tax expense between pretax income from continuing operations and other items should include deferred taxes.

The following example illustrates allocation of current and deferred tax expense. The assumptions are as follows:

a. Tax rates are 40 percent for years 1, 2, and 3 and 30 percent for year 4 and subsequent years. No valuation allowances are required for deferred tax assets.

b. At the end of year 1, there is a $500 taxable temporary difference relating to the enterprise's contracting operations and a $200 deductible temporary difference related to its other operations. Determination of the enterprise's deferred tax assets and liabilities at the end of year 1 is as follows:

	Future Years			
Temporary Differences	**Year 2**	**Year 3**	**Year 4**	**Total**
Contracting operations	$–	$–	$500	$500
Other operations	(100)	(100)	–	(200)
	$(100)	$(100)	$500	$300
Enacted tax rate for future years	40%	40%	30%	
Deferred tax liability (asset)	$(40)	$(40)	$150	$70

c. During year 2, the enterprise decides that it will sell its contracting operations in year 3. As a result, all temporary differences related to the contracting operations (the $500 taxable temporary difference that existed at the end of year 1, plus an additional $200 taxable temporary difference that arose during

[7] Those adjustments include the tax effects of (a) changes in circumstances that cause a change in judgment about the realization of deferred tax assets in future years, (b) changes in tax laws or rates, (c) changes in tax status, and (d) tax-deductible dividends paid to shareholders (except as set forth in paragraph 36 for dividends paid on unallocated shares held by an employee stock ownership plan or any other stock compensation arrangement).

year 2) are now considered to result in taxable amounts in year 3 because the contracting operations will be sold in year 3.

d. At the end of year 2, the enterprise also has $300 of deductible temporary differences ($100 of the temporary difference that existed at the end of year 1, plus an additional $200 that arose during year 2) from continuing operations.

e. For year 2, the enterprise has $50 of pretax reported income from continuing operations and $200 of pretax reported income from discontinued operations.

f. Determination of the enterprise's deferred tax asset and liability at the end of year 2 is as follows:

	Future Years		
Temporary Differences	**Year 3**	**Year 4**	**Total**
Discontinued operations	$700	$–	$700
Continuing operations	(200)	(100)	(300)
	$500	$(100)	$400
Enacted tax rate for future years	40%	30%	
Deferred tax liability (asset)	$200	$(30)	$170

Total deferred tax expense for year 2 is $100 ($170 – $70). The deferred tax benefit of the deductible temporary differences related to the enterprise's continuing operations during year 2 is determined as follows:

Deferred tax asset related to the enterprise's continuing operations at the end of year 2 (40 percent of $200 and 30 percent of $100)	$(110)
Deferred tax asset related to the enterprise's continuing operations at the beginning of year 2 (40 percent of $200)	(80)
Deferred tax benefit for year 2	$(30)

The deferred tax expense for taxable temporary differences related to the enterprise's discontinued operations during year 2 is determined as follows:

Deferred tax liability at the end of year 2 (40 percent of $700)	$280
Deferred tax liability at the end of year 1 (30 percent of $500)	(150)
Deferred tax expense for year 2	$130

Total tax expense and tax expense allocated to continuing and discontinued operations for year 2 are determined as follows:

	Discontinued Operations	Continuing Operations	Total
Pretax reported income	$200	$50	$250
Originating and reversing temporary differences, net	(200)	100	(100)
Taxable income	$–	$150	$ 150
Current tax expense (40 percent)	$–	$60	$60
Deferred tax expense (benefit) as determined above	130	(30)	100
Income tax expense	$130	$30	$160

35-7. Adjustments of Prior Interim Period's Intraperiod Tax Allocation

Question: Assume that a tax effect is allocated to an item other than income from continuing operations during the first quarter of the current fiscal year and, as a result of unanticipated events occurring in the third quarter of the same fiscal year, the tax effect allocated to that item subsequently changes (e.g., the unanticipated events change the enterprise's assessment of the need for a valuation allowance for its deferred tax assets). Should the change in tax effect in this situation be reflected in the third quarter as an adjustment of the original allocation (i.e., adjust the amount allocated to the item other than continuing operations so that, on a cumulative basis, the amount of tax allocated to that item is correct) or should that adjustment be included in the income tax allocated to continuing operations?

Response: That change in tax effect should be reflected as an adjustment of the original allocation. We believe the objective should be to properly state the intraperiod allocation of tax expense for the annual period in accordance with Statement 109 and to adjust the interim period accounting throughout the year, if necessary, to achieve that goal. This approach is consistent with the example in paragraph 58 of FASB Interpretation (FIN) No. 18, *Accounting for Income Taxes in Interim Periods*, which illustrates the accounting in interim periods for income taxes applicable to unusual, infrequently occurring, or extraordinary items. This conclusion does not apply to the interim period effects of changes in tax law or rates. As discussed in Interpretation 27-4, EITF Issue No. 93-13, "Effect of a Retroactive Change in Enacted Tax Rates That Is Included in Income from Continuing Operations," requires all effects of changes in tax law or rates on prior interim periods to be included in the current interim period as part of income from continuing operations.

(See Interpretations 5-1 and 5-2 for other examples of adjustments to prior interim period's intraperiod tax allocation.)

35-8. Intraperiod Tax Allocation of Changes in Valuation Allowances Due to Net Unrealized Losses on Available-for-Sale Securities

The FASB has developed relevant guidance on certain income tax matters as they relate to FASB Statement No. 115, *Accounting for Certain Investments in Debt and Equity Securities.*

Question (from FASB Staff Implementation Guide, *A Guide to Implementation of Statement 115 on Accounting for Certain Investments in Debt and Equity Securities,* Question 54):

> If an enterprise recognizes a deferred tax asset relating only to a net unrealized loss on available-for-sale securities and at the same time concludes that it is more likely than not that some or all of that deferred tax asset will not be realized, is the offsetting entry to the valuation allowance reported in other comprehensive income related to the unrealized loss under Statement 115 or as an item in determining income from continuing operations?

Response (from FASB Staff Implementation Guide, *A Guide to Implementation of Statement 115 on Accounting for Certain Investments in Debt and Equity Securities,* Question 54):

> The offsetting entry to the valuation allowance is reported in the Statement 115 component of other comprehensive income because the valuation allowance is directly related to the unrealized holding loss on the available-for-sale securities. The offsetting entry to the valuation allowance also would be reported in the Statement 115 component of other comprehensive income if the enterprise reaches its conclusion on the need for a valuation allowance in a later interim period of the same fiscal year in which the deferred tax asset is initially recognized.

Question (from FASB Staff Implementation Guide, *A Guide to Implementation of Statement 115 on Accounting for Certain Investments in Debt and Equity Securities,* Question 55):

> Assume an enterprise has recognized a deferred tax asset relating to other deductible temporary differences in a previous fiscal year and at the same time concluded that no valuation allowance was warranted. If in the current year an enterprise recognizes a deferred tax asset relating to a net unrealized loss on available-for-sale securities that arose in the current year and at the same time concludes that a valuation allowance is warranted, is the offsetting entry reported in the Statement 115 component of other comprehensive income or as an item in determining income from continuing operations?

Response (from FASB Staff Implementation Guide, *A Guide to Implementation of Statement 115 on Accounting for Certain Investments in Debt and Equity Securities,* Question 55):

> Management needs to determine the extent to which the valuation allowance is directly related to the unrealized loss and the other deductible temporary differences, such as an accrual for other postemployment benefits. The offsetting entry to the valuation allowance is reported in the Statement 115 component of other comprehensive income only to the extent the valuation allowance is directly related to the unrealized loss on the available-for-sale securities that arose in the current year.

Question (from FASB Staff Implementation Guide, *A Guide to Implementation of Statement 115 on Accounting for Certain Investments in Debt and Equity Securities,* Question 56):

> If an enterprise does not need to recognize a valuation allowance at the same time that it establishes a deferred tax asset relating to a net unrealized loss on available-for-sale securities but in a subsequent fiscal year concludes that it is more likely than not that some or all of that deferred tax asset will not be realized, is the offsetting entry to the valuation allowance reported in the Statement 115 component of other comprehensive income or as an item in determining income from continuing operations?

Response (from FASB Staff Implementation Guide, *A Guide to Implementation of Statement 115 on Accounting for Certain Investments in Debt and Equity Securities,* Question 56):

> If an enterprise initially decided that no valuation allowance was required at the time the unrealized loss was recognized but in a subsequent fiscal year decides that it is more likely than not that the deferred tax asset will not be realized, a valuation allowance is required to be recognized. The offsetting entry should be included as an item in determining income from continuing operations. It should not be included in other comprehensive income.

Question (from FASB Staff Implementation Guide, *A Guide to Implementation of Statement 115 on Accounting for Certain Investments in Debt and Equity Securities,* Question 57):

> If an enterprise recognizes a deferred tax asset relating to a net unrealized loss on available-for-sale securities and at the same time concludes that a valuation allowance is warranted and in a subsequent fiscal year makes a change in judgment about the level of future years' taxable income such that all or a portion of that valuation allowance is no longer warranted, is the offsetting entry reported in the Statement 115 component of other comprehensive income or as an item in determining income from continuing operations?

Response (from FASB Staff Implementation Guide, *A Guide to Implementation of Statement 115 on Accounting for Certain Investments in Debt and Equity Securities,* Question 57):

> Any reversals in the valuation allowance due to such a change in judgment in subsequent fiscal years should be included as an item in determining income from continuing operations, even though initial recognition of the valuation allowance affected the Statement 115 component of other comprehensive income. If, rather than a change in judgment about future years' taxable income, the enterprise generates taxable income in the current year that can utilize the benefit of the deferred tax asset, the elimination (or reduction) of the valuation allowance is allocated to that taxable income. Paragraphs 26 and 35–38 of FASB Statement No. 109, *Accounting for Income Taxes,* provide additional information.

35-9. Income Statement Presentation in the Consolidated Financial Statements of a Subsidiary's Deferred Tax Assets and Liabilities When That Subsidiary Is Sold

Question: When a parent sells the stock of a subsidiary, should the deferred tax assets and liabilities of the subsidiary be: (*a*) included in the cost basis of the subsidiary and thereby affect the amount of pretax gain or loss recognized or (*b*) removed from the cost basis of the subsidiary and reversed as part of the current period's income tax provision?

Response: The answer depends on the tax treatment of the sale of stock. If the sale of stock is treated for tax purposes as a sale of stock (i.e., the tax gain or loss is determined by the cost basis of the stock and the buyer inherits the tax attributes of the subsidiary), the subsidiary's deferred tax assets and liabilities should be included in the cost basis of the subsidiary. In this situation, the parent is not realizing the subsidiary's deferred tax assets nor is it settling the subsidiary's deferred tax liabilities—those tax attributes are being assumed by the buyer. Just like a parent does not treat a subsidiary's debt that is assumed by a buyer as a debt extinguishment, the parent should not treat the subsidiary's deferred tax assets and liabilities as being realized or settled.

If the sale of stock is treated for tax purposes as a sale of the underlying assets (i.e., the tax gain or loss is determined by the cost basis of the assets within the subsidiary and the buyer receives tax basis in the assets consistent with the acquisition of the underlying assets), the subsidiary's deferred tax assets and liabilities should be removed from the cost basis of the subsidiary and reversed as part of the current period's income tax provision. In this situation, the parent is realizing the subsidiary's deferred tax assets and it is settling the subsidiary's deferred tax liabilities.

It should also be noted that the anticipated tax treatment of the sale of the stock of a subsidiary can also affect accounting for income taxes in a period preceding the actual sale. That is, if the sale will be treated as a sale of stock for tax purposes and the parent has not previously provided for the tax consequence of the existing outside basis difference in the stock of the subsidiary (i.e., the difference between the parent's financial reporting and tax bases of the investment in the stock of the subsidiary), a deferred tax asset or liability should be recognized for the existing outside basis difference no later than when it becomes apparent that the reversal of the outside basis difference will have a future tax consequence. (See Interpretation 34-2 for a discussion of this issue.)

35-10. Intraperiod Tax Allocation of Income Tax Uncertainties

Question: Does FASB Interpretation (FIN) No. 48, *Accounting for Uncertainties in Income Taxes,* modify the intraperiod tax allocation provisions of Statement 109?

Response: No. Adoption of FIN 48 may change the timing of the recognition of (or the amount recognized for) tax positions, but it does not change the intraperiod tax allocation provisions of Statement 109. For example, paragraph 37 of Statement 109 requires that the tax effect of certain items be recognized in the same manner as the source of the tax effect (often referred to as "backward tracing"). FIN 48 may change the timing of the recognition of (or the amount recognized for) the tax effects of items subject to backward tracing, but it does not change the requirement to apply backward tracing to the tax effects of the items subject to paragraph 37.

Question: How should changes in estimates of amounts recognized for income tax uncertainties arising from discontinued operations be classified in the income statement?

Response: The allocation of income taxes to income or loss from discontinued operations is subject to the general intraperiod tax allocation provisions of Statement 109 (see Interpretations 35-1 and 35-2 for an explanation of the general intraperiod tax allocation provisions). However, there is diversity in practice regarding the income statement classification of changes in estimates of amounts recognized for income tax uncertainties directly related to discontinued operations when those changes in estimate are recognized in an annual period after the recognition of the related pretax income or loss. Application of the general intraperiod tax allocation provisions of Statement 109 usually would result in such changes in estimates being reflected in the income tax provision for income or loss from continuing operations. However, some have analogized to the guidance in paragraph 44 of FASB Statement No. 144, *Accounting for the Impairment or Disposal of Long-Lived Assets,* which states that "[a]djustments to amounts previously reported in discontinued operations that are directly related to the disposal of a component of an entity in a prior period shall be classified separately in the current period in discontinued operations" and classified such changes in estimates of amounts recognized for income tax uncertainties in discontinued operations.

This issue has been discussed with the FASB staff and it expressed a view that either approach is acceptable. Enterprises that have previously adopted one of these two acceptable approaches for intraperiod tax allocation of income tax uncertainties (under either FASB Statement No. 5, *Accounting for Contingencies*, or FIN 48) related to discontinued operations should continue to apply that accounting policy. Enterprises encountering this issue for the first time should make an accounting policy election and then consistently apply that accounting policy election. Any change in accounting policy should be reported as required by FASB Statement No. 154, *Accounting Changes and Error Corrections*.

EXCERPT FROM OFFICIAL TEXT

36. The tax effects of the following items occurring during the year are charged or credited directly to other comprehensive income or to related components of shareholders' equity:

    a. Adjustments of the opening balance of retained earnings for certain changes in accounting principles or a correction of an error

    b. **Gains and losses included in comprehensive income but excluded from net income** (for example, translation adjustments under Statement 52 and changes in the unrealized holding gains and losses of securities classified as available-for-sale under FASB Statement No. 115, *Accounting for Certain Investments in Debt and Equity Securities*)

    c. An increase or decrease in contributed capital (for example, deductible expenditures reported as a reduction of the proceeds from issuing capital stock)

    d. An increase in the tax basis of assets acquired in a taxable business combination accounted for as a pooling of interests[9a] and for which a tax benefit is recognized at the date of the business combination

    e. Expenses for employee share options recognized differently for financial reporting and tax purposes (refer to paragraphs 58–63 of FASB Statement No. 123 (Revised 2004), *Share-Based Payment*)*

    f. Dividends that are paid on unallocated shares held by an ESOP and that are charged to retained earnings

    g. Deductible temporary differences and carryforwards that existed at the date of a quasi reorganization (except as set forth in paragraph 39).

[9a] FASB Statement No. 141, *Business Combinations*, prohibits the use of the pooling-of-interests method for all business combinations initiated after June 30, 2001.

---

* As amended by Statement 123R.

INTERPRETATION

36-1. Tax Effects of Stock Issuance to Acquire an Asset

Question: In some situations it is possible for basis differences to arise related to assets acquired by issuing capital stock. For example, assume that: (*a*) the asset is acquired for cash and a commitment to issue a fixed number of shares of capital stock at a fixed future date; (*b*) the commitment to issue a fixed number of shares of capital stock is classified as an equity instrument; and (*c*), for tax purposes, the value of the stock issued (and thereby the tax basis of the asset acquired) is determined based on the stock's fair value at the future date at which it is legally issued. If the fair value of the capital stock at the future date at which it is legally issued is greater or less than its fair value at the time of the acquisition of the asset, a temporary difference is created. Should the tax effect of that temporary difference be recognized in income or taken directly to equity?

Response: That temporary difference is caused by a capital transaction and therefore the tax effect of that temporary difference should be taken directly to equity as an addition to, or reduction of, the proceeds from the stock issuance. If the resulting tax benefit initially requires a valuation allowance, any subsequent reduction in that valuation allowance would be reflected directly to equity in accordance with paragraph 37(b) of Statement 109.

36-2. Timing of Recognition of "Excess" Tax Benefits Related to Employee Share-Based Payments

Question: Statement 109 continues the practice of crediting directly to equity any "excess" tax benefits realized related to employee share-based payments. Excess tax benefits are the tax benefits caused by the tax deduction for employee share-based payments exceeding the recognized compensation cost due to changes in the fair value of an enterprise's shares between the measurement date for accounting purposes and a later measurement date for tax purposes. When should the excess tax benefits related to employee share-based payments be recognized?

Response: The excess tax benefits related to employee share-based payments should be credited to equity when the associated tax deduction results in a reduction in taxes payable. Footnote 82 to paragraph A94 of FASB Statement No. 123 (Revised 2004), *Share-Based Payment*, states:

> A share option exercise may result in a tax deduction prior to the actual realization of the related tax benefit

because the entity, for example, has a net operating loss carryforward. In that situation, a tax benefit and a credit to additional paid-in capital for the excess deduction would not be recognized until that deduction reduces taxes payable.

This requirement of Statement 123R is a change from prior practice. Paragraph 81 of Statement 123R provides for a prospective change in accounting for this aspect of Statement 123R.

Question: Under U.S. tax law, deductions related to stock-based payments to employees reduce the current period's taxable income and are therefore used prior to utilizing net operating loss carryforwards. How should enterprises with operating loss carryforwards determine when the excess tax deductions related to employee share-based payments result in a reduction of taxes payable?

Response: Tax effects to be allocated to items other than income from continuing operations are normally measured using an incremental "with-and-without" approach (see Interpretation 35-1). However, in this situation, enterprises are attempting to determine whether the excess tax deductions have resulted in a reduction in taxes payable, not a reduction in their total income tax provision. The FASB Statement 123R Resource Group (an informal advisory group to the FASB that addresses Statement 123R issues) concluded at its September 2005 meeting that either of two methods is acceptable and that enterprises should adopt one of the methods and then follow that method consistently. Those two methods are:

1. *Incremental approach*—Enterprises following this approach should determine the extent to which the excess tax deductions reduce taxes payable using a with-and-without approach. That is, those enterprises should compare their actual income taxes payable for the period to the amount their income tax payable would have been absent the deduction for employee share-based payments in excess of the amount of compensation cost recognized for financial reporting. Thus, net operating loss carryforwards would normally be considered "used" for financial reporting purposes before the current period's share-based deduction. Any incremental reduction in taxes payable attributable to the "excess" share-based payments deduction should be credited directly to equity. In computing the incremental reductions in taxes payable under this approach, the FASB Statement 123R Resource Group also concluded that enterprises could elect as an accounting policy to either include in or exclude from this computation the indirect effects of the excess tax deduction

(e.g., the effect of the excess deduction on the enterprise's research and development tax credit claimed for the period).

2. *Follow the tax law approach*—Under this approach, enterprises will follow the ordering provisions of the tax law (as mentioned above, current period share-based payment deductions are used prior to utilization of operating loss carryforwards) to determine when excess share-based payment deductions are considered to have reduced taxes payable and are therefore recognized for financial reporting purposes. This approach is based on an analogy to the requirements for tracking and recognizing tax benefits acquired in business combinations. Paragraph 268 of Statement 109 provides guidance about using the tax law to determine the ordering of recognition of acquired tax benefits. By analogy, that guidance also provides that, if the ordering is not determinable by looking to provisions of the tax law, the reduction in taxes payable attributable to excess deductions should be determined by prorating the reduction in taxes payable.

Question: Should the portion of the net operating loss (NOL) carryforward attributed to excess tax benefits be included in the amount of gross deferred tax assets required to be disclosed by paragraph 43 of Statement 109 with a corresponding valuation allowance or should that portion of the NOL carryforward be excluded from the amount of gross deferred tax assets required to be disclosed by paragraph 43 of Statement 109?

Response: Statement 123R precludes recognition of a deferred tax asset caused by excess tax benefits that have not yet reduced taxes payable. Accordingly, we believe the portion of the NOL carryforward attributed to excess tax benefits should not be included in the amount of gross deferred tax assets required to be disclosed by paragraph 43 of Statement 109. However, pursuant to the requirements of paragraph 48 of Statement 109, an enterprise should disclose the amounts of its NOL carryforwards and the portion of the tax benefit that, if realized, will be credited directly to equity.

36-3. Accounting for the Tax Effects of Employee Share-Based Payments Prior to Exercise

Question: Typically, compensation cost recognized for instruments classified as equity will be recognized for financial reporting purposes prior to the enterprise receiving a deduction for tax purposes. How should an enterprise recognize the expected future tax consequences of tax deductions related to such share-based payments prior to the enterprise receiving a deduction for tax purposes?

Response: Paragraph 59 of FASB Statement No. 123 (Revised 2004), *Share-Based Payment*, states, "The cumulative amount of compensation cost recognized for instruments classified as equity that ordinarily would result in a future tax deduction under existing tax law shall be considered to be a deductible temporary difference...." Accordingly, absent a need for a valuation allowance, enterprises should recognize a deferred tax benefit for the tax effect of compensation cost for equity awards that ordinarily would result in a future tax deduction (see Interpretation 36-10 for a discussion of the accounting for the tax consequences of equity awards that ordinarily would not result in a future tax deduction). The conclusion in Statement 123R to treat the cumulative amount of compensation cost recognized for instruments classified as equity as a temporary difference is consistent with the treatment of such costs for deferred tax accounting purposes prior to the adoption of Statement 123R.

Question: Some enterprises capitalize a portion of their compensation cost as part of the financial reporting cost of an asset (e.g., inventory or a self-constructed asset). Prior to the exercise of a share-based award, there is no comparable tax basis for that asset. Does the capitalization of compensation cost create a temporary difference for which deferred tax accounting is required?

Response: Consistent with the above conclusion that the cumulative amount of compensation cost recognized for instruments classified as equity that ordinarily would result in a future tax deduction should be considered a deductible temporary difference, footnote 29 to paragraph 59 of Statement 123R provides, "Compensation cost that is capitalized as part of the cost of an asset, such as inventory, shall be considered to be part of the tax basis of that asset for financial reporting purposes." In other words, the capitalization of compensation cost prior to the exercise of the award for instruments classified as equity that ordinarily would result in a future tax deduction will not create a temporary difference. However, once the award is exercised, any difference between the financial reporting and tax basis of the asset caused by capitalizing compensation cost would be a temporary difference and any excess of, or shortfall in, tax benefits would be treated as any other excess of, or shortfall in, tax benefits caused by share-based payments.

Question: Prior to the exercise of a share option by an employee, it may become evident that the enterprise will not receive a tax deduction for some or all of the amount recognized as compensation cost. Should the enterprise reduce its deferred tax asset related to compensation cost or recognize a valuation allowance for some or all of the deferred tax asset related to its compensation cost?

Response: No. Differences between the deductible temporary difference and the tax deduction inherent in the current fair value of the enterprise's stock should not be considered in measuring either the gross deferred tax asset or the need for a valuation allowance. This conclusion is consistent with the accounting required prior to the adoption of Statement 123R.

36-4. Effect on EPS Calculation of Excess Tax Benefits or Shortfalls of Tax Benefits From Stock Plans

Question: Should amounts expected to be credited (debited) to additional paid-in capital related to excess tax benefits (a shortfall of tax benefits) when employee share options are exercised in future periods be included in the computation of earnings per share (EPS)?

Response: Yes. Paragraph 21 of FASB Statement No. 128, *Earnings per Share,* indicates that in applying the treasury stock method to employee share options, the assumed proceeds are: (*a*) the sum of the amount the employee must pay on exercise, (*b*) the amount of compensation cost attributed to future services not yet recognized, and (*c*) the amount of excess tax benefits that would be credited to additional paid-in capital assuming exercise of the options. Similarly, any shortfall of tax benefits that would be charged to additional paid-in capital assuming exercise of the options should be treated as a reduction of assumed proceeds.

Question: For employee share options granted prior to the transition to FASB Statement No. 123 (Revised 2004), *Share-Based Payment,* by an enterprise that adopts Statement 123R via the modified prospective approach, should the amount of excess tax benefits (or shortfall of tax benefits) included in the proceeds be computed based on: (*a*) the amount that is expected to be recognized in equity when the options are exercised or (*b*) the pro forma amount of excess tax benefits (or shortfall of tax benefits)?

Response: The FASB Statement 123R Resource Group (an informal advisory group to the FASB that addresses Statement 123R issues) discussed this issue at its May and September 2005 meetings. No consensus on this issue was reached at those meetings and we understand there is diversity in practice with respect to this issue. If the two approaches described above produce materially different results, we believe an enterpriese should disclose the method it uses in computing its EPS.

Question: In performing the EPS calculation in periods prior to option exercise, if the enterprise believes that an excess tax benefit will not be realized, should such benefit still be reflected in the EPS calculation?

Response: Neither Statement 128 nor Statement 109 address this situation. As discussed in Interpretation 36-2, Statement 123R precludes crediting equity for excess tax benefits prior to the associated deduction reducing taxes payable. Accordingly, we believe enterprises need to assess the likelihood the tax deduction associated with the excess tax benefit will reduce taxes payable when the options are exercised. We believe that if an enterprise concludes the deduction associated with the excess tax benefits will not reduce future taxes payable, it should exclude such benefits from the EPS calculation.

36-5. Transactions Among (and With) Stockholders That Have Tax Effects for the Company

Question: Some transactions *among* stockholders affect the tax attributes of the enterprise itself. For example, in general in the United States, if over 50% of the stock of a company changes hands within a specified period, future utilization of any existing net operating loss carryforwards of the company is limited. A valuation allowance not otherwise needed now may be required for that deferred tax asset. The following are examples of such transactions:

- Heavy trading in a company's stock over a several year period;
- A 45% investor acquires an additional 10% of the company and now consolidates the company, but is precluded from using pushdown accounting;
- An investor buys 70% of a company and now consolidates the company, but is precluded from using pushdown accounting;
- An investor buys 100% of a company (in a nontaxable business combination) and now consolidates the company, but as a private company is not required to and does not use pushdown accounting; or
- An investor buys 100% of a company (in a nontaxable business combination) and now consolidates the company. Although a public company, pushdown accounting is not used because the acquired company has publicly-traded debt and preferred stock outstanding.

Transactions *with* stockholders (i.e., transactions between the enterprise and the stockholder) may have the same effect. The following are examples of such transactions:

- An initial public offering (IPO);
- A stock offering one year after an IPO;

- Conversion of convertible debt into equity pursuant to the stated terms of the debt agreement;
- Conversion of debt into equity in a troubled debt restructuring;
- A recapitalization in which preferred stock is exchanged for common stock (i.e., net no new equity is raised); or
- A recapitalization in which new debt is incurred and the proceeds are used to purchase treasury stock.

Transactions among stockholders may also change the tax bases of assets and liabilities of the company. The following are examples of such transactions:

- An investor buys 100% of the outstanding stock of a company and now consolidates the company, but as a private company is not required to and does not use pushdown accounting. The transaction is treated as the purchase of assets for tax purposes and assets are adjusted to fair value for tax purposes (this may either increase or decrease tax basis).
- An investor buys 100% of the outstanding stock of a company and now consolidates the company. Although a public company, pushdown accounting is not used because the acquired company has publicly traded debt and preferred stock outstanding. The transaction is treated as the purchase of assets for tax purposes and assets are adjusted to fair value for tax purposes (this may either increase or decrease tax basis).
- Parent Company sells 100% of the stock of Subsidiary in an IPO. The carrying amounts for financial reporting purposes of Subsidiary's assets and liabilities in its standalone financial statements will be the historical carrying amounts reflected in Parent Company's consolidated financial statements. However, the transaction is structured so that, for tax purposes, the transaction is taxable and Subsidiary adjusts its basis in its assets and liabilities to fair value (the IPO proceeds). As a result, Subsidiary now has temporary differences related to its assets and liabilities.

Should tax effects caused by transactions among (and with) stockholders be charged (or credited) to the income statement or directly to equity?

Response: EITF Issue No. 94-10, "Accounting by a Company for the Income Tax Effects of Transactions among or with Its Shareholders under FASB Statement 109," addresses both of these issues. The EITF concluded that changes in *valuation allowances* caused by transactions among (or with) stockholders should be charged (or credited) to the income statement. Statement 109 provides that, in general, all changes in valuation allowances be reflected in income from continuing operations. (See Interpretation 35-3 for the only exceptions to that rule.)

The appropriate accounting for tax effects from changes in *tax bases* of assets and liabilities caused by transactions among (or with) stockholders is also addressed in Issue 94-10. The EITF concluded that the tax effects of all changes in the tax bases of assets and liabilities caused by transactions among or with shareholders should be included in equity. The effect of valuation allowances initially required related to such an increase in tax basis should also be included in equity. Any subsequent reduction in such a valuation allowance should be reported as a reduction of income tax expense.

36-6. Effect of Dividends on Unallocated Shares Held by an ESOP on the EPS Computation

Question: Paragraph 36(f) requires that the tax benefit of dividends that are paid on unallocated shares held by an employee stock ownership plan (ESOP) and that are charged to retained earnings be credited directly to retained earnings. How should that tax benefit be treated in the earnings per share (EPS) computation? That is, is it acceptable to include that benefit in income available to common shareholders when computing EPS?

Response: The EITF reached a consensus in EITF Issue No. 92-3, "Earnings-per-Share Treatment of Tax Benefits for Dividends on Unallocated Stock Held by an Employee Stock Ownership Plan," that such tax benefits should not be included in income available to common shareholders when computing EPS.

36-7. Tax Effects of Debt With Detachable Warrants

Question: In accordance with APB Opinion No. 14, *Accounting for Convertible Debt and Debt Issued with Stock Purchase Warrants*, when an enterprise issues debt with detachable warrants, the net proceeds are allocated between the debt component and the equity (warrant) component based on the relative fair values of the two instruments at the time of issuance. In most situations, the U.S. tax law follows the same fair value allocation approach. In circumstances in which the allocation of the net proceeds between the debt and equity components are different for financial reporting and tax reporting, a temporary difference is created related to the debt (book/tax differences related to equity are not temporary differences). Should deferred taxes be recognized for that temporary difference? If so, is the associated tax benefit or charge included in income from continuing operations or allocated directly to equity?

Response: Deferred taxes should be recognized for the temporary difference related to the debt and the tax benefit or charge should be allocated directly to equity (as if it were additional proceeds for the warrants or a cost of issuing the warrants). We believe that approach is consistent with the results one would expect if the enterprise simply issued debt (i.e., the proceeds allocated to debt would be what the enterprise would have received in a straight debt offering). As a result, if the enterprise receives a larger or smaller tax benefit because the tax law allocates the net proceeds differently, this incremental tax effect is caused solely by adding the equity component to the financing transaction. Accordingly, we believe such a tax effect should be allocated to equity in accordance with paragraph 36(c) of Statement 109. If a valuation allowance is initially required for this tax effect, the effect of reducing the valuation allowance in the future will also be credited to equity in accordance with paragraph 37(b) of Statement 109.

36-8. Tax Effects of an Induced Conversion of Convertible Debt

Question: FASB Statement No. 84, *Induced Conversions of Convertible Debt*, requires the debtor enterprise to recognize an expense equal to the fair value of all securities and other consideration transferred in the transaction in excess of the fair value of securities issuable pursuant to the original conversion terms. Should a tax benefit be recognized for the inducement expense recognized for financial reporting?

Response: Yes, a tax benefit should be recognized to the extent that the inducement results in an incremental tax savings to the enterprise. For tax purposes, the excess of the tax basis of the debt over the total fair value of *all* consideration issued on conversion is a taxable gain. However, a tax deduction is not allowed for the excess of the fair value of the consideration issued over the tax basis of the debt. As a result, if a taxable gain results from a simple conversion of convertible debt (i.e., the fair value of the equity securities issued is less than the tax basis of the debt), the tax effect should be charged to equity in accordance with paragraph 36(c) of Statement 109.

As a result of the tax law regarding debt to equity conversions, the only tax effect that an inducement can have is to reduce an otherwise taxable gain. By increasing the consideration paid on conversion, the enterprise reduces the otherwise taxable gain. Note that any inducement paid that results in the total consideration paid *exceeding* the tax basis of the debt will not result in an incremental tax savings (i.e., no tax loss can result from such a transaction).

We believe that in situations in which the inducement reduces an otherwise taxable gain (i.e., absent the inducement, a straight conversion would have resulted in some taxable gain and the inducement reduces or eliminates this gain), the effect of the reduction in the taxable gain should be recognized in income from continuing operations. This calculation is in substance a "with-and-without" calculation, whereby the difference in the amount of tax due on conversion, with an inducement and without an inducement, is credited to income from continuing operations. Example 36-8A demonstrates this concept.

Example 36-8A

Example assumptions:

The Company issues a $1,000 convertible bond with a 5% coupon rate.

The bond is originally convertible into 50 shares of common stock.

When the fair value of the stock is $15 a share, Company, in anticipation of an initial public offering, wishes to reduce its current debt level and therefore offers 20 additional shares of stock to induce conversion.

The effective tax rate is 40%.

In this example, Company would record an expense for the inducement of $300 (20 shares at $15). If the debt was converted without the inducement, Company would have had a taxable gain of $250 ($1,000 – [50 × $15]). As a result of the inducement, Company would have no taxable gain as the fair value of the total consideration exchanged of $1,050 (70 shares at $15 a share) exceeds the tax basis of the debt of $1,000. Therefore, the expense for financial reporting purposes of $300 causes a reduction in taxable income of $250, resulting in a tax benefit of $100 ($250 × 40%) being reflected in the income statement and a corresponding tax charge of $100 being reflected in equity.

36-9. Classification in the Statement of Cash Flows of the Income Tax Benefit Realized on Exercise of a Nonqualified Employee Share Option

Question: Pursuant to the guidance in paragraph 36(e) of Statement 109, as amended by FASB Statement No. 123 (Revised 2004), *Share-Based Payment*, the benefit from tax deductions triggered by the exercise of nonqualified share options in excess of the associated financial reporting compensation cost is credited directly in equity.

How should the reduction in income taxes paid as a result of the excess deduction triggered by the exercise of nonqualified share options be reflected in the statement of cash flows?

Response: Statement 123R also amends FASB Statement No. 95, *Statement of Cash Flows,* and requires that such excess tax benefits be presented in the statement of cash flows as financing inflows with a corresponding operating cash outflow. It is important to note that paragraph 19(e) of Statement 95, as amended by Statement 123R, requires the excess tax benefits be computed on an award-by-award basis with no netting of amounts debited to equity from shortfalls of tax benefits.

Statement 123R requires that the amount of excess tax benefits presented in the statement of cash flows as a financing inflow be computed based on the "pro forma" amount of excess tax benefits realized during the period rather than the amount of excess tax benefit actually recognized in equity (i.e., the excess tax benefit is computed as if the enterprise had adopted FASB Statement No. 123, *Accounting for Stock-Based Compensation,* in 1995). Refer to Interpretation 36-11 for a further discussion of the pro forma computation of excess tax benefits.

As discussed in Interpretation 36-11, the FASB has issued FASB Staff Position (FSP) FAS 123R-3, "Transition Election Related to Accounting for the Tax Effects of Share-Based Payment Awards." This FSP allows enterprises to elect a simplified approach to computing the amount of cumulative excess tax benefits in equity on adoption of Statement 123R. The FSP also affects the computation of the amount reflected as a financing cash inflow for enterprises that elect to follow the alternative transition provisions of that FSP related to accounting for the tax effects of share-based payment awards. Specifically, paragraph 8 of FAS 123R-3 states:

> An entity that elects the alternative transition method described in this FSP shall classify the tax benefits related to an employee award that is fully vested prior to the adoption of Statement 123(R) that have been both (a) realized in accordance with footnote 82 of Statement 123(R) and (b) recognized in equity subsequent to the adoption of Statement 123(R) as a cash inflow from financing activities and a cash outflow from operating activities within the statement of cash flows.

Otherwise, the determination of amounts to be reflected in the statement of cash flows is the same for enterprises electing the simplified approach as it is for enterprises that do not elect to use the simplified approach.

Prior to the issuance of Statement 123R, EITF Issue No. 00-15, "Classification in the Statement of Cash Flows of the Income Tax

Benefit Received by a Company upon Exercise of a Nonqualified Employee Stock Option," required that the entire reduction in income taxes paid as a result of the deduction triggered by employee exercise of share options be classified as an operating cash flow.

The EITF also decided that the disclosure of a material income tax benefit realized is required if that benefit is not otherwise disclosed (e.g., by presenting it as a separate line item in the statement of cash flows or in the statement of changes in stockholders' equity). Issue 00-15 is superseded by Statement 123R.

36-10. Incentive Stock Options and Employee Stock Purchase Plans

Question: The cumulative amount of compensation cost recognized for instruments classified as equity that ordinarily would not result in a future tax deduction under existing tax law, such as incentive stock options (ISOs) and employee stock purchase plans (ESPPs), are not considered a deductible temporary difference under Statement 109. However, some future events, such as an employee's disqualifying disposition of stock received from exercising ISOs or through an ESPP, can result in the employer receiving a tax deduction. If a reliable estimate can be made, should enterprises treat a portion of such compensation cost as a temporary difference and provide currently for a deferred tax benefit?

Response: No. Paragraph 59 of FASB Statement No. 123 (Revised 2004), *Share-Based Payment*, states, "The tax effects of such an event shall be recognized only when it occurs."

Question: When an event occurs that gives rise to a tax deduction for compensation cost from equity instruments that ordinarily do not result in a tax deduction, such as ISOs and ESPPs, how should the resulting tax benefit be accounted for?

Response: The tax benefit of such a deduction, up to the amount of cumulative compensation cost recognized, should be recognized as a reduction of income tax expense. The tax benefit of such a deduction in excess of the amount of cumulative compensation cost recognized should be credited directly to equity. As explained in Interpretation 36-2, the amount of excess tax benefit should not be credited to equity until the associated tax deduction results in a reduction of taxes payable.

36-11. Accounting for the Shortfall in Tax Benefits Associated With an Equity Award

Question: As explained in Interpretation 36-3, the cumulative amount of compensation cost recognized for instruments classified as equity that ordinarily would result in a future tax deduction under existing tax law is considered to be a deductible temporary difference under Statement 109, even if it becomes evident that the tax deduction received will be less than the cumulative amount of compensation cost recognized. How should an enterprise account for a shortfall of tax benefits (i.e., receiving a tax benefit from a tax deduction for an equity award that is less than the deferred tax asset that has been previously recognized)?

Response: The shortfall in tax benefits from a tax deduction for an equity award that is less than the deferred tax asset that has been previously recognized should be debited to equity to the extent the enterprise has recognized cumulative amounts of "excess" tax benefits in equity in accordance with FASB Statement No. 123, *Accounting for Stock-Based Compensation,* or FASB Statement No. 123 (Revised 2004), *Share-Based Payment*. Excess tax benefits are the tax benefits caused by the tax deduction for employee share-based payments exceeding the recognized compensation cost due to changes in the fair value of an enterprise's shares between the measurement date for accounting purposes and a later measurement date for tax purposes. Excess tax benefits from all share-based awards covered by Statement 123R may be pooled together. However, excess tax benefits from arrangements outside the scope of Statement 123R, such as excess tax benefits from employee stock ownership plans, are excluded from the excess tax benefit pool. Any shortfall in tax benefits in excess of previously recognized cumulative amounts of excess tax benefits should be recognized as part of the income tax provision in the income statement.

Question: How should enterprises compute the amount of cumulative excess tax benefits on adoption of Statement 123R?

Response: On November 10, 2005, the FASB issued FASB Staff Position (FSP) FAS 123R-3, "Transition Election Related to Accounting for the Tax Effects of Share-Based Payment Awards." This FSP: (*a*) allows enterprises to elect a simplified approach to computing the amount of cumulative excess tax benefits in equity on adoption of Statement 123R and (*b*) limits the need to compute a pro forma excess tax benefit for periods subsequent to the adoption of Statement 123R to awards that were partially vested at the adoption of Statement 123R. Accordingly, enterprises have a choice between computing that transitional amount: (*a*) pursuant to Statement 123R as originally issued and (*b*) following the simplified alternative approach described in the FSP. These two methods of computing the amount of cumulative excess tax benefits on adoption of Statement 123R will produce different amounts for most enterprises. Accordingly, enterprises will need to carefully consider which method to use.

Paragraph 81 of Statement 123R provides the following transition guidance on computing the amount of cumulative excess tax benefits when adopting Statement 123R:

> For purposes of calculating the available excess tax benefits if deferred tax assets need to be written off in subsequent periods, an entity shall include as available for offset only the net excess tax benefits that would have qualified as such had the entity adopted Statement 123 for recognition purposes for all awards granted, modified, or settled in cash for fiscal years beginning after December 15, 1994.

Consistent with the guidance on transition in paragraph 81, paragraph 63 of Statement 123R states the following:

> An entity that continued to use Opinion 25's intrinsic value method as permitted by Statement 123 shall calculate the amount available for offset as the net amount of excess tax benefits that would have qualified as such had it instead adopted Statement 123 for recognition purposes pursuant to Statement 123's original effective date and transition method.

Accordingly, most enterprises using this method will need to develop a year-by-year rollforward of their "pro forma" excess tax benefits and shortfalls of tax benefits from 1995 (i.e., computed as if the enterprise had adopted Statement 123 on the effective date therein) to the adoption of Statement 123R.

Points to keep in mind when developing this pro forma computation of excess tax benefits include the following:

- Options granted prior to the effective date of Statement 123 (and not modified subsequent to the effective date of Statement 123) should be excluded from the analysis.
- Consistent with the guidance in Interpretation 36-2, excess tax benefits should not be included in the memo computation until the associated tax deduction results in a reduction of taxes payable.
- Disqualifying dispositions of stock received from exercising incentive stock options or through an employee stock purchase plan may create excess tax benefits, but cannot cause a tax benefit shortfall.
- Vested nonqualifying stock options that expire unexercised will cause a tax benefit shortfall equal to the entire amount of the deferred tax asset associated with those vested nonqualifying stock options.

Paragraphs 5 through 7 of FSP FAS 123R-3 describe the allowed simplified alternative method:

> Upon adoption of Statement 123(R), the beginning balance of the APIC pool related to employee compensation shall be calculated as follows:
>
> > The sum of all net increases of additional paid-in capital recognized in an entity's annual financial statements related to tax benefits from stock-based employee compensation during fiscal periods subsequent to the adoption of Statement 123 but prior to the adoption of Statement 123(R).
> >
> > Less:
> >
> > The cumulative incremental pretax employee compensation costs that would have been recognized if Statement 123 had been used to account for stock-based employee compensation costs, multiplied by the entity's blended statutory tax rate upon adoption of Statement 123(R), inclusive of federal, state, local, and foreign taxes. Cumulative incremental compensation costs are the total stock-based employee compensation costs included in pro forma net income as if the fair-value-based method had been applied to all awards pursuant to the provisions of Statement 123,[1,2] less the stock-based compensation costs included in the entity's determination of net income as reported.
>
> Tax benefits related to an employee award that is fully vested prior to the adoption of Statement 123(R) that have been both (a) realized in accordance with footnote 82 of Statement 123(R) and (b) recognized in equity subsequent to the adoption of Statement 123(R) shall increase the APIC pool.

---

1 In calculating cumulative incremental compensation costs, entities shall exclude compensation costs associated with an award that ordinarily does not result in tax deductions under existing tax law (as described in paragraph 59 of Statement 123(R)) unless the award has resulted in a tax deduction prior to the adoption of Statement 123(R) or the entity is unable to obtain the information necessary to determine the amount of such cost.

2 In calculating cumulative incremental compensation costs, entities shall exclude compensation costs associated with awards that are partially vested upon the adoption of Statement 123(R).

The impact on the APIC pool of an employee award that is partially vested upon or granted after the adoption of Statement 123(R) should be determined in accordance with the guidance in Statement 123(R). That is, the compensation deduction for tax purposes for a partially vested award should be compared with the sum of compensation cost recognized or disclosed for that award under Statement 123 and Statement 123(R). The tax effect of any resulting excess deduction for tax purposes should increase the APIC pool; the tax effect of any resulting deficient deduction for tax purposes should be deducted from the APIC pool.

36-12. Income Tax Consequences of Issuing Convertible Debt With a Beneficial Conversion Feature

Question: Pursuant to the requirements of EITF Issue No. 00-27, "Application of Issue No. 98-5 to Certain Convertible Instruments," an enterprise that issues a convertible debt security with a nondetachable conversion feature that is "in-the-money" bifurcates the instrument and accounts separately for the conversion feature. The portion of the proceeds assigned to the conversion feature is credited directly to equity and the remainder of the proceeds is assigned to the liability. For U.S. federal tax purposes, the conversion feature is not accounted for separately and the entire amount of proceeds received at issuance of the convertible debt instrument is its tax basis. Is the difference between the book and tax basis of the liability in this situation a temporary difference?

Response: The EITF concluded in EITF Issue No. 05-8, "Income Tax Consequences of Issuing Convertible Debt with a Beneficial Conversion Feature," that the difference between the book and tax basis of the liability in this situation is a temporary difference. Accordingly, a deferred tax liability should be recognized at the time the convertible security with the nondetachable, in-the-money, conversion feature is issued. Because the taxable temporary difference is caused by a direct entry to equity, the EITF also concluded that paragraph 36(c) of Statement 109 applies and that the offset to the deferred tax liability (i.e., the tax consequence of that direct entry to equity) should be charged directly to the "related components of shareholders' equity."

EXCERPT FROM OFFICIAL TEXT

37. The tax benefit of an operating loss carryforward or carryback (other than those carryforwards referred to at the end of this paragraph) shall be reported in the same manner as the source of the income or loss in the current year and not in the same manner as (a) the source of the operating loss carryforward or taxes paid in a prior year or (b) the source of expected future income that will result in realization of a deferred tax asset for an operating loss carryforward from the current year. The only exceptions are as follows

    a. Tax effects of deductible temporary differences and carryforwards that existed at the date of a purchase business combination and for which a tax benefit is initially recognized in subsequent years in accordance with the provisions of paragraph 30
    b. Tax effects of deductible temporary differences and carryforwards that are allocated to shareholders' equity in accordance with the provisions of paragraph 36 (items (c) and (e)–(g)).

INTERPRETATION

37-1. Recognition of Pre-Quasi Reorganization Tax Benefits

Question (from FASB Staff Implementation Guide, Question 9):

An enterprise charged losses directly to contributed capital at the date of a quasi reorganization. At that date, the deferred tax asset for the enterprise's deductible temporary differences and carryforwards was offset by a valuation allowance. Part of those deductible temporary differences and carryforwards related to losses that were included in determining income in prior years. The remainder were attributable to losses that were charged directly to contributed capital as a result of the quasi reorganization. When recognized (by reducing or eliminating the valuation allowance) subsequent to the date of the quasi reorganization, how should the tax benefit of such deductible temporary differences and carryforwards be reported?

Response (from FASB Staff Implementation Guide, Question 9):

> All unrecognized tax benefits of deductible temporary differences and carryforwards that existed at the date of a quasi reorganization, except as provided in paragraph 39, should be reported as a direct addition to contributed capital when recognized subsequent to the date of the quasi reorganization.
>
> ARB No. 43, Chapter 7, "Capital Accounts," states that after a quasi reorganization, the enterprise's accounting should be substantially similar to that appropriate for a new enterprise. As such, any subsequently recognized tax benefit of an operating loss or tax credit carryforward that existed at the date of a quasi reorganization should not be included in the determination of income of the "new" enterprise, regardless of whether losses that gave rise to an operating loss carryforward were charged to income prior to the quasi reorganization or directly to contributed capital as part of the quasi reorganization. A new enterprise would not have tax benefits attributable to operating losses or tax credits that arose prior to its organization date.
>
> A charge to income should be recorded, however, if subsequent to a quasi reorganization an enterprise concludes that due to a change in circumstances a valuation allowance should be recognized or increased to reduce the amount of tax benefits that were recognized at the time of the quasi reorganization.
>
> Quasi reorganizations for companies that adopted Statement 96 and that only eliminated a deficit in retained earnings by a concurrent reduction in contributed capital qualify for special treatment as described in paragraph 39.

(See Interpretation 37-4 for ordering of recognition of pre- and post-quasi reorganization deferred tax benefits.)

37-2. Quasi Reorganization That Results in a Net Gain Being Credited to Capital

Question (from FASB Staff Implementation Guide, Question 10):

> Some enterprises have credited a net gain directly to contributed capital at the date of a prior quasi reorganization. Does the answer to Question 9 [Interpretation 37-1] change for those enterprises?

Response (from FASB Staff Implementation Guide, Question 10):

> No. The accounting for any subsequently recognized tax benefit of deductible temporary differences and carryforwards that existed at the date of a quasi reorganization does not change based on whether gains were credited directly to contributed capital or losses were charged directly to contributed capital. As noted in the answer to Question 9, the purpose of a quasi reorganization is to create a new basis of accounting. That is the reason ARB 43, Chapter 7 permits the adjustment of assets to their fair value.

37-3. Subsequent Recognition of Tax Benefits Existing at the Date of Emerging From Bankruptcy

Question: If an enterprise has a valuation allowance for deferred tax assets at the time it emerges from bankruptcy, should subsequent reductions in that valuation allowance be credited to income, directly to equity, or in some other manner?

Response: AICPA Statement of Position (SOP) 90-7, *Financial Reporting by Entities in Reorganization Under the Bankruptcy Code*, provides the appropriate guidance for this question. If the enterprise qualifies for "fresh-start" accounting under SOP 90-7, any subsequent reduction in the deferred tax asset valuation allowance that exists at the date of the fresh-start is first credited to "reorganization value in excess of amounts allocable to identifiable assets," then credited to other identifiable intangible assets existing at the date of the fresh-start, and, once those assets are reduced to zero, credited directly to equity.

If the enterprise does not qualify for fresh-start accounting under SOP 90-7, any subsequent reduction in the deferred tax valuation allowance would be accounted for pursuant to the guidance in paragraphs 26 and 35 of Statement 109 (generally as a reduction of income tax expense).

37-4. Order of Recognition of Pre- and Post-Fresh-Start Tax Benefits

Question: Enterprises emerging from bankruptcy or electing a quasi reorganization often have valuation allowances established to offset some or all of their deferred tax assets. Interpretations 37-3 and 39-1 address the requirements for subsequent recognition of those tax benefits (i.e., the subsequent reduction in the valuation allowance that existed at the date of emerging from bankruptcy or electing a quasi reorganization). What is the order of recognition of reductions in valuation allowances if an enterprise has both a valuation allowance established at the date of fresh-start accounting and a valuation allowance related to tax benefits generated since the date of fresh-start accounting?

Response: The FASB staff announced at an EITF meeting (see *EITF Abstracts*, Topic D-33, "Timing of Recognition of Tax Benefits for Pre-reorganization Temporary Differences and Carryforwards,") that enterprises should follow the Statement 109 rules for the subsequent recognition of acquired tax benefits described in paragraphs 268 and 269 of the statement. That is, if it can be determined by the provisions in the tax law which tax benefits are being recognized (e.g., the sequence in which net operating loss carryforwards are utilized in the tax return), the financial reporting should reflect the recognition of those tax benefits. If not determinable by provisions in the tax law, a tax benefit recognized for financial reporting (i.e., the reduction in the valuation allowance) should be prorated between the pre- and post-fresh-start tax benefits.

37-5. Tax Effects of Gains and Losses Included in Comprehensive Income but Excluded From Net Income

Question: Statement 109 provides that tax effects of gains and losses included in comprehensive income but excluded from net income (e.g., translation adjustments under FASB Statement No. 52, *Foreign Currency Translation*, changes in the carrying amount of securities classified as available for sale under FASB Statement No. 115, *Accounting for Certain Investments in Debt and Equity Securities*, and adjustments from recognizing certain minimum pension obligations under FASB Statement No. 87, *Employers' Accounting for Pensions*) are to be charged or credited directly to the related components of shareholders' equity. Statement 109 provides that, with certain exceptions (see paragraph 37 of Statement 109 for a list of the exceptions), the tax benefit from a reduction in a valuation allowance that is solely the result of income or loss in the current year should be reported in the same manner as the source of the income or loss that allows for the reduction in valuation allowance (however, note that income from continuing operations is always calculated first—see Interpretation 35-1). Those provisions can result in the situation set forth in Example 37-5A.

Example 37-5A

Enterprise recognizes an unrealized loss on a marketable equity security with a charge directly to equity in Year 1. The reduction in the net carrying amount of the asset creates a deductible temporary difference; however, the deferred tax asset created by that deductible

Continued on page 217

Continued from page 216

> temporary difference is fully offset by a valuation allowance. In Year 2, the net carrying amount of the marketable equity security does not change, but Enterprise's facts and circumstances change such that a valuation allowance for the deferred tax asset related to the marketable equity security is no longer needed. The valuation allowance is reversed with a credit to income tax expense related to continuing operations. In Year 3, the marketable equity security recovers in value and thereby eliminates the deferred tax asset.

Should the elimination of the deferred tax asset in Year 3 be charged to income or directly to equity?

Response: Determining how the elimination of the deferred tax asset should be charged depends on whether the enterprise elects to account for the tax effects of such transactions using an individual security approach or a portfolio approach. (We believe enterprises have the option to elect to use either method; however, a change from one method to the other would be a change in accounting method.) Under the individual security approach, the tax effects in equity are tracked on a security-by-security basis. If the enterprise is using an individual security approach in this example, there is no pretax unrealized gain or loss in equity related to that marketable security at the end of Year 3 and therefore there should not be any tax effect remaining in equity related to that marketable security at the end of Year 3. Because there was no tax benefit originally reflected in equity, there is no benefit to reverse to the income statement and the net effect of the elimination of the deferred tax asset in Year 3 is charged to income.

Under the portfolio approach, an enterprise should follow a strict period-by-period (not cumulative) incremental allocation of income taxes to the *change* in unrealized gains and losses reflected in equity and disregard the net cumulative tax effect that is reflected in equity. The net cumulative tax effects of marketable securities' unrealized gains and losses reflected in equity would only be "cleaned up" when substantially the entire category of "gains and losses" is eliminated (e.g., if the entire marketable equity security portfolio were sold). If the enterprise uses a portfolio approach in this example (and assuming that the enterprise has not disposed of substantially its entire marketable security portfolio), the elimination of the deferred tax asset in Year 3 should be charged directly to equity. The mechanics of intraperiod tax allocation in Statement 109 require that the difference between total income tax expense and income tax expense attributable to income from continuing operations be allocated to the items other than income from continuing operations. In this example, total income tax expense exceeds income tax expense attributable to income from continuing operations in Year 3 by the amount of the eliminated deferred tax asset and therefore that amount should be charged directly to equity.

Example 37-5B is another example of the mechanics of intraperiod tax allocation under Statement 109.

Example 37-5B

In Year 1, Enterprise that follows FASB Statement No. 115, *Accounting for Certain Investments in Debt and Equity Securities*: (*a*) recognizes unrealized appreciation in its investment securities directly to equity, (*b*) recognizes the appropriate deferred tax liability for that taxable temporary difference (the book basis of the investment security exceeds its tax basis), and (*c*) charges the resulting tax expense directly to equity. In Year 2, Enterprise incurs an operating loss for book and tax (no change in temporary differences) in the same amount as the taxable temporary difference related to the unrealized appreciation and does not establish a valuation allowance for that deferred tax asset due to the existence of that taxable temporary difference. The tax benefit of the operating loss is credited to net income. In Year 3, the value of the investment security declines to its original cost (thereby eliminating the taxable temporary difference) and Enterprise breaks even from operations for book and tax (no other changes in temporary differences). Enterprise concludes it needs a valuation allowance at the end of Year 3 for the deferred tax asset.

If there was a change in circumstances that caused a change in judgment about the realization of deferred tax assets in future years (e.g., the current year's income from operations was significantly below projections and Enterprise's future earnings from operations are now considered less assured), the charge for increasing the valuation allowance should be charged to income from continuing operations. However, if the increase in the valuation allowance is due *solely* to the loss charged directly to equity (the decline in value of the marketable securities), the charge for increasing the valuation allowance should be charged directly to equity.

The first situation noted above could also occur at transition to Statement 109 if the tax benefit of the temporary difference was initially recognized as part of the cumulative effect of the change in accounting.

37-6. Tax Effects of Gains and Losses Included in Comprehensive Income but Excluded From Net Income When There Is a Change in Tax Rates or Laws

Question: Paragraph 27 of Statement 109 requires that the effect of a change in tax laws or rates on deferred tax liabilities and assets be included in income from continuing operations for the period that includes the enactment date. If a deferred tax asset or liability related to a gain or loss included in comprehensive income but excluded from net income (e.g., an unrealized gain on an investment under FASB Statement No. 115, *Accounting for Certain Investments in Debt and Equity Securities*) is adjusted for a tax rate change by a charge or credit to the income statement, how is the tax effect recognized when the unrealized gain or loss is subsequently realized and reflected in the income statement?

Response: The manner in which the tax effect is recognized when the unrealized gain or loss is realized and reflected in the income statement depends on whether the enterprise specifically identifies the investments or not as discussed in Interpretation 37-5. Assume: (*a*) the old tax rate was 35% and the new rate is 37%, (*b*) the incremental effect in prior periods of all prior unrealized gains was 35%, and (*c*) the enterprise specifically tracks its investments for Statement 109 purposes such that it identifies which investments have tax effects reflected in equity at the old rate and which have tax effects reflected in equity at the new rates. When one of the investments that has been tax effected in equity at 35% is subsequently sold, the entity would reverse the tax effect out of equity (and reflect it in its tax provision) at the 35% rate. Thus, in this situation, the cumulative provision reflected in the income statement is at a 37% rate (2% recognized when the rate changed and 35% recognized when the gain was realized).

Alternatively, if it is not feasible for the enterprise to track its investments separately or the enterprise elects not to do so for Statement 109 purposes, when the gain is realized, the enterprise allocates the current period's incremental tax effect of the realized gain to equity (absent unusual conditions, such as a valuation allowance, the incremental effect should be a 37% rate). For those investments that have been tax effected in equity at 35%, this will create a 2% differential in equity. That differential will not be cleared out of equity until such time as the entire category of gains or losses is substantially eliminated (e.g., if the entire marketable equity securities portfolio were sold).

37-7. Tax Benefit Substitution

Question: Paragraph 37 requires that certain tax benefits be reported in the same manner as the source of the tax benefit (e.g., the initial recognition of an acquired tax benefit first reduces goodwill related to that acquisition). However, sometimes an operating loss carryforward is used on a tax return without changing the enterprise's net tax position (e.g., the transaction creating the taxable income that utilizes the operating loss carryforward also creates a deductible temporary difference). If a valuation allowance was needed for the operating loss carryforward at the beginning of the period and a valuation allowance is needed for the deductible temporary difference at the end of the period, should the benefit from utilization of an operating loss carryforward covered by paragraphs 37(a) or (b) be credited to goodwill or stockholders' equity?

Response: In that situation, an operating loss carryforward was simply converted into a deductible temporary difference and therefore no amount should be credited to goodwill or equity. Paragraph 243 of Statement 109 states:

> Under those circumstances, the reduction in taxable income and taxes payable from utilization of the operating loss or tax credit carryforward gives no cause for recognition of a tax benefit because, in effect, the operating loss or tax credit carryforward has been replaced by temporary differences that will result in deductible amounts when a nontax liability is settled in future years. The requirements for recognition of a tax benefit for deductible temporary differences and for operating loss carryforwards are the same, and the manner of reporting the eventual tax benefit recognized (that is, in income or as required by paragraph 37) is not affected by the intervening transaction reported for tax purposes.

Paragraph 244 of Statement 109 contains an example of such a transaction:

> The following example illustrates the interaction of loss carryforwards and temporary differences that will result in net deductible amounts in future years. The assumptions are as follows:
>
> a. The financial loss and the loss reported on the tax return for an enterprise's first year of operations are the same.
>
> b. In year 2, a gain of $2,500 from a transaction that is a sale for tax purposes but a sale and leaseback for financial reporting is the only difference between pretax financial income and taxable income.

	Financial Income	**Taxable Income**
Year 1: Income (loss) from operations	$(4,000)	$(4,000)
Year 2: Income (loss) from operations	$–	$–

Taxable gain on sale	2,500
Taxable income before loss carryforward	2,500
Loss carryforward from year 1	(4,000)
Taxable income	$–

The $4,000 operating loss carryforward at the end of year 1 is reduced to $1,500 at the end of year 2 because $2,500 of it is used to reduce taxable income. The $2,500 reduction in the loss carryforward becomes $2,500 of deductible temporary differences that will reverse and result in future tax deductions when lease payments are made. The enterprise has no deferred tax liability to be offset by those future tax deductions, the future tax deductions cannot be realized by loss carryback because no taxes have been paid, and the enterprise has had pretax losses for financial reporting since inception. Unless positive evidence exists that is sufficient to overcome the negative evidence associated with those losses, a valuation allowance is recognized at the end of year 2 for the full amount of the deferred tax asset related to the $2,500 of deductible temporary differences and the remaining $1,500 of operating loss carryforward.

EXCERPT FROM OFFICIAL TEXT

38. If there is only one item other than continuing operations, the portion of income tax expense or benefit for the year that remains after the allocation to continuing operations is allocated to that item. If there are two or more items other than continuing operations, the amount that remains after the allocation to continuing operations shall be allocated among those other items in proportion to their individual effects on income tax expense or benefit for the year. When there are two or more items other than continuing operations, the sum of the separately calculated, individual effects of each item sometimes may not equal the amount of income tax expense or benefit for the year that remains after the allocation to continuing operations. In those circumstances, the procedures to allocate the remaining amount to items other than continuing operations are as follows:

    a. Determine the effect on income tax expense or benefit for the year of the total net loss for all net loss items
    b. Apportion the tax benefit determined in (a) ratably to each net loss item
    c. Determine the amount that remains, that is, the difference between (1) the amount to be allocated to all items other than continuing operations and (2) the amount allocated to all net loss items
    d. Apportion the tax expense determined in (c) ratably to each net gain item.

Refer to paragraphs 273–276 for additional guidance.

Certain Quasi Reorganizations

EXCERPT FROM OFFICIAL TEXT

Certain Quasi Reorganizations

39. The tax benefits of deductible temporary differences and carryforwards as of the date of a quasi reorganization as defined and contemplated in ARB No. 43, Chapter 7, "Capital Accounts," ordinarily are reported as a direct addition to contributed capital if the tax benefits are recognized in subsequent years. The only exception is for enterprises that have previously both adopted Statement 96 and effected a quasi reorganization that involves only the elimination of a deficit in retained earnings by a concurrent reduction in contributed capital prior to adopting this Statement. For those enterprises, subsequent recognition of the tax benefit of prior deductible temporary differences and carryforwards is included in income and reported as required by paragraph 37 (without regard to the referenced exceptions) and then reclassified from retained earnings to contributed capital. Those enterprises should disclose (a) the date of the quasi reorganization, (b) the manner of reporting the tax benefits and that it differs from present accounting requirements for other enterprises and (c) the effect of those tax benefits on income from continuing operations, income before extraordinary items, and on net income (and on related per share amounts).

INTERPRETATION

39-1. Quasi Reorganizations

Question: If an enterprise has a valuation allowance for deferred tax assets at the time of a quasi reorganization, should subsequent reductions in that valuation allowance be credited to income, directly to equity, or in some other manner?

Response: Statement 109 allows enterprises that adopted Statement 96 and effected a "deficit-only-reclassification quasi reorganization" prior to adopting Statement 109 to recognize tax benefits that existed and were not recognized at the date of the quasi reorganization as reductions of income tax expense when subsequently recognized. All other enterprises should report such tax benefits as direct additions to contributed capital.

In SEC Staff Accounting Bulletin (SAB) Topic 5S, "Miscellaneous Accounting—Quasi-Reorganization," (SAB 86) Question 4, the SEC staff states its view that existing SEC accounting requirements preclude deficit-only-reclassification quasi reorganizations (i.e., in the SEC staff's view, all quasi reorganizations are based on a "fresh-start" concept). Therefore, for public companies, only those few public companies that adopted Statement 96 before the SEC staff issued SAB 86 and were effectively "grandfathered" by the SEC staff are allowed to recognize tax benefits that existed and were not recognized at the date of a deficit-only-reclassification quasi reorganization as reductions of tax expense when subsequently recognized.

PARAGRAPH 40: SEPARATE FINANCIAL STATEMENTS OF A SUBSIDIARY

EXCERPT FROM OFFICIAL TEXT

Separate Financial Statements of a Subsidiary

40. The consolidated amount of current and deferred tax expense for a group that files a consolidated tax return shall be allocated among the members of the group when those members issue separate financial statements. This Statement does not require a single allocation method. The method adopted, however, shall be systematic, rational, and consistent with the broad principles established by this Statement. A method that allocates current and deferred taxes to members of the group by applying this Statement to each member as if it were a separate taxpayer[10] meets those criteria. Examples of methods that are not consistent with the broad principles established by this Statement include:

a. A method that allocates only current taxes payable to a member of the group that has taxable temporary differences

b. A method that allocates deferred taxes to a member of the group using a method fundamentally different from the asset and liability method described in this Statement (for example, the Opinion 11 deferred method)

c. A method that allocates no current or deferred tax expense to a member of the group that has taxable income because the consolidated group has no current or deferred tax expense.

Certain disclosures are also required (paragraph 49).

---

10 In that situation, the sum of the amounts allocated to individual members of the group may not equal the consolidated amount. That may also be the result when there are intercompany transactions between members of the group. The criteria are satisfied, nevertheless, after giving effect to the type of adjustments (including eliminations) normally present in preparing consolidated financial statements.

INTERPRETATION

40-1. Allocating Taxes Among Members of the Consolidated Group

Question: Statement 109 requires that the method of allocating taxes among members of a group that file a consolidated tax return be "systematic, rational, and consistent with the broad principles established by this Statement." How many methods have been identified that meet that definition?

Response: We have identified two methods that meet the requirements in Statement 109—the "separate return" method and the "pro rata" method:

1. The separate return method is fairly self-explanatory. The allocation of tax expense (benefit) is based on what the subsidiary's current and deferred tax expense would have been had the subsidiary filed a separate tax return.
2. The pro rata method allocates tax expense/benefit to the members of the group filing a consolidated tax return based on each member's relative contribution to the group's consolidated tax liability. For example, assume a consolidated group has taxable income of $100 and taxes payable of $33. Subsidiary A generated taxable income of $30 and therefore is allocated $10 of the consolidated group's tax liability. Subsidiary B generated a taxable loss of $60 and therefore is allocated $20 of tax benefits. Each member of the consolidated group computes its deferred tax assets and liabilities in the same manner. In most situations, the amount of tax expense allocated to profitable members of the consolidated group will be similar under both the separate return and pro rata methods. However, the amounts allocated to loss companies could be significantly different under the separate return method than the pro rata method.

If the enterprise's tax-sharing agreement is consistent with either of those methods, that method should be used. If the enterprise does not have a formal tax-sharing agreement or its tax-sharing agreement is inconsistent with both of the previous methods, either of those methods may be used to allocate tax expense to members of the group filing a consolidated tax return. Generally, any differences between tax expense (or benefit) so allocated and payments to be made to (or received from) the parent for tax expense should be treated as capital transactions (i.e., as dividends or capital contributions). Consider Example 40-1A.

Example 40-1A

Assume that Parent and Subsidiary file a consolidated tax return. For purposes of remitting taxes to Parent, there is an informal tax-sharing agreement under which Subsidiary pays Parent an amount each month that is computed simply by multiplying pretax accounting income by 50%. Tax expense for the year, however, should be computed using one of the previous methods (i.e., separate return or pro rata). In most situations, tax expense would be pretax accounting income added to or subtracted from permanent differences multiplied by the enacted regular tax rate (the answer could differ, e.g., because of a change in enacted tax law during the period or changes in valuation allowances). The difference between the computed tax expense and the amount paid to Parent for taxes would be treated as a capital transaction (in this case, a dividend). Subsidiary would have no deferred tax assets or liabilities because those amounts are being currently paid to or received from Parent. In its footnotes, Subsidiary should disclose the types of any significant temporary differences and the fact that the tax effects of those temporary differences have been paid to or received from Parent. If Subsidiary is a public enterprise, it should also quantify the approximate tax effect of each significant type of temporary difference. (See Interpretation 49-1 for a discussion of other required disclosures.)

We believe the method used for allocation of income taxes among members of a consolidated group should be consistently applied to all members of that consolidated group. We understand that the SEC staff agrees with this position.

We are aware of only one exception to this rule that occurs when a consolidated group uses the pro rata method of income tax allocation and is planning to divest a subsidiary by taking that subsidiary public for the first time. In cases in which the subsidiary will become a separate taxpaying entity, we believe it is acceptable to present the subsidiary's historical financial statements in its initial public offering using the separate return method.

40-2. Examples of Separate Return and Pro Rata Allocation Approaches

Question: Interpretation 40-1 states that there are two acceptable alternatives for allocating the consolidated tax provision (in separate company financial statements) among entities that file a consolidated tax return. How do these approaches work in practice and what effect does a different funding approach (to or from the parent) have on the calculations?

Response: The two approaches discussed in Interpretation 40-1 appear straightforward on the surface. They can be complicated at times; however, especially when the consolidated entity has a valuation allowance or the subsidiary funds the tax liability to the parent on a different method than it used to allocate tax expense.

The separate return method is fairly self-explanatory. The allocation of tax expense (benefit) is based on what the subsidiary's current and deferred tax provision would have been had the subsidiary filed a separate tax return.

The pro rata method can be somewhat more complicated. The pro rata method allocates tax expense/benefit to the members of the group filing a consolidated tax return based on each member's relative contribution to the group's consolidated tax liability (both current and deferred). The following guidelines should be followed in applying the pro rata method:

- In general, the consolidated current provision and deferred provision should be allocated to the subsidiaries based on each subsidiary's relative amount of taxable income/loss and changes in temporary differences to the consolidated taxable income/loss and changes in temporary differences, respectively.
- If the consolidated entity does not require a valuation allowance, no subsidiary should reflect a valuation allowance in its separate company statements.
- If there is a valuation allowance required at the consolidated level, it should all be allocated to the subsidiary whose deferred tax assets required the valuation. If there is more than one subsidiary with deferred tax assets, the valuation allowance generally should be allocated to those subsidiaries based on the relative amount of their deferred tax assets. When there is evidence that the valuation allowance clearly relates to specific deferred tax assets of one subsidiary (e.g., one subsidiary has deferred tax assets that are expected to turn on a short-term basis and therefore are deemed realizable while another subsidiary has longer term deferred tax assets, of which realization is uncertain), it should be allocated to the specific deferred tax assets.
- Although the separate return method will sometimes result in the sum of the subsidiaries provisions not equaling the consolidated provision (requiring an entry in consolidation as allowed by footnote 10 to paragraph 40 of Statement 109), this should not be the case with the pro rata approach. The sum of all of the provisions must equal the consolidated provision.

Example 40-2A demonstrates the two approaches.

Example 40-2A

Example assumptions:

	Pretax Book Income (Loss)	**20X1 Results Change in Temporary Differences**	**Taxable Income (Loss)**
Sub A	$100	$(60)	$40
Sub B	(200)	60	(140)
Consolidated	$(100)	$0	$(100)

Beginning of 20X1: (1) no temporary differences and (2) no carryforwards/carrybacks.

Tax rate is 40%.

On a consolidated basis, the company recognizes 50% of the resulting net deferred tax asset of $40 (tax net operating loss [NOL] carryforward of $100 at 40% assuming the temporary differences of Sub A and B will offset for tax purposes) or $20, resulting in a valuation allowance of $20.

On a separate return method, Sub B does not recognize any of its net deferred tax asset of $80 (tax NOL carryforward of $140 plus deductible temporary differences of $60, all at 40%). The partial recognition of the consolidated loss is based solely on a qualifying tax planning strategy, which will generate taxable income of $50 for Sub A.

The resulting consolidated tax provision is as follows:

Deferred tax asset	$20	
Deferred tax benefit		$20

Scenario A: Separate Return Approach—Funding to Parent Based on Currently Payable

Sub A's tax provision would be as follows:

Tax provision	$40	
Tax currently payable		$16
Deferred tax liabilities		24

Sub A would pay the $16 of currently payable to its parent and recognize a deferred tax liability (payable to parent) of $24.

Continued on page 230

Continued from page 229

Sub B's tax provision would be as follows:

> No entry, because on a separate return method Sub B is not more-likely-than-not to realize its net deferred tax asset of $80. Sub B would disclose deferred tax assets of $80 and a valuation allowance of $80.

As a result of the above, the following entry is required in consolidation:

Tax currently payable	$16	
Deferred tax liabilities	24	
Deferred tax assets	20	
Tax provision		$60

Scenario B: Pro Rata Approach—Funding to Parent Based on Currently Payable

Sub A contributed a combined $100 of taxable income ($40) and taxable temporary differences ($60) to the consolidated provision. Therefore, its provision is based on this $100 and results in the same provision as the separate return method as follows:

Tax provision	$40	
Tax currently payable		$16
Deferred tax liabilities		24

Sub B contributed a combined $200 of operating loss ($140) and deductible temporary differences ($60). Of this amount, $100 was benefited against Sub A's taxable items and $50 was benefited based on the future taxable income of the Sub A tax planning strategy. Therefore, Sub B will reflect a benefit for $150 of the $200 and the consolidated valuation allowance of $20 will all be allocated to Sub B to cover the remaining $50 of its tax deductible items whose realization is not considered more-likely-than-not. The following tax provision results for Sub B:

Deferred tax assets	$44	
Tax currently receivable	16	
Tax provision		$60

Sub B's provision was zero under the separate return method while Sub B reflects a tax benefit of $60 under the pro rata approach.

Generally, any differences between tax expense (benefit) allocated using one of the two approaches and payments made to, or received from, the parent for that expense using a different approach should

Continued on page 231

Continued from page 230

be treated as capital transactions. The following scenarios demonstrate this situation using the same assumptions from above.

Scenario C: Separate Return Approach—Funding to Parent Based on 50% of Pretax Book Income (Parent Does Not Pay Sub for Losses)

Sub A: Pretax income was $100; therefore, Sub A paid its parent $50. The net entry required to record the provision and resulting dividend would be as follows:

Tax provision	$40	
Dividend (retained earnings)	10	
Cash		$50

Sub B: Pretax loss was $200 that the parent will not pay B for even though the parent was able to benefit $150 of this NOL. As no provision was made, no entry is required related to the non-funding (see Scenario E for subsequent accounting).

Scenario D: Pro Rata Approach—Funding to Parent Based on 50% of Pretax Book Income (Parent Does Not Pay Sub for Losses)

Sub A: Same entry as Scenario C.

Sub B: While Sub B recognizes a deferred tax benefit of $60 related to its NOL and deductible temporary differences, it will never receive payment from the parent for those tax benefits. Therefore, this tax benefit is "dividended" to the parent. The net provision entry is as follows:

Dividend (retained earnings)	$60	
Tax provision		$60

Scenario E: Separate Return Approach—Funding to Parent Based on 50% of Pretax Book Income (Parent Does Not Pay Sub for Losses)—(Same as Scenario C)

Now assume Sub B has book and taxable income in 20X2 of $240, which was not expected at December 31, 20X1.

On a separate return approach, Sub B has a tax NOL carryforward of $140 from 20X1. Therefore, this will be realized against 20X2's taxable income of $240.

However, Sub B must pay its parent $120 (50% of pretax income of $240) since the parent gives no credit for NOLs (either in the year generated or in the year "utilized" by the subsidiary). Therefore, assuming Sub B's $60 of deductible temporary differences from 20X1 are still not considered realizable at December 31, 20X2, the

Continued on page 232

Continued from page 231

following entry is required to reflect the provision and resulting payments to parent:

Tax provision	$40*	
Dividend (retained earnings)	80**	
Cash		$120

In all cases, the subsidiary should disclose in its footnote the types (and if public, the related tax effects) of any significant temporary differences and carryforwards and whether the tax effects of those temporary differences and carryforwards have been paid to or received from the parent. We believe such disclosure is especially important in the financial statements of a subsidiary that: (*a*) has paid the deferred tax expense related to significant taxable temporary differences to its parent currently (and therefore does not reflect a deferred tax liability in its separate company financial statements) and (*b*) would become primarily liable for the deferred tax consequences of those taxable temporary differences if the subsidiary were no longer a member of the group filing a consolidated tax return.

---

* 20X2 taxable income ($240) less 20X1 NOL ($140) at 40%.

** Reflects "lost" NOL from 20X1 of $140 at 50% payment rate ($70) and excess of payment rate over tax rate on 20X2 net taxable income ($240 – 140) × (50% – 40%) = $10.

40-3. Valuation Allowances in Separate Company Financial Statements

Question: In situations in which deferred tax assets are recognized by a member of a group filing a consolidated tax return in its separate financial statements, how should the enterprise determine whether a valuation allowance is needed?

Response: The manner in which the enterprise determines whether a valuation allowance is needed depends on the tax-sharing agreement among the members of the group filing the consolidated tax return. If the tax-sharing agreement is based on the tax expense or benefit the subsidiary would pay or receive if it filed a separate tax return, the evaluation of the need for a valuation allowance would be the same as if the subsidiary filed a separate tax return (assuming that the parent has the ability to honor its obligation under the tax-sharing agreement).

If the tax-sharing agreement provides for a "pro rata" allocation of the group's tax liability, the subsidiary's valuation allowance for deferred tax assets should be consistent with the consolidated group's accounting for income taxes. That is, if the consolidated group does not need a valuation allowance for deferred tax assets, neither should any subsidiary in its separate company financial statements.

If there is no formal tax-sharing agreement or the tax-sharing agreement is inconsistent with both of the previous methods, the evaluation of the need for a valuation allowance should be consistent with the tax allocation method used (see Interpretation 40-2). The notes to the financial statements should contain adequate disclosure of the basis used to determine the valuation allowance.

40-4. Change in Method of Intercorporate Tax Allocation

Question: Statement 109 does not prescribe a single method of allocating taxes among members of a group that file a consolidated tax return. In the separate financial statements of a subsidiary that is a member of a group that files a consolidated tax return, is a change from one acceptable method of allocating taxes to another acceptable method a change in accounting?

Response: Yes. The requirements of FASB Statement No. 154, *Accounting Changes and Error Corrections,* should be followed. Further, if the subsidiary is an SEC registrant, a preferability letter will be required.

40-5. Subpart F Income

Question: A U.S. shareholder is taxed currently on its share of a controlled foreign corporation's (as defined in the Internal Revenue Code [IRC]) subpart F income (also as defined in the IRC—primarily passive income) whether the income is distributed or not. Does Statement 109 require allocation of the U.S. tax expense attributable to a subsidiary's subpart F income to that subsidiary when separate financial statements of that subsidiary are prepared?

Response: No. Statement 109 requires allocation of tax expense among members of a group that file a consolidated tax return. In this situation, the subsidiary is not part of the U.S. federal consolidated tax return. An enterprise may elect to have that subsidiary treated as a domestic subsidiary and included in the U.S. federal consolidated tax return (in some situations, this results in a better tax answer for the enterprise). In that situation, current and deferred taxes would need to be allocated to the subsidiary pursuant to Statement 109.

40-6. Tax Effects of Push Down of Debt in an Acquisition

Question: Company A acquires Company B in a business combination (taxable or nontaxable). Subsequent to the acquisition, Company B will be included in the consolidated tax return of Company A. Company B guarantees the debt incurred by Company A in the acquisition and Company A will only be able to service the debt through dividends from Company B. Therefore, Company A is required to "push down" the acquisition debt to the Company B separate company financial statements. As a result, the debt is reflected in Company B's financial statements but Company B has no tax basis in that debt and will receive no tax deductions for the interest expense it recognizes for financial reporting purposes.

Does the acquisition debt that is pushed down to Company B create a temporary difference in the separate company financial statements of Company B?

Response: No. From a U.S. federal tax standpoint, in general, the payments made from Company B to Company A to service the debt are treated as dividends (Company A's investment in Company B's stock will increase by Company B's taxable earnings and profits and decrease by these dividends). Therefore, although there is a basis difference related to the acquisition debt, there is no future tax consequence to the reversal of that basis difference and therefore no temporary difference.

Question: Should a tax effect for interest expense on the pushed down debt be reflected in the separate company financial statements of Company B (Company A will receive the tax deduction for the interest paid on the debt)?

Response: Yes. The group filing the consolidated tax return receives a tax deduction for the interest paid and we believe that Company B should reflect whatever tax benefit is recognized from that deduction in its separate company financial statements (if Company B is not paid for this benefit under its tax sharing agreement with Company A, the other side of Company B's journal entry is to equity).

40-7. [Not Used]

40-8. Presenting Income Taxes in Carveout Financial Statements

Question: It is sometimes necessary for enterprises to prepare financial statements of a business that is a part of a larger consolidated group, but that is not a legal entity (e.g., in an SEC registrant's filing related to the acquisition of a division of another company). Such financial statements are commonly referred to as "carveout" financial statements. The SEC staff, in SEC Staff Accounting Bulletin (SAB) Topic 1B, "Financial Statements—Allocation of Expenses and Related Disclosure in Financial Statements of Subsidiaries, Divisions or Lesser Business Components of Another Entity," (SAB 55) provides some guidance on the preparation of carveout financial statements.

Should income tax expense or benefit be allocated to a business that is a part of a larger consolidated group when preparing carve-out financial statements for that business, if that business is not a legal entity?

Response: To the extent that the carveout financial statements include a tax-paying entity, such as a corporate subsidiary, current and deferred taxes should be allocated to that tax-paying entity in preparing the carveout financial statements of the business. To the extent that the carveout financial statements include non-tax-paying entities, such as a division of a corporation, practice has been diverse.

The SEC staff expresses its preference in SAB 55 that any carved out subsidiary present its income tax expense computed on a separate return basis and requires certain pro forma disclosures if income tax expense has been allocated on another basis:

> When the historical income statements in the filing do not reflect the tax provision on the separate return basis, the staff has required a pro forma income statement for the most recent year and interim period reflecting a tax provision calculated on the separate return basis.

SAB 55 does not explicitly address the allocation of income taxes to a business that is not a legal entity, such as a division. However, in a meeting with the AICPA SEC Regulations Committee in June 2001, the SEC staff did state the following:

> As stated in SAB Topic 1B, the staff believes that financial statements are more useful to investors if they reflect all costs of doing business. As the transactions reported in the carveout financial statements have income tax implications to the taxable entity of which the reporting entity is a part, the staff believes that carveout financial statements should reflect income tax expense and deferred tax assets/liabilities attributable to the reporting entity.

40-9. Presenting Income Taxes in the Separate Financial Statements of a Single Member LLC

Question: Flow-through entities, such as most partnerships, by definition, "flow through" their tax attributes to their owners and are not, as an entity, subject to income taxes. Accordingly, income taxes are not reflected in the financial statements of flow-through entities.[1] Because most partnerships and limited liability companies (LLCs) that are treated as partnerships for tax purposes are flow-through entities, income taxes are not reflected in most partnership and LLC financial statements.

However, a single member LLC is treated as a "disregarded entity" for tax purposes rather than a flow-through entity (unless an election is made to treat the single member LLC as a corporation). In other words, most single member LLCs are treated no differently for tax purposes than a division of a taxpayer.

Assuming the parent of the single member LLC is a taxable entity, should income taxes be reflected in the financial statements of a single member LLC that is treated as a disregarded entity for tax purposes?

Response: This question is not addressed in the authoritative literature and we believe that reasonable arguments can be made for both reflecting and not reflecting income taxes in the financial statements of a single member LLC that is treated as a disregarded entity for tax purposes as long as the parent of the single member LLC is a taxable entity.

Arguments for including income taxes in single member LLC financial statements primarily focus on the fact that single member LLCs that are disregarded entities for tax purposes are treated no differently for tax purposes than a division and practice accepts reflecting a tax provision in the carveout financial statements of a division (see Interpretation 40-8). Arguments against including income taxes in single member LLC financial statements are primarily based on an analogy to the accounting required for tax flow-through entities. Proponents of this view argue that there is no substantive difference, from the LLC's perspective, between being a disregarded entity vs. being a flow-through entity—in both situations, the owners of the LLC, not the LLC, are obligated with respect to any taxes due resulting from the operations of the LLC.

If the single member LLC's financial statements will be included in a public filing, refer to Interpretation 40-8 for the SEC staff's views on allocation of income taxes in carveout financial statements.

1 It is possible for a LLC that is treated as a flow-through entity for federal income tax purposes to be taxed as an entity by a state. In such a situation, the LLC should reflect current and deferred state income taxes in its financial statements in accordance with Statement 109.

PARAGRAPHS 41–42: FINANCIAL STATEMENT PRESENTATION

EXCERPT FROM OFFICIAL TEXT

Financial Statement Presentation

41. In a classified statement of financial position, an enterprise shall separate deferred tax liabilities and assets into a current amount and a noncurrent amount. Deferred tax liabilities and assets shall be classified as current or noncurrent based on the classification of the related asset or liability for financial reporting. A deferred tax liability or asset that is not related to an asset or liability for financial reporting (paragraph 15), including deferred tax assets related to carryforwards, shall be classified according to the expected reversal date of the temporary difference pursuant to FASB Statement No. 37, *Balance Sheet Classification of Deferred Income Taxes*. The valuation allowance for a particular tax jurisdiction shall be allocated between current and noncurrent deferred tax assets for that tax jurisdiction on a pro rata basis.

INTERPRETATION

41-1. Current/Noncurrent Classification of Tax Carryforwards

Question: How should the current/noncurrent classification of deferred tax assets and liabilities that do not relate to financial statement assets or liabilities (e.g., a net operating loss [NOL] carryforward for tax purposes) be determined?

Response: Classification of deferred tax assets and liabilities that do not relate to financial statement assets or liabilities should be based on the expected "reversal date" of the temporary difference or carryforward. For example, if one-third of a NOL carryforward ($100 of a $300 deferred tax asset related to the NOL carryforward) is expected to be utilized next year, $100 normally should be classified as current and $200 as noncurrent. However, if the utilization of one-third of the

NOL next year is expected to result in a $20 reduction in taxes payable and an $80 alternative minimum tax credit carryforward, only $20 of the deferred tax asset should be classified as current.

41-2. Effect of a Valuation Allowance on Financial Statement Classification

Question: Statement 109 requires that deferred tax liabilities and assets should be classified as current or noncurrent based on the classification of the related asset or liability for financial reporting. It also requires that the valuation allowance for a particular jurisdiction should be allocated between current and noncurrent deferred tax assets for that jurisdiction on a *pro rata* basis. Finally, it requires that all current deferred tax liabilities and assets within a jurisdiction should be offset and presented as a single amount and all noncurrent deferred tax liabilities and assets within a jurisdiction should be offset and presented as a single amount. Does this mean that if a company has a valuation allowance for its entire net deferred tax asset that it would not report any tax assets or liabilities in its balance sheet?

Response: No. In most cases, the company will still report some deferred tax assets or liabilities even if its net deferred tax asset is fully reserved. This is due to the fact that the financial statement classification is a three-step procedure that must be performed in the order that the steps are presented in the previous question. Example 41-2A demonstrates this point.

Example 41-2A

Example assumptions:

Company A has temporary differences (all in the same tax jurisdiction) related to the following assets and liabilities. The dollar amounts represent the tax effects, before consideration of a valuation allowance, of the temporary differences:

Deferred Tax Assets

Accrued expenses (current)	$100
Long-term warranty accrual	50
	$150

Deferred Tax Liabilities

Installment receivable (current)	$80
Fixed assets	20
	$100

Continued on page 239

Continued from page 238

The taxable temporary differences reverse in the same time period as the deductible temporary differences and therefore assure the realization of a part of the deferred tax asset. Company A then needs to assess the realizability of the balance of its deferred tax asset of $50 ($150 – $100). It concludes that it needs a $50 valuation allowance (i.e., its net deferred taxes, including the valuation allowance, is zero).

The $50 valuation allowance must be allocated on a pro rata basis using the gross deferred tax assets. Therefore, 67% ($100/$150) or $33 of the valuation allowance will be included in the current deferred tax classification and 33% or $17 of the valuation allowance will be included in the noncurrent deferred tax classification.

Current deferred tax assets are now netted against current deferred tax liabilities and noncurrent deferred tax assets are now netted against noncurrent deferred tax liabilities as follows:

Current deferred tax assets	$100
Current portion of valuation allowance	(33)
Current deferred tax liabilities	(80)
Net current deferred tax liability	($13)

Noncurrent deferred tax assets	$50
Noncurrent portion of valuation allowance	(17)
Noncurrent deferred tax liability	(20)
Net noncurrent deferred tax asset	$13

In this case, Company A will report in its balance sheet a noncurrent deferred tax asset of $13 and a current deferred tax liability of $13 even though it has a valuation allowance for the entire amount of its net deferred tax assets. Note that the order in which the three steps are performed is very important. If the deferred tax liabilities were incorrectly netted against the deferred tax assets first and then the valuation allowance were allocated, in the case of Company A there would be no deferred tax assets or liabilities to report in the balance sheet.

41-3. Classification of Deferred Taxes Related to LIFO Inventory

Question: Some temporary differences, although relating to current assets, have tax effects that will not be payable for several years or longer. One example is a temporary difference related to last-in, first-out (LIFO) inventory. The LIFO inventory is classified as a current asset, whereas the deferred tax effect of any related temporary difference will not become payable as long as the base level of LIFO inventory is maintained. Should such deferred taxes be classified as current or noncurrent in the statement of financial position?

Response: The FASB considered several different approaches to financial statement classification of deferred tax assets and liabilities. However, it ultimately settled on the approach previously followed under Opinion 11 whereby classification is dependent on the classification of the asset or liability that gives rise to the temporary difference. The FASB did not make any exceptions to this requirement. As a result, any deferred taxes resulting from a LIFO temporary difference are classified as current.

41-4. Presentation of Deferred Taxes Related to Intercompany Profits

Question: Paragraph 9(e) of Statement 109 creates an exception to the statement's general rules for taxes paid by the seller on intercompany profits on assets remaining within a consolidated group and the temporary differences created in the buyer's tax jurisdiction related to those assets. Under this exception, the seller's tax expense (current and deferred) related to the sale is deferred and amortized to tax expense as the asset is realized (through depreciation or sale) and no deferred tax asset is recognized for the temporary difference in the buyer's tax jurisdiction. That treatment is consistent with the treatment of taxes on intercompany profits under Opinion 11.

Under Opinion 11, such deferred tax assets could be included with other deferred tax assets or could be netted against the related asset. How should the deferred taxes related to intercompany profits be displayed in the *consolidated* financial statements under Statement 109? That is, should those deferred taxes be included with other deferred tax assets or should those deferred taxes be netted against the related asset or is either presentation acceptable?

Response: Because Statement 109 specifically prohibits net-of-tax accounting and reporting (see paragraph 29(a)), we believe deferred tax assets related to intercompany profits should be included with other deferred tax assets.

EXCERPT FROM OFFICIAL TEXT

42. For a particular tax-paying component of an enterprise and within a particular tax jurisdiction, (a) all current deferred tax liabilities and assets shall be offset and presented as a single amount and (b) all noncurrent deferred tax liabilities and assets shall be offset and presented as a single amount. However, an enterprise shall not offset deferred tax liabilities and assets attributable to different tax-paying components of the enterprise or to different tax jurisdictions.

PARAGRAPHS 43–49: FINANCIAL STATEMENT DISCLOSURE

EXCERPT FROM OFFICIAL TEXT

Financial Statement Disclosure

43. The components of the net deferred tax liability or asset recognized in an enterprise's statement of financial position shall be disclosed as follows:

    a. The total of all deferred tax liabilities measured in procedure (b) of paragraph 17
    b. The total of all deferred tax assets measured in procedures (c) and (d) of paragraph 17
    c. The total valuation allowance recognized for deferred tax assets determined in procedure (e) of paragraph 17.

    The net change during the year in the total valuation allowance also shall be disclosed. A **public enterprise** shall disclose the approximate tax effect of each type of temporary difference and carryforward that gives rise to a significant portion of deferred tax liabilities and deferred tax assets (before allocation of valuation allowances). A **nonpublic enterprise** shall disclose the types of significant temporary differences and carryforwards but may omit disclosure of the tax effects of each type. A public enterprise that is not subject to income taxes because its income is taxed directly to its owners shall disclose that fact and the net difference between the tax bases and the reported amounts of the enterprise's assets and liabilities.

INTERPRETATION

43-1. Classification of Liabilities for Tax Contingencies

Question: Should liabilities for tax contingencies (sometimes referred to as uncertain tax positions) be included in deferred tax liabilities?

Response: No. Liabilities for tax contingencies should not be included in deferred tax liabilities or as part of the valuation allowance. FASB Interpretation (FIN) No. 48. *Accounting for Uncertainty in Income Taxes,* provides specific guidance on recognizing and measuring the effect of uncertain tax positions (see Interpretation 10-1 and Appendix I). In brief, FIN 48 provides that any additional currently payable (or reduction in amounts refundable) recognized from its application should be classified as a current liability (or reduction in current refund receivable) to the extent the enterprise expects payment (or receipt) of cash within one year or the operating cycle, if longer. Otherwise, the additional liability should be classified as a long-term liability.

There was diversity in practice prior to the issuance of FIN 48. Some accountants believed such liabilities, if expected to be paid in the next year, should be included in taxes currently payable and, if expected to be paid after one year, should be shown as long-term liabilities (similar to contingent liabilities recognized pursuant to FASB Statement No. 5, *Accounting for Contingencies*). Other accountants believed that all such liabilities should be included in taxes currently payable because the creditor (the taxing authority) has the ability to demand immediate payment.

43-2. Level of Detail in Determining Deductible and Taxable Temporary Differences

Question: Paragraph 43 of Statement 109 requires disclosure of gross deferred tax assets and gross deferred tax liabilities. What level of detail is required when separately quantifying deductible and taxable temporary differences for this disclosure? That is, should temporary differences be quantified by looking to financial statement captions (e.g., property, plant, and equipment) or by subgroup (e.g., tractors, trailers, and terminals for a trucking company) or by individual asset?

Response: There is no definitive answer regarding whether differences should be quantified by looking to financial statement captions, subgroup, or individual asset. We believe enterprises should look to the level of detail available in their general accounting records (e.g., by property subgroup), but are not required to quantify temporary differences by individual asset. The level of detail used should not affect an enterprise's *net* deferred tax position, but will affect its footnote disclosure of *gross* deferred tax assets and liabilities.

43-3. Level of Detail of Types of Temporary Differences

Question: Paragraph 43 of Statement 109 requires public enterprises to disclose the approximate tax effect of each type of temporary difference and carryforward that gives rise to a "significant" portion of deferred tax liabilities and deferred tax assets. Does Statement 109 or Regulation S-X define significant?

Response: Neither Statement 109 nor Regulation S-X defines the term "significant" for this purpose. We believe a reasonable threshold for significant in this situation is 5% of the greater of gross deferred tax assets (before valuation allowance) or gross deferred tax liabilities.

43-4. Disclosure of Carryforwards

Question: Paragraph 43 of Statement 109 requires public companies to disclose the approximate tax effect of each type of temporary difference and carryforward that gives rise to a significant portion of deferred tax liabilities and deferred tax assets (nonpublic companies are required to disclose the types of such items; the tax effects may be omitted). If a company has a deductible temporary difference or carryforward (and an offsetting valuation allowance) that it clearly will never realize (e.g., a loss carryforward in a jurisdiction in which operations have been terminated) couldn't it be considered misleading to continue disclosure of such deferred tax asset? If so, when should a company stop disclosing such a deferred tax asset and the related valuation allowance?

Response: Some respondents to the exposure draft on Statement 109 raised this issue. The FASB believed that it need not and should not develop detailed guidance for when to cease disclosure of the existence of a worthless asset (see paragraph 156 of Statement 109). We believe that if it is determined to be *remote* that the asset will ever be realized, nondisclosure of the gross asset and related valuation allowance would be acceptable. In the example discussed in the previous question, if the carryforward can only be realized through starting a new operation in that tax jurisdiction and the enterprise has no plans to do this, nondisclosure would be acceptable.

43-5. Direct Financing or Sales-Type Lease Temporary Differences

Question: Assume a lessor has a lease that is accounted for as a direct financing or sales-type lease for financial reporting purposes, but qualifies as an operating lease for tax purposes. For purposes of disclosing the tax effects of temporary differences, does the lessor have one or two temporary differences under Statement 109?

Response: Neither Statement 109 nor the FASB staff implementation guide on Statement 109 specifically addresses this question. However, question and answer (Q&A) 11 of the FASB Staff

Implementation Guide, *A Guide to Implementation of Statement 96 on Accounting for Income Taxes,* does address the question and concludes that there are two temporary differences. Q&A 11 states that one temporary difference relates to the investment in the lease (for financial reporting), which has a zero tax basis and the other temporary difference relates to the depreciable asset (for tax purposes), which has a zero basis for financial reporting. We believe following such an approach under Statement 109 is required except in the circumstances stated in the next paragraph.

Because Q&A 11 dealt primarily with determining the reversal patterns of temporary differences, it was not carried forward to the FASB staff implementation guide on Statement 109. Some have argued that the grossing up of the footnote disclosures that occurs if the logic in Q&A 11 is followed is misleading. They believe there is only one temporary difference—the difference between the carrying amount of the lease for financial reporting (a lease receivable) and for tax reporting (a depreciable asset). However, it is possible for the temporary difference related to the receivable to be settled without affecting the temporary difference related to the depreciable asset (e.g., if the enterprise sells the lease revenue stream, but retains the asset). We believe the one temporary difference approach for purposes of disclosure of tax effects of temporary differences in the notes to financial statements of enterprises is acceptable only in situations in which the enterprise does not have any intentions of disposing of the lease revenue stream while retaining the asset.

43-6. Disclosure of Public Partnership Basis Differences

Question: Paragraph 43 of Statement 109 states:

> A public enterprise that is not subject to income taxes because its income is taxed directly to its owners shall disclose that fact and the net difference between the tax bases and the reported amounts of the enterprise's assets and liabilities.

What types of entities does this requirement apply to and is the reference to "tax bases" an aggregation of the partners' tax bases in the partnership assets or the partnership's tax bases in the assets?

Response: This provision applies to any public entity for which income is taxed directly to its owners, including public partnerships, public real estate investment trusts, and regulated investment companies (mutual funds). The reference to tax bases is to the partnership's tax bases in its assets.

43-7. Disclosure of Certain Significant Risks and Uncertainties

Question: Does AICPA Statement of Position (SOP) 94-6, *Disclosure of Certain Significant Risks and Uncertainties,* require additional disclosures related to the realizability of deferred tax assets?

Response: Paragraph 13 of SOP 94-6 requires disclosure regarding significant estimates when both of the following criteria are met:

- It is at least reasonably possible that the estimate of the effect on the financial statements of a condition, situation, or set of circumstances that existed at the date of the financial statements will change in the near term due to one or more future confirming events.
- The effect of the change would be material to the financial statements.

The disclosure should indicate the nature of the uncertainty and include an indication that it is at least reasonably possible that a change in the estimate will occur in the near term. Disclosure of the factors that cause the estimate to be sensitive to change is encouraged but not required.

One example given in SOP 94-6 of a significant estimate is an estimate of future taxable income considered when assessing the need for a deferred tax asset valuation allowance. Accordingly, for enterprises that need to consider future taxable income in assessing the need for a deferred tax asset valuation allowance, if such an enterprise determines that its estimate of future tax income meets the two criteria above, SOP 94-6 does require the enterprise to make additional disclosures.

43-8. SEC Schedule of Valuation Allowances

Question: Rule 12-09 of Regulation S-X requires information about "all valuation and qualifying accounts and reserves not included in specific schedules." Should the valuation allowance for deferred tax assets be included on that schedule?

Response: We understand the SEC staff has concluded that the valuation allowance for deferred tax assets need not be included on the valuation and qualifying accounts and reserves schedule.

43-9. Additional Disclosures for SEC Registrants

Question: For public companies, Regulation S-X (Rule 4-08(h)), SEC Staff Accounting Bulletin (SAB) Topic 6I, "Interpretations of

Accounting Series Releases and Financial Reporting Releases—Accounting Series Release 149—Improved Disclosure of Income Tax Expense," (SABs 1 and 8) and SAB Topic 11C, "Miscellaneous Disclosure—Tax Holidays," (SAB 1) contain specific disclosure requirements related to income taxes. Are those disclosures in addition to those required by Statement 109?

Response: Yes.

For public companies, the following disclosures are required in addition to the disclosures required by Statement 109:

- The components of income (loss) before tax expense (benefit) as either domestic or foreign; and
- The amounts applicable to U.S. federal income taxes, foreign income taxes, and other income taxes stated separately for each major component of income tax expense (i.e., current and deferred);[1]
- A brief description of any temporary tax exemptions or "tax holidays," including the aggregate dollar and per share amounts, and the date on which the special tax status will terminate;
- Whenever the tax components of an equity method investee are known and material to the investor's financial position or result of operations, "appropriate disclosure should be made," including disclosures of tax holidays afforded equity method investees; and
- A reconciliation of the tax effect of items reported on a net of tax basis (e.g., extraordinary items and discontinued operations) to the applicable statutory federal income tax rate.

Statement 109 requires disclosure of all "significant" reconciling items between reported income tax expense and the amount that would have resulted from applying domestic federal statutory tax rates to pretax income from continuing operations. For public companies, Regulation S-X effectively defines the term "significant" by requiring disclosure of all reconciling items that are more than 5% of

[1] Paragraph 45 of Statement 109 requires disclosure of the significant components of income tax expense related to income from continuing operations. In order to comply with the requirements of paragraph 45 of Statement 109 as well as this SEC staff position, public companies for which income tax expense is allocated to items in addition to income from continuing operations will need to disclose: (*a*) the significant components of income tax expense related to income from continuing operations and (*b*) the significant components of income tax expense related to the items other than the income from continuing operations to which income tax expense was allocated.

the amount computed by multiplying pretax income by the statutory tax rate.

Finally, Section 811 of the American Jobs Creation Act of 2004, requires entities that are required to file periodic reports (e.g., Forms 10-K and 10-KSB) under Section 13 or 15(d) of the Securities and Exchange Act of 1934, to provide certain disclosures in their Forms 10-K and 10-KSB (Item 3, "Legal Proceedings") if they have been penalized for using tax-avoidance transactions. This nonfinancial, Internal Revenue Service disclosure requirement is documented in Internal Revenue Code (IRC) Section 6707A. In summary, registrants are required to disclose the amount of the penalty, a description of the penalty, whether the penalty has been paid, and the specific IRC section under which the penalty was determined. The penalties covered by this legislation are:

- A penalty under IRC Section 6707A for failure to disclose a listed transaction;
- The 30% penalty under IRC Section 6662A for an understatement attributable to an undisclosed listed transaction or undisclosed reportable avoidance transaction;
- The 40% penalty under IRC Section 6662 for a gross valuation misstatement if the 30% penalty under IRC Section 6662A would have applied, but for the application of IRC Section 6662A(e)(2)(c)(ii); and
- The penalty under IRC Section 6707A(e) for failure to make the required disclosure in SEC reports of the penalties enumerated above (i.e., new separate penalties will continue to accumulate for each successive failure to disclose until disclosure is made).

A company that may be subject to the reporting requirements under IRC Section 811 of the American Jobs Creation Act of 2004, should consult with appropriate tax, SEC, and other corporate counsel to determine whether any disclosure is required.

EXCERPT FROM OFFICIAL TEXT

44. The following information shall be disclosed whenever a deferred tax liability is not recognized because of the exceptions to comprehensive recognition of deferred taxes for any of the areas addressed by Opinion 23 (as amended by this Statement) or for deposits in statutory reserve funds by U.S. steamship enterprises:

    a. A description of the types of temporary differences for which a deferred tax liability has not been recognized and the types of events that would cause those temporary differences to become taxable
    b. The cumulative amount of each type of temporary difference
    c. The amount of the unrecognized deferred tax liability for temporary differences related to investments in foreign subsidiaries and foreign corporate joint ventures that are essentially permanent in duration if determination of that liability is practicable or a statement that determination is not practicable
    d. The amount of the deferred tax liability for temporary differences other than those in (c) above (that is, undistributed domestic earnings, the bad-debt reserve for tax purposes of a U.S. savings and loan association or other qualified thrift lender, the policyholders' surplus of a life insurance enterprise, and the statutory reserve funds of a U.S. steamship enterprise) that is not recognized in accordance with the provisions of paragraphs 31 and 32.

INTERPRETATION

44-1. Opinion 23 Disclosure of Outside Basis Differences

Question: Assume an enterprise has two foreign subsidiaries operating in different tax jurisdictions and has a "taxable" outside basis difference (i.e., an outside basis difference that, absent APB Opinion No. 23, *Accounting for Income Taxes—Special Areas,* would require the accrual of a deferred tax liability) related to one subsidiary and a "deductible" outside basis difference related to the other. Is it acceptable to net the outside basis differences for purposes of meeting the paragraph 44 disclosure requirements of Statement 109?

Response: No. The disclosures required by paragraph 44 for unrecognized deferred tax liabilities related to foreign subsidiaries should include only subsidiaries with "taxable" outside basis differences.

EXCERPT FROM OFFICIAL TEXT

45. The significant components of income tax expense attributable to continuing operations for each year presented shall be disclosed in the financial statements or notes thereto. Those components would include, for example:

    a. **Current tax expense or benefit**
    b. Deferred tax expense or benefit (exclusive of the effects of other components listed below)
    c. Investment tax credits
    d. Government grants (to the extent recognized as a reduction of income tax expense)
    e. The benefits of operating loss carryforwards
    f. Tax expense that results from allocating certain tax benefits either directly to contributed capital or to reduce goodwill or other noncurrent intangible assets of an acquired entity
    g. Adjustments of a deferred tax liability or asset for enacted changes in tax laws or rates or a change in the tax status of the enterprise
    h. Adjustments of the beginning-of-the-year balance of a valuation allowance because of a change in circumstances that causes a change in judgment about the realizability of the related deferred tax asset in future years.

INTERPRETATION

45-1. Disclosure of the Significant Components of Income Tax Expense

Question (from FASB Staff Implementation Guide, Question 18):

Paragraph 45 requires disclosure of the significant components of income tax expense attributable to continuing operations. Should the sum of the amounts disclosed for the components of tax expense equal the amount of income tax expense that is reported in the statement of earnings? Also, should the amounts disclosed for current tax expense and for deferred tax expense be before or after reduction for the tax benefit of operating loss carryforwards and tax credits?

Response (from FASB Staff Implementation Guide, Question 18):

The sum of the amounts disclosed for the components of tax expense should equal the amount of tax expense that is reported in the statement of earnings for continuing operations. Insignificant components that are not separately disclosed should be combined and disclosed as a single amount so that the sum of the amounts disclosed will equal total income tax expense attributable to continuing operations.

Separate disclosure of (a) the tax benefit of operating loss carryforwards and (b) tax credits and tax credit carryforwards that have been recognized as a reduction of current tax expense and deferred tax expense is required. There are a number of ways to satisfy that disclosure requirement. Three acceptable approaches are illustrated below. All three illustrations are based on the following assumptions:

An enterprise has $1,588 of taxable income and $100 of investment tax credits for the current year. The $100 deferred tax asset for $295 of operating loss carryforwards was fully reserved at the beginning of the current year.

Pretax financial income from continuing operations	$5,000
Income tax expense from continuing operations	$1,500
Effective tax rate	30%
Statutory tax rate	34%

1. Components of Income Tax Expense from Continuing Operations (*Gross Method*)

	Current	Deferred
Tax expense before application of investment tax credits and operating loss carryforwards	$540	$1,160
Investment tax credits	(100)	–
Tax benefit of operating loss carryforwards	(100)	–
Tax expense from continuing operations	$340	$1,160

2. Components of Income Tax Expense from Continuing Operations (*Net Method*)

Current tax expense (net of $100 investment tax credits and $100 tax benefit of operating loss carryforwards)	$ 340
Deferred tax expense	1,160
Tax expense from continuing operations	$1,500

3. Components of Income Tax Expense from Continuing Operations (*Statutory Tax Rate Reconciliation Method*)

Current tax expense	$ 340
Deferred tax expense	1,160
Tax expense from continuing operations	$1,500
Tax expense at statutory rate	$1,700
Benefit of investment tax credits	(100)
Benefit of operating loss carryforwards	(100)
Tax expense from continuing operations	$1,500

Statement 109 defines income tax expense as the sum of current and deferred tax expense, and the amount to be disclosed under any of the above approaches is only the amount by which total income tax expense from continuing operations has been reduced by tax credits or an operating loss carryforward. For example, assume that a tax benefit is recognized for an operating loss or tax credit carryforward by recognizing a deferred tax asset in year 1, with no valuation allowance required because of an existing deferred tax liability. Further, assume that the carryforward is realized on the tax return in year 2. For financial reporting in year 2:

a. Current tax expense will be reduced for the tax benefit of the operating loss or tax credit carryforward realized on the tax return.
b. Deferred tax expense will be larger (or a deferred tax benefit will be smaller) by the same amount.

In those circumstances, the operating loss or tax credit carryforward affects only income tax expense (the sum of current and deferred tax expense) in year 1 when a tax asset (with no valuation allowance) is recognized. There is no effect on income tax expense in year 2 because the separate effects on current and deferred tax expense offset each other. Accordingly, the requirement for separate disclosure of the effects of tax credits or an operating loss carryforward is not applicable for year 2. However, that disclosure requirement applies to financial statements for year 1 that are presented for comparative purposes.

45-2. Interest and Penalties

Question: Does Statement 109 preclude the reporting of interest and penalties assessed on income tax deficiencies as part of income tax expense?

Response: Paragraph 19 of FASB Interpretation (FIN) No. 48, *Accounting for Uncertainty in Income Taxes,* permits companies to classify interest as either a component of income tax expense or as interest expense. Further, penalties may be classified within income tax expense or another expense classification, based on the company's elective accounting policy which must be consistently applied. FIN 48 also requires a company to disclose the total amount of interest and penalties recognized in its income statement and balance sheet.

45-3. Disclosure of the Effect of the Change in Tax Rates on Deferred Tax Liabilities and Assets

Question: Paragraph 45(g) of Statement 109 requires that "[a]djustments of a deferred tax liability or asset for enacted changes in tax laws or rates or a change in the tax status of the enterprise" be disclosed. Should that disclosure be based on temporary differences that existed as of the first day of the corporation's fiscal year or on temporary differences that exist as of the enactment date?

Response: For both conceptual and practical reasons, we believe the disclosure should be based on temporary differences that exist as of the first day of the corporation's fiscal year. Conceptually, we believe it is potentially misleading to disclose the amount computed using temporary differences as of the enactment date.

For example, consider the disclosures in Example 45-3A for two companies when a 1% increase in income tax rates is enacted August 10, 20X3, and that increase is retroactive to January 1, 20X3.

Example 45-3A

Company A is a calendar year corporation and had no temporary differences as of January 1, 20X3. Company A's financial reporting income from January 1, 20X3, to August 10, 20X3, is $100 million and it created no temporary differences during this time period. Company B is identical to Company A except that Company B created a taxable temporary difference of $100 million during the period from January 1, 20X3, to August 10, 20X3, and therefore had zero current taxable income during that period. Therefore, if the disclosure is based on temporary differences as of the enactment date, Company A would report that the change in tax rates had no effect on its deferred tax liabilities or assets and Company B would report a $1 million increase in deferred tax liabilities as a result of the tax rate change. Both companies are similarly affected by the change in tax rates (in fact, Company A is economically more adversely affected because it will need to make the actual increased tax payment before Company B) and yet the disclosure infers that

Continued on page 255

Continued from page 254

Company B is much more significantly affected by the change in tax rates than Company A.

Further, *neither* company will report an effect of the tax law change in its effective tax rate reconciliation. However, if Company B bases its paragraph 45(g) disclosure on temporary differences that exist at the enactment date, Company B would need to somehow reconcile its disclosure of a $1 million increase in deferred tax liabilities as a result of the tax law change with its disclosure in its effective tax rate reconciliation. Finally, we believe the intent of paragraph 45(g) is to disclose the "out-of-period" effect of the change in tax law or rates on deferred tax liabilities or assets.

From a practical standpoint, we believe it is very difficult to determine temporary differences as of an interim date (in other than the simplest fact situation) because of the integral (rather than discrete) approach to accounting for income taxes in interim periods.

45-4. Disclosures Related to Tax Benefits From Share-Based Payments

Question: Does FASB Statement No. 123 (Revised 2004), *Share-Based Payment*, contain any disclosure requirements related to tax benefits derived from share-based payments?

Response: Yes. Paragraph A240 of Statement 123R contains two disclosure requirements related to tax benefits: (1) enterprises are required to disclose, for each year for which an income statement is presented, total recognized tax benefits related to total compensation cost for share-based payment arrangements and (2) enterprises are required to disclose the tax benefit realized from stock options exercised during the current year.

EXCERPT FROM OFFICIAL TEXT

46. The amount of income tax expense or benefit allocated to continuing operations and the amounts separately allocated to other items (in accordance with the provisions of paragraphs 35–39) shall be disclosed for each year for which those items are presented.

47. A public enterprise shall disclose a reconciliation using percentages or dollar amounts of (a) the reported amount of income tax expense attributable to continuing operations for the year to (b) the amount of income tax expense that would result from applying domestic federal statutory tax rates to pretax income from continuing operations. The "statutory" tax rates shall be the regular tax rates if there are alternative tax systems. The estimated amount and the nature of each significant reconciling item shall be disclosed. A nonpublic enterprise shall disclose the nature of significant reconciling items but may omit a numerical reconciliation. If not otherwise evident from the disclosures required by this paragraph and paragraphs 43–46, all enterprises shall disclose the nature and effect of any other significant matters affecting comparability of information for all periods presented.

INTERPRETATION

47-1. Effective Tax Rate Reconciliation: Change in Valuation Allowance

Question: Does the realization of a net operating loss (NOL) carryforward affect the effective tax rate reconciliation under Statement 109?

Response: The realization of an NOL carryforward does not directly affect the effective tax rate reconciliation. Under Statement 109, an NOL carryforward is recognized as a deferred tax asset in the period it arises. If a valuation allowance is not required, the NOL carryforward has no affect on the effective tax rate reconciliation in the period in which it arises or in the period in which it is utilized. However, if a valuation allowance is required for all or part of an NOL carryforward and, for example, due to the realization of the NOL carryforward in the tax return, the valuation allowance is reduced, the reduction in the valuation allowance will affect the effective tax rate reconciliation. Under Statement 109, it will be the increases and decreases in the valuation allowance that affects the effective tax rate, not the creation or realization of carryforwards.

47-2. Disclosure of Future Taxable Income Assumptions

Question: Does Statement 109 require disclosure of the amount of income from future operations that is assumed in determining the amount of a valuation allowance (or that no valuation allowance is needed)?

Response: No. However, in situations in which a valuation allowance is not provided for a material amount of deferred tax assets based on an assessment of future taxable income from future operations or qualifying tax-planning strategies, we encourage disclosure in the notes to the financial statements of the significant assumptions underlying the conclusion that a valuation allowance is not required in order to enhance the reader's understanding of the risk as to realization of the deferred tax asset.

For public companies, such disclosures may be required in their management's discussion & analysis of financial condition and results of operations (MD&A). The SEC staff stated the following in a May 1, 1999 release, "Frequently Requested Accounting and Financial Reporting Interpretations and Guidance":

> If a registrant has recognized a net deferred tax asset that is material, it may be necessary to discuss uncertainties surrounding realization of the asset and material assumptions underlying management's determination that the net asset will be realized. If the asset's realization is dependent on material improvements over present levels of consolidated pre-tax income, material changes in the present relationship between income reported for financial and tax purposes, or material asset sales or other non-routine transactions, a description of these assumed future events, quantified to the extent practicable, should be furnished in the MD&A. For example, the minimum annualized rate by which taxable income must increase during the tax NOL carryforward period should be disclosed if realization of the benefit is dependent on taxable income higher than currently reported. Also, if significant objective negative evidence indicates uncertainty regarding realization of the deferred asset, the countervailing positive evidence relied upon by management in its decision not to establish a full allowance against the asset should be identified.

47-3. Disclosures Related to Safe Harbor Leases

Question: The Economic Recovery Act of 1981 allowed certain tax benefits to be transferred via leases (see Interpretation 9-1, "Safe Harbor Leases"). What disclosures are required for sales and purchases of tax benefits through safe harbor leases?

Response: FASB Technical Bulletin (FTB) No. 82-1, *Disclosure of the Sale or Purchase of Tax Benefits through Tax Leases*, provides certain required disclosures. Disclosures required for safe harbor leases can be summarized as follows:

- The accounting policies or practices followed for safe harbor leases, including the method of accounting for those transactions and the methods of recognizing revenue and allocating income tax benefits and asset costs to current and future periods.
- Transactions involving the sale or purchase of tax benefits through tax leases may give rise to a significant reconciling item that should be disclosed pursuant to the requirements of paragraph 47 of Statement 109.
- If material and unusual or infrequent to the enterprise, the nature and financial effects of transactions involving the sale or purchase of tax benefits through tax leases should be disclosed on the face of the income statement in accordance with APB Opinion No. 30, *Reporting the Results of Operations—Reporting the Effects of Disposal of a Segment of a Business, and Extraordinary, Unusual and Infrequently Occurring Events and Transactions.*
- Any other disclosure that may be appropriate, depending on the circumstances involved. For example, if significant contingencies exist with respect to the sale or purchase of tax benefits, disclosures in accordance with FASB Statement No. 5, *Accounting for Contingencies*, may be warranted. Also, as referred to in paragraph 2 of Chapter 2A of Accounting Research Bulletin (ARB) No. 43, *Restatement and Revision of Accounting Research Bulletins*, if comparative financial statements are presented, disclosure should be made of any change in practice that significantly affects comparability.

47-4. Disclosure of the Effect of a Change in Tax Law or Rates on Leveraged Leases

Question: In EITF Issue No. 86-43, "Effect of a Change in Tax Law or Rates on Leveraged Leases," the EITF addressed issues related to the calculation and reporting of adjustments to net investments in leveraged leases required by a change in tax law or rates. What type of disclosure would be required for such a change?

Response: In connection with that issue, the SEC Observer stated that in SEC filings, the SEC staff will expect the cumulative effect on pretax income and income tax expense, if material, to be reported as separate line items in the lessor's income statement. The SEC Observer also stated that the SEC staff would not object to exclusion of an unfavorable pretax adjustment from the "earnings" component of the ratio of earnings to fixed charges, in cases in which the after-tax effect is favorable, provided that: (*a*) such exclusion is adequately identified and explained in connection with all disclosures and discussions relating to the ratio and (*b*) supplemental disclosure is made of the ratio as calculated in accordance with the applicable instructions (i.e., with the unfavorable pretax adjustment).

For all companies, private and public, any significant variation from the customary relationship between income tax expense and pretax accounting income resulting from the effect of a tax law or rate change would be disclosed in accordance with paragraph 47 of Statement 109.

EXCERPT FROM OFFICIAL TEXT

48. An enterprise shall disclose (a) the amounts and expiration dates of operating loss and tax credit carryforwards for tax purposes and (b) any portion of the valuation allowance for deferred tax assets for which subsequently recognized tax benefits will be allocated to reduce goodwill or other noncurrent intangible assets of an acquired entity or directly to contributed capital (paragraphs 30 and 36).

49. An entity that is a member of a group that files a consolidated tax return shall disclose in its separately issued financial statements:

    a. The aggregate amount of current and deferred tax expense for each statement of earnings presented and the amount of any tax-related balances due to or from affiliates as of the date of each statement of financial position presented

    b. The principal provisions of the method by which the consolidated amount of current and deferred tax expense is allocated to members of the group and the nature and effect of any changes in that method (and in determining related balances to or from affiliates) during the years for which the disclosures in (a) above are presented.

INTERPRETATION

49-1. Required Disclosures in Separate Company Financial Statements

Question: Paragraph 49 of Statement 109 lists disclosures required in separate company financial statements. Are those disclosures in addition to or in lieu of the disclosure requirements set forth in paragraphs 43 through 48 of Statement 109?

Response: Practice has generally interpreted the disclosures required by paragraph 49 as being in lieu of, rather than in addition to, the disclosures required by paragraphs 43 through 48 of Statement 109. We strongly encourage public companies in particular to provide the disclosures required by paragraphs 43 through 48. In some situations (e.g., a member of a consolidated tax group that anticipates becoming a separate taxpayer), we believe those disclosure are necessary to provide users with an adequate understanding of relevant income tax-related information.

PARAGRAPHS 50–59: EFFECTIVE DATE AND TRANSITION

EXCERPT FROM OFFICIAL TEXT

Effective Date and Transition

50. This Statement shall be effective for fiscal years beginning after December 15, 1992. Earlier application is encouraged. Financial statements for any number of consecutive fiscal years before the effective date may be restated to conform to the provisions of this Statement. Initial application of this Statement shall be as of the beginning of an enterprise's fiscal year (that is, if the Statement is adopted prior to the effective date and during an interim period other than the first interim period, all prior interim periods of that fiscal year shall be restated). Application of the requirements for recognition of a deferred tax liability or asset for a restated interim or annual period shall be based on the facts and circumstances as they existed at that prior date and without the benefit of hindsight.

51. The effect of initially applying this Statement shall be reported as the effect of a change in accounting principle in a manner similar to the cumulative effect of a change in accounting principle (APB Opinion No. 20, *Accounting Changes,* paragraph 20) except for initially recognized tax benefits of the type required by this Statement to be excluded from comprehensive income. If the earliest year restated is not presented in the financial statements, the beginning balance of retained earnings and, if necessary, any other components of shareholders' equity for the earliest year presented shall be adjusted for the effect of the restatement as of that date. Paragraph 30 addresses the manner of reporting acquired tax benefits initially recognized subsequent to a business combination and paragraph 36 identifies five items ((c)–(g)) for which tax benefits are excluded from comprehensive income and allocated directly to contributed capital or retained earnings. Pro forma effects of retroactive application (Opinion 20, paragraph 21) are not required if statements of earnings presented for prior years are not restated.

51-1. [Not Used]

51-2. Determining the Amount of Acquired Tax Benefits at Transition to Statement 109

Question (from FASB Staff Implementation Guide, Question 17B [formerly Question 23]):

The tax benefit of acquired deductible differences and carryforwards that are initially recognized at the date of transition is one of the effects referred to in paragraphs 30 and 51 of Statement 109 for which part of the transition adjustment to the Statement might have to be excluded from net income. Those tax benefits are excluded from net income when initially recognized after the purchase business combination, either at the transition date or in subsequent periods, until first goodwill and then other noncurrent intangible assets related to that acquisition are reduced to zero.

If a purchase business combination occurred in a prior year that is not restated when Statement 109 is initially applied, the remaining balances of any assets and liabilities recognized in that business combination are adjusted to pretax amounts unless impracticable. In either case, how should an enterprise determine the amount of acquired deductible temporary differences and operating loss or tax credit carryforwards from a prior purchase business combination for which any subsequently recognized tax benefits first should be applied to reduce to zero any goodwill and other noncurrent intangible assets related to that business combination?

Response (from FASB Staff Implementation Guide, Question 17B [formerly Response 23]):

At the date of the purchase business combination, the amount of acquired deductible temporary differences and carryforwards for which any subsequently recognized tax benefit first should be applied to reduce goodwill and other noncurrent intangible assets related to that business combination is the total of:

a. Any operating loss or tax credit carryforwards for which a tax benefit was not recognized

b. Any excess of the tax basis over the pretax fair value of the net assets acquired (assets, excluding goodwill, minus liabilities) for which a tax benefit was not reflected in assigning values (net-of-tax) to those net assets. For this purpose, tax benefits were not reflected in assigning net-of-tax values if those tax benefits were discounted to zero.

Any remainder at the transition date of such acquired deductible temporary differences and carryforwards is the amount for which any tax benefits that are recognized either at the transition date or in subsequent periods are excluded from net income until goodwill and other noncurrent intangible assets related to that acquisition are reduced to zero. That remainder is the sum of the following:

1. The amount in (*a*) above at the acquisition date minus the portion recognized in periods subsequent to the business combination as an adjustment of goodwill in accordance with either Statement 96 or paragraph 88 of Opinion 16 (before its amendment by Statements 109 and 96). Thus, the amount in (*a*) above is not reduced for any portion that was recognized in income in periods subsequent to the business combination pursuant to the guidance in EITF Issue No. 86-1, "Recognizing Net Operating Loss Carryforwards," and prior to adoption of Statement 96 or 109.
2. The amount in (*b*) above minus the portion recognized in periods subsequent to the business combination as a retroactive adjustment of the purchase price allocation or as a reduction of income tax expense.

51-3. Determining the Amount of Acquired Tax Benefits at Transition to Statement 109 When Information Is Lacking

Question (from FASB Staff Implementation Guide, Question 17C [formerly Question 24]):

Information about a prior business combination that is needed to determine the amount of acquired deductible temporary differences and carryforwards for which subsequently recognized tax benefits are excluded from net income until goodwill and other noncurrent intangible assets related to that acquisition are reduced to zero might not be available, or the cost to develop it might be excessive. If so, how much, if any, of those tax benefits should be excluded from net income at the transition date and in subsequent periods?

Response (from FASB Staff Implementation Guide, Question 17C [formerly Response 24]):

> In those circumstances, no portion of the transition adjustment is allocated to reduce goodwill and other noncurrent intangible assets. However, immediately after the transition date, the amount of any deductible temporary differences and carryforwards for which a tax benefit has not been recognized should be presumed to have been acquired in the prior purchase business combination. That presumption may be overcome to the extent that some or all of the deductible temporary differences and carryforwards are clearly attributable to events that occurred after the date of the purchase business combination. To the extent that amounts are not clearly attributable to events that occurred after the combination date, any related tax benefits recognized after the transition date first should be applied to reduce to zero any goodwill and noncurrent intangible assets related to that acquisition. Any additional tax benefits recognized should be applied to reduce income tax expense.

EXCERPT FROM OFFICIAL TEXT

52. When initially presented, the financial statements for the year this Statement is first adopted shall disclose:

    a. The effect, if any, of adopting this Statement on pretax income from continuing operations (for example, the effect of adjustments for prior purchase business combinations and for regulated enterprises) for the year of adoption if restated financial statements for the prior year are not presented

    b. The effect of any restatement on income from continuing operations, income before extraordinary items, and net income (and on related per share amounts) for each year for which restated financial statements are presented.

PRIOR BUSINESS COMBINATIONS

EXCERPT FROM OFFICIAL TEXT

Prior Business Combinations

53. If financial statements for prior years are restated, all purchase business combinations that were consummated in those prior years shall be remeasured in accordance with the requirements of this Statement.

54. For a purchase business combination consummated prior to the beginning of the year for which this Statement is first applied, any balance remaining as of that date for goodwill or negative goodwill shall not be adjusted to equal the amount it would be if financial statements for the year of the combination and subsequent years were restated. However, except for leveraged leases and except as provided in paragraph 55, (a) remaining balances as of the date of initially applying this Statement for assets and liabilities acquired in that combination shall be adjusted from their net-of-tax amounts to their pretax amounts and (b) any differences between those adjusted remaining balances and their tax bases are temporary differences. A deferred tax liability or asset shall be recognized for those temporary differences pursuant to the requirements of this Statement as of the beginning of the year for which this Statement is first applied.

55. If, for a particular business combination, determination of the adjustment for any or all of the assets and liabilities referred to in paragraph 54 is impracticable, either because the necessary information is no longer available or because the cost to develop that information is excessive, none of the remaining balances of any assets and liabilities acquired in that combination shall be adjusted to pretax amounts, that is, all remaining amounts that were originally assigned on a net-of-tax basis pursuant to paragraph 89 of Opinion 16 shall not be adjusted. Any differences between those unadjusted remaining balances and their tax bases are temporary differences, and a deferred tax liability or asset shall be recognized for those temporary differences pursuant to the requirements of this Statement as of the beginning of the year for which this Statement is first applied.

INTERPRETATION

55-1. Potential Impairments Caused by Prior Net-of-Tax Accounting

Question (from FASB Staff Implementation Guide, Question 17A [formerly Question 22]):

An enterprise adopts Statement 109 without restating the financial statements of prior years and because it is impracticable, does not adjust (as permitted by paragraph 55) any remaining amounts that were originally assigned on a net-of-tax basis pursuant to paragraph 89 of APB Opinion No. 16, *Business Combinations*. Instead, the enterprise records deferred tax assets and liabilities for the difference between the tax bases and the remaining balances for financial reporting of the acquired assets and liabilities, including those assets and liabilities reported on a net-of-tax basis.

After transition to Statement 109, the future recovery or settlement of the pretax amount of assets and liabilities that are reported on a net-of-tax basis will often result in an after-tax gain or loss. For example, assume that although an enterprise was unable, because information was not available, to gross up all assets and liabilities reported net-of-tax for an acquired entity, for *certain* assets and liabilities the following information is available at transition to Statement 109:

	Note Receivable	Accrued Liability
Pretax amount of receivable or payable	$1,200	$100
Tax basis	$1,000	$0
Net-of-tax reported amount	$1,120	$60
Taxable (deductible) temporary difference	$120	$(60)
Deferred tax liability (asset) at transition (40 percent)	$48	$(24)

The future recovery and settlement of the pretax amounts of that note receivable and accrued liability would result in the following:

	Note Receivable	Accrued Liability
Amount received or paid	$1,200	$100
Less: reported amount	1,120	60

Pretax gain (loss)	80	(40)
Current tax expense (benefit):		
0 percent of ($1,200 – $1,000)	80	
40 percent of ($100 – $0)		(40)
Deferred tax expense (benefit)	(48)	24
Net income (loss)	$48	$(24)

At transition to Statement 109, should an asset or liability reported net-of-tax that is expected to result in an after-tax loss when it is recovered or settled in future years be (*a*) remeasured (that is, adjusted to a pretax amount rather than a net-of-tax amount and a corresponding deferred tax asset recognized for the related temporary difference) or (*b*) otherwise adjusted because that asset is deemed impaired or that liability is deemed understated?

Response (from FASB Staff Implementation Guide, Question 17A [formerly Response 22]):

No. Remeasurement or adjustment of certain purchased assets or liabilities when *other* assets or liabilities acquired in the same business combination are stated at net-of-tax amounts because of impracticability is not permitted in adopting Statement 109. If an asset becomes impaired or a liability becomes understated after adopting Statement 109, any adjustment of that asset or liability should exclude the effect of reporting that asset or liability at a net-of-tax rather than a pretax amount. (Statement 109 nullifies the consensus in EITF Issue No. 86-42, "Effect of a Change in Tax Rates on Assets and Liabilities Recorded Net-of-Tax in a Purchase Business Combination.")

EXCERPT FROM OFFICIAL TEXT

56. The net effect of the adjustments required by paragraphs 54 and 55 shall be included in the effect of initially applying this Statement and reported in accordance with the provisions of paragraph 51.

Assets of Regulated Enterprises Reported on a Net-of-Tax or After-Tax Basis

EXCERPT FROM OFFICIAL TEXT

Assets of Regulated Enterprises Reported on a Net-of-Tax or After-Tax Basis

57. Some regulated enterprises that apply Statement 71 have accounted for certain components of construction in progress on either a net-of-tax or after-tax basis, or both. Upon initial application of this Statement, those enterprises shall make appropriate adjustments required by this Statement to account for the net-of-tax and after-tax components of construction in progress as if the requirements of this Statement were applied to that construction in progress in all prior years. Except as provided in paragraph 58, the reported amount of plant in service at the beginning of the year for which this Statement is first applied shall be similarly adjusted.

58. If determination of the adjustment to plant in service referred to in paragraph 57 is impracticable, either because the necessary information is no longer available or because the cost to develop that information is excessive, any difference between the reported amount and the tax basis of that plant in service is a temporary difference, and a deferred tax liability shall be recognized for that temporary difference. If, as a result of an action by a regulator, it is probable that amounts required for settlement of that deferred tax liability will be recovered from customers through future rates, an asset and the related deferred tax liability for that additional temporary difference shall be recognized for that probable future revenue.

59. The net effect of the adjustments required by paragraphs 57 and 58 shall be included in the effect of initially applying this Statement and reported in accordance with the provisions of paragraph 51.

SECTION II
FUTURE EXPECTATIONS AND PROJECTS

RECENT DEVELOPMENTS

The FASB issued FASB Interpretation (FIN) No. 48, *Accounting for Uncertainty in Income Taxes,* in June 2006. FIN 48 is effective for fiscal years beginning after December 15, 2006. Earlier adoption is permitted as of the beginning of an enterprise's fiscal year, provided the enterprise has not yet issued financial statements (including financial statements for any interim period) for that fiscal year. (See Interpretation 10-1 and Appendix I for an analysis of FIN 48.) This publication incorporates the guidance contained in FIN 48, its amendments to Statement 109, and other authoritative literature.

The Emerging Issues Task Force (EITF), at its November 16, 2006, meeting, tentatively concluded in EITF Issue No. 06-11, "Accounting for Income Tax Benefits of Dividends on Share-Based Payment Awards," that any tax benefit of dividends on restricted stock and option awards should be accounted for as a credit to additional paid-in capital (APIC). If the EITF finalizes this consensus at a future meeting (scheduled for the March 15, 2007, EITF meeting) and the consensus is ratified by the FASB, the consensus is expected to be effective prospectively for fiscal years beginning after September 15, 2007.

In addition, the FASB has two projects underway that could affect accounting for income taxes over the next few years. The following is a summary of those projects and their expected effect on accounting for income taxes.

Business Combinations

The FASB issued an exposure draft (ED) of proposed FASB Statement, *Business Combinations,* in July 2005. This proposed statement, which is currently scheduled to be issued in its final form in 2007, retains the existing fundamental concepts of accounting for the income tax consequences of business combinations. However, it would result in the following changes related to accounting for income taxes in a business combination:

- Currently, when acquired tax benefits are initially recognized subsequent to the date of acquisition, the benefit from the reduction in valuation allowance is recognized by: first, reducing to zero any goodwill related to the acquisition; second, reducing to zero other noncurrent intangible assets related to the acquisition; and third, reducing income tax expense (see Interpretation 30-21). Under the proposed statement, there is a rebuttable presumption that all acquired tax benefits initially recognized within 12 months of the date of acquisition first reduce to zero any goodwill related to the acquisition and then reduce income tax expense. Acquired tax benefits initially recognized after that 12-month period reduce income tax expense.

At its January 31, 2007, meeting, the FASB decided that companies should apply the same guidance for subsequent adjustments of acquired tax benefits and tax uncertainties as for other assets and liabilities acquired in the business combination. That is, all qualifying adjustments recognized within the measurement period will be recognized as adjustments to goodwill with any other adjustments being recognized in income.

- Currently, any reduction in the acquirer's valuation allowance for deferred tax assets as a result of a business combination is recognized as part of the business combination (see Interpretation 30-2). Under the proposed statement, any reduction in the acquirer's valuation allowance for deferred tax assets as a result of a business combination is recognized as a reduction of the acquirer's income tax provision in the period of the business combination.
- Currently, Statement 109 precludes recognizing a deferred tax asset related to an excess of tax basis of tax deductible goodwill over financial reporting basis of goodwill (see Interpretation 30-19). The proposed statement eliminates that exception to the general principles of Statement 109.

In addition, the International Accounting Standards Board (IASB), which is addressing accounting for business combinations at the same time as the FASB, has tentatively decided that an excess of financial reporting basis over tax basis of goodwill should be accounted for as a taxable temporary difference and has requested that the FASB consider making the same change to Statement 109. At its January 31, 2007, meeting, the FASB decided to not change the current Statement 109 treatment of an excess of financial reporting basis over tax basis of goodwill.

Short-Term Convergence With the IASB

Statement 109 and International Accounting Standard (IAS) No. 12, *Income Taxes*, are based on similar principles. However, the standards have differing exceptions to their general principles and, over time, there have been different interpretations of certain aspects of those standards. The FASB and the IASB have decided to work jointly to make changes to both Statement 109 and IAS 12 to eliminate as many of the currently existing differences between the two standards as possible. The FASB's current schedule calls for an ED of the changes to Statement 109 to be issued in the first half of 2007. The FASB currently has no stated timeframe for the issuance of a final statement. The FASB has tentatively decided to amend Statement 109 in the following areas:

- *Exception in paragraph 9(e) of Statement 109 related to intercompany transfers of assets.* Currently, paragraph 9(e) of Statement 109 provides that: (*a*) the seller's net current and deferred tax effect of any sale of assets to another member of the consolidated financial reporting group be deferred and (*b*) the buyer should not recognize a deferred tax asset for the tax effect of the difference between the financial reporting basis and tax basis of the assets in the buyer's tax jurisdiction. If that exception is eliminated, enterprises will recognize the current and deferred tax consequences of the sale of assets between members of the consolidated financial reporting group at the time of the intercompany sale of assets.
- *Exception in paragraph 9(f) of Statement 109 related to foreign nonmonetary assets and liabilities that are remeasured from the local currency into the functional currency.* Currently, paragraph 9(f) of Statement 109 prohibits recognition of deferred tax assets or liabilities for differences related to assets and liabilities that are remeasured from the local currency into the functional currency using historical exchange rates (i.e., nonmonetary assets and liabilities of operations for which the local currency is not the functional currency) and that result from changes in exchange rates and indexing for tax purposes (see Interpretation 9-6). If that exception is eliminated, enterprises will recognize the deferred tax consequences of changes in exchange rates and indexing for tax purposes in the period in which such changes occur.
- *Temporary differences created by the acquisition of an asset (or group of assets) when the asset (or group of assets) acquired is not a business.* Currently, the accounting for the tax consequences of such transactions is addressed in EITF Issue No. 98-11, "Accounting for Acquired Temporary Differences in Certain Purchase Transactions That Are Not Accounted for as Business Combinations" (see Interpretation 16-1). The FASB has tentatively concluded: (*a*) to nullify Issue 98-11 and (*b*) that (i) assets acquired should be recognized at fair value and (ii) any excess of fair value of assets acquired, plus deferred tax assets recognized, over consideration paid should be recognized as a purchase discount allowance on the deferred tax asset acquired.

- *Timing of recognition of changes in tax law or rates outside of the United States.* Currently, paragraph 27 of Statement 109 provides that changes in tax law or rates in all jurisdictions are to be recognized in the period in which all steps in the process of the legislation becoming law have been completed (see Interpretation 27-9). The FASB has tentatively concluded that, in taxing jurisdictions outside of the United States, changes in tax law or rates will be recognized in the period in which the changes have been substantially enacted.
- *Measurement of deferred tax assets and liabilities if income is taxed at different rates depending on whether that income is distributed to shareholders.* This issue is currently addressed in a series of EITF issues (i.e., EITF Issue No. 95-9, "Accounting for Tax Effects of Dividends in France in Accordance with FASB Statement No. 109," EITF Issue No. 95-10, "Accounting for Tax Credits Related to Dividend Payments in Accordance with FASB Statement No. 109," and EITF Issue No. 95-20, "Measurement in the Consolidated Financial Statements of a Parent of the Tax Effects Related to the Operations of a Foreign Subsidiary That Receives Tax Credits Related to Dividend Payments" [see Interpretations 4-7 and 18-8]). The FASB has tentatively concluded to nullify those EITF issues and to require that deferred tax assets and liabilities be measured based on the undistributed tax rate. However, to the extent that there is an obligation to distribute a portion of that income, deferred tax assets and liabilities related to that portion of income should be measured using the distributed rate.

SECTION III
APPENDICES

SECTION III
APPENDICES

CONTENTS

APPENDIX I: INTERPRETATIONS OF FIN 48, *ACCOUNTING FOR UNCERTAINTY IN INCOME TAXES*

This appendix reflects material that is quoted directly from FASB Interpretation (FIN) No. 48, *Accounting for Uncertainty in Income Taxes,* together with our commentary and interpretation. Refer to the Preface of this publication for other information and copyright details.

EXCERPT FROM OFFICIAL TEXT

INTRODUCTION

1. This Interpretation clarifies the accounting for uncertainty in income taxes recognized in an enterprise's financial statements in accordance with FASB Statement No. 109, *Accounting for Income Taxes.* Statement 109 does not prescribe a recognition threshold or measurement attribute for the financial statement recognition and measurement of a tax position taken in a tax return. Consistent with Statement 109, the term *enterprise* is used throughout this Interpretation because accounting for income taxes is primarily an issue for business enterprises. However, the requirements of this Interpretation apply to not-for-profit organizations. This Interpretation also applies to pass-through entities and entities whose tax liability is subject to 100 percent credit for dividends paid (for example, real estate investment trusts and registered investment companies) that are potentially subject to income taxes.
2. Diversity in practice exists in the accounting for income taxes. To address that diversity, this Interpretation clarifies the application of Statement 109 by defining a criterion that an individual tax position must meet for any part of the benefit of that position to be recognized in an enterprise's financial statements. Additionally, this Interpretation provides guidance on measurement, derecognition, classification, interest and penalties, accounting in interim periods, disclosure, and transition.

INTERPRETATION

Scope

3. This Interpretation applies to all tax positions accounted for in accordance with Statement 109.
4. The term *tax position* as used in this Interpretation refers to a position in a previously filed tax return or a position expected to be taken in a future tax return that is reflected in measuring current or deferred income tax assets and liabilities for interim or annual periods. A tax position can result in a permanent reduction of income taxes payable, a deferral of income taxes otherwise currently payable to future years, or a change in the expected realizability of deferred tax assets. The term *tax position* also encompasses, but is not limited to:

   a. A decision not to file a tax return

   b. An allocation or a shift of income between jurisdictions

   c. The characterization of income or a decision to exclude reporting taxable income in a tax return

Continued on page 283

Continued from page 282

d. A decision to classify a transaction, entity, or other position in a tax return as tax exempt.

Recognition

5. The appropriate unit of account for determining what constitutes an individual tax position, and whether the more-likely-than-not recognition threshold is met for a tax position, is a matter of judgment based on the individual facts and circumstances of that position evaluated in light of all available evidence. The determination of the unit of account to be used in applying the provisions of this Interpretation shall consider the manner in which the enterprise prepares and supports its income tax return and the approach the enterprise anticipates the taxing authority will take during an examination.

INTERPRETATION

FIN 48 5-1. Unit of Account

Question: The definition of a unit of account in FIN 48 seems to be a matter of judgment. Did the FASB provide any additional guidance or examples of how to determine a unit of account?

Response: The FASB intentionally left the definition of a unit of account to be a matter of judgment to allow enterprises flexibility in determining what units of account are most meaningful in their individual situations. The primary factors affecting the determination of a unit of account should be: (*a*) the manner in which the enterprise prepares and supports its income tax return and (*b*) the approach the enterprise anticipates the taxing authority will take during an examination. In determining the unit of account, enterprises should presume that the taxing authority, with full knowledge of all of the relevant information, will evaluate the position. Once a unit of account has been determined, that unit of account should be consistently applied to similar positions from period to period unless a change in facts and circumstances indicates that a different unit of account is more appropriate.

Paragraphs A5 through A9 of FIN 48 contain an example of the determination of a unit of account related to an enterprise's plan to claim a research and experimentation credit on its tax return for the current year. That example illustrates that different facts and circumstances can result in a different determination of the unit of account for the same type of deduction or credit.

EXCERPT FROM OFFICIAL TEXT

6. An enterprise shall initially recognize the financial statement effects of a tax position when it is more likely than not, based on the technical merits, that the position will be sustained upon examination. As used in this Interpretation, the term *more likely than not* means a likelihood of more than 50 percent; the terms *examined* and *upon examination* also include resolution of the related appeals or litigation processes, if any. The more-likely-than-not recognition threshold is a positive assertion that an enterprise believes it is entitled to the economic benefits associated with a tax position. The determination of whether or not a tax position has met the more-likely-than-not recognition threshold shall consider the facts, circumstances, and information available at the reporting date.
7. In assessing the more-likely-than-not criterion as required by paragraph 6 of this Interpretation:

   a. It shall be presumed that the tax position will be examined by the relevant taxing authority that has full knowledge of all relevant information.

   b. Technical merits of a tax position derive from sources of authorities in the tax law (legislation and statutes, legislative intent, regulations, rulings, and case law) and their applicability to the facts and circumstances of the tax position. When the past administrative practices and precedents of the taxing authority in its dealings with the enterprise or similar enterprises are widely understood, those practices and precedents shall be taken into account.

   c. Each tax position must be evaluated without consideration of the possibility of offset or aggregation with other positions.

INTERPRETATION

FIN 48 7-1. Administrative Practices and Precedents

Question: How should a taxing authority's past administrative practices and precedents affect the more-likely-than-not assessment of the technical merits of a tax position?

Response: A taxing authority may have administrative practices or precedents of not objecting to a limited number of tax positions that may be deemed technical violations of the tax law. The FASB decided to allow enterprises to consider "widely understood" administrative practices and procedures when determining whether, based on its technical merits, a tax position is more likely than not of being sustained if examined by the taxing authority. Paragraph B36 of FIN 48 gives the following explanation for determining whether a particular widely understood administrative practice or precedent should be considered:

> In determining whether a particular administrative practice or precedent will be applicable, an enterprise should presume that the tax position will be examined and that the taxing authority has the same information on the tax position that is available to the enterprise when asserting that a particular administrative practice or precedent would be applied by the taxing authority.

Paragraphs A12 through A15 of FIN 48 provide two examples of possible administrative practices and precedents. The first example relates to an enterprise's practice of immediately deducting routine equipment purchases below a specified threshold. Because the tax law of this jurisdiction has no capitalization threshold, an enterprise's tax position of immediately expensing small equipment purchases could be viewed as a violation of the tax law. The second example relates to how many years back a tax authority might look when determining whether a tax return is due and a deficiency owed (i.e., an issue of nexus in a particular jurisdiction). Because the statute of limitations never begins to run if a tax return is not filed, an enterprise with an uncertain nexus tax position is potentially subject to an ever increasing tax liability. Paragraphs A12 through A15 explain how the FASB believes widely understood administrative practices and precedents could affect an enterprise's more-likely-than-not assessment of those tax positions.

EXCERPT FROM OFFICIAL TEXT

Measurement

8. A tax position that meets the more-likely-than-not recognition threshold shall initially and subsequently be measured as the largest amount of tax benefit that is greater than 50 percent likely of being realized upon ultimate settlement with a taxing authority that has full knowledge of all relevant information. Measurement of a tax position that meets the more-likely-than-not recognition threshold shall consider the amounts and probabilities of the outcomes that could be realized upon ultimate settlement[1] using the facts, circumstances, and information available at the reporting date. As used in this Interpretation, the term *reporting date* refers to date of the enterprise's most recent statement of financial position.

---

1 For further explanation and illustration, see the illustrative examples in paragraphs A19–A30.

INTERPRETATION

FIN 48 8-1. Example of How to Measure the Tax Benefits to Be Recognized Under FIN 48

Question: How should tax positions that meet the more-likely-than-not criterion be measured?

Response: The benefit recognized from a tax position that meets the more-likely-than-not criterion should be the largest amount that is greater than 50% likely of being realized upon ultimate settlement with a taxing authority that has full knowledge of all of the relevant information. Paragraphs A21 and A22 of FIN 48 provide the following example of applying this measurement guidance:

> In applying the recognition criterion of this Interpretation, an enterprise has determined that a tax position resulting in a benefit of $100 qualifies for recognition and should be measured. The enterprise has considered the amounts and probabilities of the possible estimated outcomes as follows:

Possible Estimated Outcome	Individual Probability of Occurring (%)	Cumulative Probability of Occurring (%)
$100	5	5
80	25	30
60	25	55
50	20	75
40	10	85
20	10	95
0	5	100

Because $60 is the largest amount of benefit that is greater than 50 percent likely of being realized upon ultimate settlement, the enterprise would recognize a tax benefit of $60 in the financial statements.

In some circumstances, there will be a greater than 50% likelihood that the entire benefit will be realized. In these situations, the entire amount of the benefit should be recognized.

FIN 48 8-2. All Income Tax Uncertainties Need to Be Accounted for Pursuant to FIN 48

Question: Some tax positions may involve uncertainty only with respect to the timing of the deduction or income. For example, assume there is no uncertainty as to the ultimate deductibility of a particular expenditure, only uncertainty as to the appropriate period in which to deduct that expenditure for tax purposes. Does FIN 48 apply to income tax positions that are simply uncertainties about timing?

Response: Yes. For tax positions in which there is little or no uncertainty that an expenditure is deductible in some period, the more-likely-than-not recognition criterion has been met. However, the measurement provisions of FIN 48 need to be applied to appropriately determine the various components of income tax related assets and liabilities.

Assume an enterprise purchases an asset with a five-year life for financial reporting purposes for $120 (to be depreciated on a straight-line basis—$24 per year). There is no uncertainty that the cost of the asset is deductible for income tax purposes, but there is some uncertainty about when the cost of the asset is deductible. Assume there is a 25% likelihood that the cost of the asset is deductible in Year 1, a 35% likelihood it is deductible ratably over three years, and a 40% likelihood it is deductible ratably over a five-year period.

Assume the enterprise intends to deduct the entire cost of the asset in its Year 1 tax return.

In this example, the largest deduction that is greater than 50% likely of being realized in Year 1 upon ultimate settlement with the taxing authority is $40 (i.e., there is a 60% likelihood in this example that the deduction in Year 1 will be no less than $40—a ratable deduction of the cost of the asset over a three-year period). The journal entries for Year 1 are shown in Example FIN 48 8-2A.

Example FIN 48 8-2A

Example assumptions:

There are no other temporary differences or tax uncertainties.

There is financial reporting income of $1,000.

The tax rate is 40%.

For simplicity, this example ignores interest and penalties.

Dr.	Current tax expense	393.60	
Cr.	Taxes currently payable		361.60
Cr.	Liability for unrecognized tax benefits		32.00
Dr.	Deferred tax expense	6.40	
Cr.	Deferred tax liability		6.40

Computations:

- Current tax expense: $(1{,}000 + 24 - 40) \times 40\%$
- Taxes currently payable: $(1{,}000 + 24 - 120) \times 40\%$
- Liability for unrecognized tax benefits: $(120 - 40) \times 40\%$
- Deferred tax liability: $(96 - 80) \times 40\%$

Absent new information, the enterprise should continue to base its FIN 48 analysis in future years on the asset being deductible ratably over a three-year period.

Paragraphs A26 through A30 of FIN 48 contain further examples applying FIN 48 to uncertainties related to the timing of the deductibility of costs.

EXCERPT FROM OFFICIAL TEXT

Tax-Planning Strategies

9. When a tax-planning strategy is contemplated as a source of future taxable income to support the realizability of a deferred tax asset under paragraph 21(d) of Statement 109, paragraphs 5–8 of this Interpretation shall be applied in determining the amount of available future taxable income.

Subsequent Recognition, Derecognition, and Measurement

10. If the more-likely-than-not recognition threshold is not met in the period for which a tax position is taken or expected to be taken, an enterprise shall recognize the benefit of the tax position in the first interim period that meets any one of the following three conditions:

    a. The more-likely-than-not recognition threshold is met by the reporting date.

    b. The tax matter is ultimately settled through negotiation or litigation.

    c. The statute of limitations for the relevant taxing authority to examine and challenge the tax position has expired.

INTERPRETATION

FIN 48 10-1. Ultimately Settled Through Negotiation or Litigation

Question: Paragraph 10(b) of FIN 48 refers to a tax matter being "ultimately settled through negotiation or litigation." How should that phrase be interpreted when a taxing authority has completed its examination of a specific year but there is not a formal agreement between the taxing authority and the enterprise closing that year?

Response: In early February 2007, the FASB instructed its staff to prepare a FASB staff position (FSP) for exposure that would amend paragraph 10(b) of FIN 48. The exposure draft (ED) is expected to propose changing paragraph 10(b) from an ultimate settlement approach to an effective settlement approach. The ED is expected to be issued in February 2007 with a 30-day comment period. If ultimately issued in final form, the FSP is expected to be effective with the adoption of FIN 48. Enterprises should follow this FASB project for the latest information on the issue.

In the absence of additional FASB guidance, we believe the criterion in paragraph 10(b) is not met until the taxing authority can no longer reopen the year for reasons other than fraud or misrepresentation. We believe interpreting paragraph 10(b) otherwise involves consideration of detection risk and therefore would be inconsistent with the requirement in paragraph 7(a) that states, "[i]t shall be presumed that the tax position will be examined by the relevant taxing authority that has full knowledge of all relevant information" and the definition in paragraph 6 of "examined" ("the terms *examined* and *upon examination* also include resolution of the related appeals or litigation processes"). This interpretation of paragraph 10(b) is also consistent with our belief that the term "*ultimately* settled through negotiation or litigation" is intended to convey a finality to the resolution of the tax position similar to the expiration of the statute of limitations.

In the U.S. federal tax jurisdiction, we believe a Closing Agreement meets the criterion in paragraph 10(b). However, the issuance of a Form 870 or Form 870AD[1] does not preclude the taxing authority from reopening the period examined for reasons other than fraud or misrepresentation[2] and therefore we believe the issuance of a Form 870 or Form 870AD does not meet the criterion in paragraph 10(b). However, the completion of the tax authority's examination may produce new evidence that causes the enterprise to conclude that the criterion in paragraph 10(a) has been met. For example, assume a tax position that was initially judged to be less than more likely than not of being sustained was specifically reviewed by senior persons within the taxing authority as part of the examination and the tax position was not challenged by the taxing authority. Through discussions with the taxing authority during the examination, the enterprise may develop a better

---

1 Form 870 is prepared by the revenue agent and lists all of the agent's proposed adjustments. Form 870AD is a determination by the IRS appeals division of any revenue agent proposed adjustments the enterprise elected to appeal to the IRS appeals division.

2 IRS Policy Statement 8-3 (issued January 5, 2007) states "a case closed by Appeals on the basis of concessions made by both Appeals and the taxpayer will not be reopened by actions initiated by the Service unless the disposition involved fraud, malfeasance, concealment or misrepresentation of material fact, an important mistake in mathematical calculations, or discovery that a return contains unreported income, unadjusted deductions, credits, gains, losses, etc. resulting from the taxpayer's participation in a listed transaction. . . ." That Policy Statement further states "a case closed by Appeals on a basis not involving concessions made by both Appeals and the taxpayer will not be reopened by action initiated by the Service unless the prior disposition involved fraud, malfeasance, concealment or misrepresentation of material fact, an important mistake in mathematical calculation, or such other circumstances that indicate that failure to take such action would be a serious administrative omission. . . ."

understanding of the taxing authority's view of this specific tax position and, as a result of this new information, the enterprise might conclude that the tax position now meets the more-likely-than-not recognition threshold.

In addition, the taxing authority may have administrative practices or precedents regarding reopening periods once an examination is complete[3] that would also have an effect on an enterprise's assessment of paragraph 10(a). (See Interpretation FIN 48 7-1 for a discussion of administrative practices and precedents that may be considered in assessing the more-likely-than-not recognition criterion.) In our view, the question with respect to administrative practices and precedents once the examination is complete is *not* "does the enterprise expect the taxing authority to reopen the period previously examined?" That question inherently includes consideration of detection risk. Rather, we believe the appropriate question is "if the taxing authority has the same information on the tax position that is available to the enterprise, would the taxing authority reopen the period previously examined?" If not, that administrative practice or precedent should be considered in assessing the more-likely-than-not recognition threshold under paragraph 10(a) in the same manner it would be considered under paragraph 7(b) of FIN 48.

For tax positions that meet the more-likely-than-not criterion, the completion of an examination by the taxing authority may produce new evidence that changes an enterprise's conclusion about the largest amount of tax benefit that is greater than 50% likely of being realized upon ultimate settlement with the taxing authority. Just as with initial measurement, any subsequent measurement of the benefit from a tax position needs to be computed assuming ultimate settlement with a taxing authority that has full knowledge of all of the relevant information.

To reiterate, even though the examination is complete and the enterprise judges it unlikely that the taxing authority will open the period that has been examined: (*a*) the enterprise must presume the tax position will be examined by the relevant taxing authority that has full knowledge of all of the relevant information (i.e., detection risk cannot be considered) when assessing the recognition of a tax benefit (the more-likely-than-not test) or the measurement of the benefit from the tax position and (*b*) changes in judgment should result from the evaluation of new information and not simply from a new evaluation or new interpretation of information that was available in a prior period.

---

[3] See footnote [2] for a summary of certain administrative practices in the US Federal tax jurisdiction regarding periods previously examined.

EXCERPT FROM OFFICIAL TEXT

11. An enterprise shall derecognize a previously recognized tax position in the first period in which it is no longer more likely than not that the tax position would be sustained upon examination. Use of a valuation allowance[2] is not a permitted substitute for derecognizing the benefit of a tax position when the more-likely-than-not recognition threshold is no longer met.

12. Subsequent recognition, derecognition, and measurement shall be based on management's best judgment given the facts, circumstances, and information available at the reporting date. A tax position need not be legally extinguished and its resolution need not be certain to subsequently recognize or measure the position. Subsequent changes in judgment that lead to changes in recognition, derecognition, and measurement should result from the evaluation of new information and not from a new evaluation or new interpretation by management of information that was available in a previous financial reporting period.

---

[2] The term *valuation allowance* in this Interpretation has the same meaning as in Statement 109.

INTERPRETATION

FIN 48 12-1. Consideration of Subsequent Events Differs From Statement 5

Question: Should information that only becomes available after the date of the balance sheet, but before the issuance of the financial statements, be considered when assessing the recognition of tax positions or measuring tax positions in the not-yet-issued financial statements?

Response: No. When assessing the recognition of tax positions or measuring tax positions, enterprises should consider all of the facts, circumstances, and information available at the balance-sheet date. Unlike the guidance in FASB Statement No. 5, *Accounting for Contingencies,* the facts, circumstances, and information that only becomes available after the date of the balance sheet should not be considered in making this more-likely-than-not recognition assessment or when measuring tax positions under FIN 48. However, material subsequent events should be disclosed in the footnotes to the financial statements.

FIN 48 only applies to income tax uncertainties. All other contingencies should continue to be accounted for pursuant to other applicable accounting literature (primarily Statement 5).

EXCERPT FROM OFFICIAL TEXT

Change in Judgment

13. A change in judgment that results in subsequent recognition, derecognition, or change in measurement of a tax position taken in a prior annual period (including any related interest and penalties) shall be recognized as a discrete item in the period in which the change occurs. The provisions of paragraphs 35 and 38 in Statement 109 that pertain to intraperiod tax allocation are not changed by this Interpretation.
14. A change in judgment that results in subsequent recognition, derecognition, or change in measurement of a tax position taken in a prior interim period within the same fiscal year is an integral part of an annual period and, consequently, shall be reflected pursuant to the provisions of paragraph 19 of APB Opinion No. 28, *Interim Financial Reporting,* and FASB Interpretation No. 18, *Accounting for Income Taxes in Interim Periods.*

Interest and Penalties

15. When the tax law requires interest to be paid on an underpayment of income taxes, an enterprise shall begin recognizing interest expense in the first period the interest would begin accruing according to the provisions of the relevant tax law. The amount of interest expense to be recognized shall be computed by applying the applicable statutory rate of interest to the difference between the tax position recognized in accordance with this Interpretation and the amount previously taken or expected to be taken in a tax return.

INTERPRETATION

FIN 48 15-1. Capitalization of Interest

Question: Does interest expense related to underpayments of income taxes qualify for capitalization pursuant to FASB Statement No. 34, *Capitalization of Interest Costs*?

Response: In our view, no. Paragraph 12 of Statement 34 states, "[t]he amount of interest cost to be capitalized for qualifying assets is intended to be that portion of the interest cost incurred during the assets' acquisition periods that theoretically could have been avoided (for example, by avoiding additional borrowings or by using the funds expended for the assets to repay existing borrowings) if expenditures for the assets had not been made." Statement 34 refers repeatedly to interest costs related to an enterprise's *borrowings* when providing guidance on the amount of interest costs to be capitalized. Accordingly, we do not believe that interest expense related to underpayments of income taxes should be considered interest costs within the context of Statement 34. This view is also consistent with the decisions made by the FASB with respect to accretion expense associated with asset retirement obligations (i.e., paragraph 14 of FASB Statement No. 143, *Accounting for Asset Retirement Obligations*) and accretion expense associated with one-time termination benefits (i.e., footnote 6 to paragraph 6 of FASB Statement No. 146, *Accounting for Costs Associated with Exit or Disposal Activities*).

EXCERPT FROM OFFICIAL TEXT

16. If a tax position does not meet the minimum statutory threshold to avoid payment of penalties (considering the factors in paragraph 7 of this Interpretation), an enterprise shall recognize an expense for the amount of the statutory penalty in the period in which the enterprise claims or expects to claim the position in the tax return. If penalties were not recognized when the position was initially taken, the expense shall be recognized in the period in which the enterprise's judgment about meeting the minimum statutory threshold changes. Previously recognized interest and penalties associated with tax positions that subsequently meet one of the conditions in paragraph 10 of this Interpretation shall be derecognized in the period that condition is met.

Classification

17. As a result of applying this Interpretation, the amount of benefit recognized in the statement of financial position may differ from the amount taken or expected to be taken in a tax return for the current year. These differences represent unrecognized tax benefits, which are the differences between a tax position taken or expected to be taken in a tax return and the benefit recognized and measured pursuant to this Interpretation. A liability is created (or the amount of a net operating loss carryforward or amount refundable is reduced) for an unrecognized tax benefit because it represents an enterprise's potential future obligation to the taxing authority for a tax position that was not recognized pursuant to this Interpretation. An enterprise that presents a classified statement of financial position shall classify a liability associated with an unrecognized tax benefit as a current liability (or the amount of a net operating loss carryforward or amount refundable is reduced) to the extent the enterprise anticipates payment (or receipt) of cash within one year or the operating cycle, if longer. The liability for unrecognized tax benefits (or reduction in amounts refundable) shall not be combined with deferred tax liabilities or assets.

INTERPRETATION

FIN 48 17-1. Determining the Current Portion of the Liability for Unrecognized Tax Benefits

Question: How should the liability for unrecognized tax benefits be classified in the statement of financial position?

Response: The accounting treatment required by FIN 48 for uncertain tax positions may affect: (*a*) the amount recognized for financial reporting as due on tax returns (the currently payable and [or] refundable amount), (*b*) the amount of deferred tax assets and liabilities recognized (by affecting the presumed tax basis of an asset or liability and thereby affecting the associated temporary difference or by affecting the presumed amount of a carryforward), or (*c*) both. Any liability for unrecognized tax benefits (or a reduction in amounts refundable) recognized as a result of applying FIN 48 should be classified as a current liability (or a reduction in the current refund receivable) to the extent the enterprise expects payment (or receipt) of cash within: (*a*) one year or (*b*) the operating cycle, if longer. Otherwise, the liability for unrecognized tax benefits is classified as a long-term liability. Such liabilities should not be combined with deferred tax liabilities or assets.

Changes in deferred tax assets and liabilities caused by the application of FIN 48 should be classified as current or long-term in the same manner as any other deferred tax asset or liability (see paragraph 41 of Statement 109 for guidance on the classification of deferred tax assets and liabilities).

FIN 48 17-2. Balance Sheet Classification of Long-Term Liabilities for Unrecognized Tax Benefits

Question: How should long-term liabilities for unrecognized tax benefits be characterized in the statement of financial position?

Response: FIN 48 states in paragraph 17 that liabilities for unrecognized tax benefits should not be combined with deferred tax assets or liabilities. Otherwise, it has no explicit guidance regarding the presentation of long-term liabilities for unrecognized tax benefits in the statement of financial position. For public companies, Rule 5-02 of Regulation S-X contains the SEC requirements for the presentation of liabilities in the statement of financial position for commercial and industrial companies. The SEC staff has expressed its view that long-term liabilities for unrecognized tax benefits should be classified as "other long-term liabilities" rather than as "contingent liabilities" in the statement of financial position.

Further, the SEC staff, at the 2006 AICPA National Conference on Current SEC and PCAOB Developments, stated its view that liabilities for unrecognized tax benefits should be included in the tabular disclosure of contractual obligations required by Item 303(a)(5) of Regulation S-K. In our view, liabilities for unrecognized tax benefits have more attributes of contingent liabilities than contractual obligations. We are unsure whether the SEC staff plans to issue guidance with respect to its view on including liabilities for unrecognized tax benefits in the table of contractual obligations or what approach public companies will take with respect to this issue.

EXCERPT FROM OFFICIAL TEXT

> 18. A tax position recognized in the financial statements as a result of applying this Interpretation may also affect the tax bases of assets or liabilities and thereby change or create temporary differences. A taxable and deductible temporary difference is a difference between the reported amount of an item in the financial statements and the tax basis of an item as determined by applying the recognition threshold and measurement provisions of this Interpretation. A liability recognized as a result of applying this Interpretation shall not be classified as a deferred tax liability unless it arises from a taxable temporary difference.

INTERPRETATION

FIN 48 18-1. Interaction Between Net Operating Loss Carryforwards and Liabilities for Unrecognized Tax Benefits

Question: Should deferred tax assets recognized for carryforwards be based on the carryforwards in the tax returns as filed or should deferred tax assets for carryforwards be based on the carryforwards as determined by the recognition threshold and measurement provisions of FIN 48?

Response: Paragraph 18 requires the tax basis used for measuring temporary differences to be "the tax basis of an item as determined by applying the recognition threshold and measurement provisions of [FIN 48]." The same principle applies in determining the amount of a carryforward used as a basis for recognizing and measuring a deferred tax asset. In other words, deferred tax assets for carryforwards should be based on carryforward amounts that are determined on a basis that is internally consistent with the enterprise's determination of the liability for unrecognized tax benefits and temporary differences.

As stated in paragraph 17 of FIN 48, "[t]he liability for unrecognized tax benefits . . . shall not be combined with deferred tax liabilities or assets."

EXCERPT FROM OFFICIAL TEXT

> 19. Interest recognized in accordance with paragraph 15 of this Interpretation may be classified in the financial statements as either income taxes or interest expense, based on the accounting policy election of the enterprise. Penalties recognized in accordance with paragraph 16 of this Interpretation may be classified in the financial statements as either income taxes or another expense classification, based on the accounting policy election of the enterprise. Those elections shall be consistently applied.

INTERPRETATION

FIN 48 19-1. Changing Accounting Policies for Penalties and Interest

Question: Is a change in the financial statement classification of penalties and interest a change in accounting under FASB Statement No. 154, *Accounting Changes and Error Corrections*?

Response: Yes. Paragraph 19 of FIN 48 states that the financial statement classification of penalties and interest is an accounting policy election. Paragraph 14 of APB Opinion No. 22, *Disclosure of Accounting Policies*, makes it clear that changes in accounting policy are subject to Statement 154. Accordingly, any change in the financial statement presentation of penalties and interest needs to be a change to a preferable financial statement presentation (and, for public enterprises, a preferability letter would be required) and the change should be reported through a retrospective application to all prior periods since the date of the adoption of FIN 48.

Question: Is a change in the financial statement presentation of penalties and interest at the date of the adoption of FIN 48 a change in accounting that is subject to the guidance in Statement 154?

Response: Because the accounting model for tax contingencies and interest has fundamentally changed with the adoption of FIN 48, it appears that practice will not treat a change in the financial statement presentation of penalties and interest at the adoption of FIN 48 as a voluntary change in accounting subject to the requirements of Statement 154. For example, in the minutes to the September 2006 meeting between the AICPA SEC Regulations Committee and the SEC staff, the SEC staff states it will not require justification on the basis of preferability or a preferability letter for changes in the financial statement presentation of penalties and interest upon the adoption of FIN 48. The SEC staff also states its view in those minutes that the financial statement presentation of penalties and interest in periods prior to the date of the adoption of FIN 48 should not be changed. Finally, in those minutes, the SEC staff expresses its view that any registrant that changes its classification policy "should disclose, in annual financial statements that include any period prior to the adoption of FIN 48, both the classification and amount of interest and penalties on uncertain tax positions reflected in each income statement."

Changes in the financial statement presentation of penalties and interest after the adoption of FIN 48 are subject to the requirements of Statement 154 and would require a preferability letter.

Question: Both of the above responses indicate that the financial statement presentation of penalties and interest in periods prior to the adoption of FIN 48 should not be changed. Why wouldn't the retrospective application requirement of Statement 154 apply and require the application of the new accounting policy to all periods presented?

Response: Because FIN 48 changes the fundamental accounting model for income tax contingencies and interest, some accountants (most importantly, the SEC staff) believe the prohibition in FIN 48 against any form of retroactive application of the requirements of FIN 48 also applies to the financial statement presentation of penalties and interest.

We believe enterprises that want to change their accounting policy for the financial statement presentation for penalties and interest for periods prior to the adoption of FIN 48 will need to apply the guidance in Statement 154 separately to those prior periods. That is, those enterprises will need to assess the preferability of the change in those prior periods in the context of their accounting policies for the periods prior to the adoption of FIN 48 and public companies will need to obtain preferability letters that apply to the accounting policy change for those prior periods.

EXCERPT FROM OFFICIAL TEXT

Disclosures

20. An enterprise shall disclose its policy on classification of interest and penalties in accordance with paragraph 19 of this Interpretation in the footnotes to the financial statements.

21. An enterprise shall disclose the following at the end of each annual reporting period presented:

    a. A tabular reconciliation of the total amounts of unrecognized tax benefits at the beginning and end of the period, which shall include at a minimum:

        (1) The gross amounts of the increases and decreases in unrecognized tax benefits as a result of tax positions taken during a prior period

        (2) The gross amounts of increases and decreases in unrecognized tax benefits as a result of tax positions taken during the current period

        (3) The amounts of decreases in the unrecognized tax benefits relating to settlements with taxing authorities

        (4) Reductions to unrecognized tax benefits as a result of a lapse of the applicable statute of limitations

    b. The total amount of unrecognized tax benefits that, if recognized, would affect the effective tax rate

    c. The total amounts of interest and penalties recognized in the statement of operations and the total amounts of interest and penalties recognized in the statement of financial position

    d. For positions for which it is reasonably possible that the total amounts of unrecognized tax benefits will significantly increase or decrease within 12 months of the reporting date:

        (1) The nature of the uncertainty

        (2) The nature of the event that could occur in the next 12 months that would cause the change

        (3) An estimate of the range of the reasonably possible change or a statement that an estimate of the range cannot be made

    e. A description of tax years that remain subject to examination by major tax jurisdictions.

INTERPRETATION

FIN 48 21-1. Disclosures Required for Public Companies in Interim Period of Adoption

Question: What disclosures are required of public companies in the interim period of adopting FIN 48 and the subsequent interim periods of the year of adoption?

Response: The AICPA SEC Regulations Committee prepared the following table that was discussed with the SEC staff at a meeting in September 2006, and reflects revisions made by the SEC staff in February 2007:

FIN 48 Disclosures	Disclosure as of date of adoption[1]	Disclosure as to interim periods post adoption[2]
20. An enterprise shall disclose its policy on classification of interest and penalties in accordance with paragraph 19 of this Interpretation in the footnotes to the financial statements.	**Yes[4]**	**Disclose any change in classification**
21. An enterprise shall disclose the following at the end of each annual reporting period presented:		
a. A tabular reconciliation of the total amounts of unrecognized tax benefits at the beginning and end of the period, which shall include at a minimum:	**Total amount of unrecognized tax benefits as of date of adoption**	**Tabular reconciliation not required for interim periods**
(1) The gross amounts of the increases and decreases in unrecognized tax benefits as a result of tax positions taken during a prior period	**N/A**	**Disclose any material changes**
(2) The gross amounts of increases and decreases in unrecognized tax benefits as a result of tax positions taken during the current period	**N/A**	**Disclose any material changes[3]**
(3) The amounts of decreases in the unrecognized tax benefits relating to settlements with taxing authorities	**N/A**	**Disclose any material changes[3]**

FIN 48 Disclosures	Disclosure as of date of adoption[1]	Disclosure as to interim periods post adoption[2]
(4) Reductions to unrecognized tax benefits as a result of a lapse of the applicable statute of limitations	**N/A**	**Disclose any material changes[3]**
b. The total amount of unrecognized tax benefits that, if recognized, would affect the effective tax rate	**Yes, amount of as of date of adoption**	**Disclose any material changes**
c. The total amounts of interest and penalties recognized in the statement of operations and the total amounts of interest and penalties recognized in the statement of financial position[4]	**Total amount of accrued interest and penalties as of date of adoption**	**Disclose any material changes[4]**
d. For positions for which it is reasonably possible that the total amounts of unrecognized tax benefits will significantly increase or decrease within 12 months of the reporting date:	**Yes, amount of as of date of adoption**	**Disclose any material changes[5]**
(1) The nature of the uncertainty	**Yes, as of date of adoption**	**Disclose any material changes**
(2) The nature of the event that could occur in the next 12 months that would cause the change	**Yes, as of date of adoption**	**Disclose any material changes**
(3) An estimate of the range of the reasonably possible change or a statement that an estimate of the range cannot be made	**Yes, estimate of as of date of adoption**	**Disclose any material changes**
e. A description of tax years that remain subject to examination by major tax jurisdictions.	**Yes, as of date of adoption**	**Disclose any material changes**

1 Disclose in all interim financial statements in the year of adoption.

2 Regarding interim balances or activity during the current and year-to-date interim periods.

3 If material amounts are recognized during the quarter, disclosure in management's discussion and analysis may be required.

4 See SEC Staff Position [discussed in Interpretation 19-1] regarding supplemental disclosures for interest and penalties in pre-adoption periods.

5 If material amounts are updated during the quarter, disclosure in management's discussion and analysis may be required and critical accounting policies may need to be updated.

The SEC staff agreed that the above approach to disclosure in the year of the adoption of FIN 48 was reasonable.

FIN 48 21-2. Amounts Included in the Tabular Rollforward

Question: Does the "total amounts of unrecognized tax benefits" required to be disclosed in a tabular rollforward pursuant to paragraph 21(a) equate to the liability for unrecognized tax benefits discussed in Interpretations FIN 48 17-1 and FIN 48 17-2?

Response: No. The total amount of unrecognized tax benefits includes the effect of unrecognized tax benefits on refunds claimed, temporary differences, and carryforwards as well as the liability for unrecognized tax benefits. Exactly which tax-related assets or liabilities are affected by unrecognized tax benefits depends on each enterprise's specific tax situation.

For example, assume an enterprise immediately deducts for tax purposes the cost of an asset that is capitalized and amortized over five years for financial reporting purposes. Further assume the enterprise has concluded that the appropriate accounting under the recognition and measurement principles of FIN 48 is to recognize a tax benefit for the pro rata amortization of the asset over a five-year period (i.e., the same treatment as for financial reporting). In this situation, there is no temporary difference and hence no deferred tax asset or liability recognized with respect to a temporary difference. The way in which this unrecognized tax benefit affects other income tax-related amounts depends on the enterprise's specific tax situation:

- Assume that the effect of immediately deducting the full cost of this asset in Year 1 simply reduces, but does not eliminate, the enterprise's tax liability for Year 1. In this situation, the unrecognized tax benefit would be a liability for unrecognized tax benefits.
- Assume that the effect of immediately deducting the full cost of this asset in Year 1 increases the amount of a refund of income taxes due the enterprise. In this situation, the amount of the tax refund asset recognized would be reduced by the amount of unrecognized tax benefit.
- Assume that the effect of immediately deducting the full cost of this asset in Year 1 increases the amount of operating loss carryforward reported in the tax return. In this situation, the deferred tax asset for the operating loss carryforward would be reduced by the amount of unrecognized tax benefit.

FIN 48 21-3. Effective Tax Rate Disclosure

Question: Paragraph 21(b) states that enterprises should disclose the total amount of unrecognized tax benefits that, if recognized, would affect the effective tax rate. What is the purpose of this disclosure requirement?

Response: The total amount of unrecognized tax benefits disclosed pursuant to paragraph 21(a) of FIN 48 includes amounts that are simply timing differences as well as amounts that, if ultimately recognized, will be: (*a*) credited directly to equity, (*b*) used to reduce the carrying amount of acquired intangible assets or goodwill, or (*c*) recognized as immediate reductions in the enterprise's provision for income taxes. We believe the FASB was concerned that users of financial statements, absent this disclosure, might mistakenly assume that the total amount of unrecognized tax benefits disclosed pursuant to paragraph 21(a) could potentially provide the enterprise with a reduction in reported tax expense related to continuing operations in some future period. In addition to disclosing the total amount of unrecognized tax benefits that, if recognized, would affect the effective tax rate, we believe enterprises should consider disclosing any material amounts of unrecognized tax benefits that, if recognized, would be: (*a*) credited directly to equity, (*b*) used to reduce acquired intangible assets or goodwill, or (*c*) otherwise recognized outside of income from continuing operations (e.g., discontinued operations).

FIN 48 21-4. Example Disclosure From FIN 48

Question: Does FIN 48 provide any examples of disclosures that comply with its requirements?

Response: Yes. Paragraph A33 of FIN 48 contains the following illustrative disclosure example:

> The following example illustrates disclosures about uncertainty in income taxes. In this illustrative example, the reporting entity has adopted the provisions of this Interpretation for the year ended December 31, 2007:
>
> > The Company or one of its subsidiaries files income tax returns in the U.S. federal jurisdiction, and various states and foreign jurisdictions. With few exceptions, the Company is no longer subject to U.S. federal, state and local, or non-U.S. income tax examinations by tax authorities for years before 2001. The Internal Revenue Service (IRS) commenced an examination of the Company's U.S. income tax returns for 2002 through 2004

in the first quarter of 2007 that is anticipated to be completed by the end of 2008. As of December 31, 2007, the IRS has proposed certain significant adjustments to the Company's transfer pricing and research credits tax positions. Management is currently evaluating those proposed adjustments to determine if it agrees, but if accepted, the Company does not anticipate the adjustments would result in a material change to its financial position. However, the Company anticipates that it is reasonably possible that an additional payment in the range of $80 to $100 million will be made by the end of 2008.

The Company adopted the provisions of FASB Interpretation No. 48, *Accounting for Uncertainty in Income Taxes,* on January 1, 2007. As a result of the implementation of Interpretation 48, the Company recognized approximately a $200 million increase in the liability for unrecognized tax benefits, which was accounted for as a reduction to the January 1, 2007, balance of retained earnings. A reconciliation of the beginning and ending amount of unrecognized tax benefits is as follows:

	(in millions)
Balance at January 1, 2007	$370,000
Additions based on tax positions related to the current year	10,000
Additions for tax positions of prior years	30,000
Reductions for tax positions of prior years	(60,000)
Settlements	(40,000)
Balance at December 31, 2007	$310,000

Included in the balance at December 31, 2007, are $60 million of tax positions for which the ultimate deductibility is highly certain but for which there is uncertainty about the timing of such deductibility. Because of the impact of deferred tax accounting, other than interest and penalties, the disallowance of the shorter deductibility period would not affect the annual effective tax rate but would accelerate the payment of cash to the taxing authority to an earlier period.

The Company recognizes interest accrued related to unrecognized tax benefits in interest expense and penalties in operating expenses. During the years ended December 31, 2007, 2006, and 2005, the Company recognized approximately $10, $11, and $12 million in interest and penalties. The Company had approximately $60 and $50 million for the payment of interest and penalties accrued at December 31, 2007, and 2006, respectively.

EXCERPT FROM OFFICIAL TEXT

EFFECTIVE DATE AND TRANSITION

22. This Interpretation shall be effective for fiscal years beginning after December 15, 2006. Earlier adoption is permitted as of the beginning of an enterprise's fiscal year, provided the enterprise has not yet issued financial statements, including financial statements for any interim period, for that fiscal year.

23. The provisions of this Interpretation shall be applied to all tax positions upon initial adoption of this Interpretation. Only tax positions that meet the more-likely-than-not recognition threshold at the effective date may be recognized or continue to be recognized upon adoption of this Interpretation. The cumulative effect of applying the provisions of this Interpretation shall be reported as an adjustment to the opening balance of retained earnings (or other appropriate components of equity or net assets in the statement of financial position) for that fiscal year, presented separately. The cumulative-effect adjustment does not include items that would not be recognized in earnings, such as the effect of adopting this Interpretation on tax positions related to business combinations. The amount of that cumulative-effect adjustment is the difference between the net amount of assets and liabilities recognized in the statement of financial position prior to the application of this Interpretation and the net amount of assets and liabilities recognized as a result of applying the provisions of this Interpretation.

INTERPRETATION

FIN 48 23-1. Treatment of Subsequent Events at Transition to FIN 48

Question: Is it possible that the effect of events occurring subsequent to the balance-sheet date, but prior to the date the financial statements are issued, that changes the recognition or measurement of income tax contingencies could be recognized in both the tax provision of: (*a*) the period immediately preceding the adoption of FIN 48 and (*b*) the period of the adoption of FIN 48?

Response: Given the change in treatment of subsequent events in accounting for income tax contingencies from FASB Statement No. 5, *Accounting for Contingencies,* to FIN 48, such an outcome seems possible (with the effect of the subsequent event being recognized in the period immediately preceding the adoption of FIN 48, then being reversed as part of the cumulative effect of adopting FIN 48, and then being recognized again in the period of the adoption of FIN 48). Refer to Interpretation FIN 48 12-1 for an explanation of the difference in consideration of subsequent events between Statement 5 to FIN 48.

However, we understand the FASB and SEC staffs have been consulted on this question and have expressed the view that either of the following two alternatives (but only these two alternatives) is an acceptable treatment of subsequent events at the time of the adoption of FIN 48:

1. Consider the effect of the subsequent event in measuring the liability for tax contingencies at the balance-sheet date immediately preceding the adoption of FIN 48 and also consider the effect of the subsequent event in determining the cumulative effect of adopting FIN 48 on the first day of the period of adoption.
2. Do not consider the effect of the subsequent event in measuring the liability for tax contingencies at the balance-sheet date immediately preceding the adoption of FIN 48 and also do not consider the effect of the subsequent event in determining the cumulative effect of adopting FIN 48 on the first day of the period of adoption.

Applying either of the above alternatives results in the subsequent event being recognized only once in the tax provision—in the period immediately preceding the adoption of FIN 48 under the first alternative or in the period of adoption of FIN 48 under the second alternative. If the effect of such subsequent events is material, we believe enterprises should disclose which alternative accounting treatment they elected to use and the effect on the financial statements of electing that alternative treatment.

The transition to new accounting standards is often more a practical than a theoretical exercise. We believe the above view of the FASB and SEC staffs to be a practical answer to a transition situation some accountants believe could otherwise produce a counterintuitive result. As such, we do not believe enterprises should analogize to this guidance.

EXCERPT FROM OFFICIAL TEXT

24. An enterprise shall disclose the cumulative effect of the change on retained earnings in the statement of financial position as of the date of adoption. This disclosure is required only in the year of adoption.

APPENDIX II: GLOSSARY

The information in this appendix is taken from Appendix E of Statement 109.

This appendix contains definitions of certain terms or phrases used by the FASB in the preparation of Statement 109.

Carrybacks

Deductions or credits that cannot be utilized on the tax return during a year that may be carried back to reduce taxable income or taxes payable in a prior year. An operating loss carryback is an excess of tax deductions over gross income in a year; a tax credit carryback is the amount by which tax credits available for utilization exceed statutory limitations. Different tax jurisdictions have different rules about whether excess deductions or credits may be carried back and the length of the carryback period.

Carryforwards

Deductions or credits that cannot be utilized on the tax return during a year that may be carried forward to reduce taxable income or taxes payable in a future year. An operating loss carryforward is an excess of tax deductions over gross income in a year; a tax credit carryforward is the amount by which tax credits available for utilization exceed statutory limitations. Different tax jurisdictions have different rules about whether excess deductions or credits may be carried forward and the length of the carryforward period. The terms *carryforward, operating loss carryforward,* and *tax credit carryforward* refer to the amounts of those items, if any, reported in the tax return for the current year.

Current tax expense or benefit

The amount of income taxes paid or payable (or refundable) for a year as determined by applying the provisions of the enacted tax law to the taxable income or excess of deductions over revenues for that year.

Deductible temporary difference

Temporary differences that result in deductible amounts in future years when the related asset or liability is recovered or settled, respectively. Also refer to **Temporary difference.**

Deferred tax asset

The deferred tax consequences attributable to deductible temporary differences and carryforwards. A deferred tax asset is measured using the applicable enacted tax rate and provisions of the enacted tax law. A deferred tax asset is reduced by a valuation allowance if, based on the weight of evidence available, it is more likely than not that some portion or all of a deferred tax asset will not be realized.

Deferred tax consequences

The future effects on income taxes as measured by the applicable enacted tax rate and provisions of the enacted tax law resulting from temporary differences and carryforwards at the end of the current year.

Deferred tax expense or benefit

The change during the year in an enterprise's deferred tax liabilities and assets. For deferred tax liabilities and assets acquired in a purchase business combination during the year, it is the change since the combination date. Income tax expense or benefit for the year is allocated among continuing operations, discontinued operations, extraordinary items, and items charged or credited directly to shareholders' equity.

Deferred tax liability

The deferred tax consequences attributable to taxable temporary differences. A deferred tax liability is measured using the applicable enacted tax rate and provisions of the enacted tax law.

Event

A happening of consequence to an enterprise. The term encompasses both transactions and other events affecting an enterprise.

Gains and losses included in comprehensive income but excluded from net income

Under present practice, gains and losses included in comprehensive income but excluded from net income include certain changes in market values of investments in marketable equity securities classified as noncurrent assets, certain changes in market values of investments in industries having specialized accounting practices for marketable securities, adjustments from recognizing certain additional pension liabilities, and foreign currency translation adjustments. Future changes to generally accepted accounting principles may change what is included in this category.

Income taxes

Domestic and foreign federal (national), state, and local (including franchise) taxes based on income.

Income taxes currently payable (refundable)

Refer to **Current tax expense or benefit**.

Income tax expense (benefit)

The sum of current tax expense (benefit) and deferred tax expense (benefit).

Nonpublic enterprise

An enterprise other than one (*a*) whose debt or equity securities are traded in a public market, including those traded on a stock exchange or in the over-the-counter market (including securities quoted only locally or regionally), or (*b*) whose financial statements are filed with a regulatory agency in preparation for the sale of any class of securities.

Public enterprise

An enterprise (*a*) whose debt or equity securities are traded in a public market, including those traded on a stock exchange or in the over-the-counter market (including securities quoted only locally or regionally), or (*b*) whose financial statements are filed with a regulatory agency in preparation for the sale of any class of securities.

Taxable income

The excess of taxable revenues over tax deductible expenses and exemptions for the year as defined by the governmental taxing authority.

Taxable temporary difference

Temporary differences that result in taxable amounts in future years when the related asset or liability is recovered or settled, respectively. Also refer to **Temporary difference**.

Tax consequences

The effects on income taxes—current or deferred—of an event.

Tax-planning strategy

An action (including elections for tax purposes) that meets certain criteria (paragraph 22) and that would be implemented to realize a tax benefit for an operating loss or tax credit carryforward before it expires. Tax-planning strategies are considered when assessing the need for and amount of a valuation allowance for deferred tax assets.

Temporary difference

A difference between the tax basis of an asset or liability computed pursuant to FASB Interpretation No. 48, *Accounting for Uncertainty in Income Taxes,* and its reported amount in the financial statements that will result in taxable or deductible amounts in future years when the reported amount of the asset or liability is recovered or settled, respectively. Paragraph 11 cites 8 examples of temporary differences. Some temporary differences cannot be identified with a particular asset or liability for financial reporting (paragraph 15), but those temporary differences (*a*) result from events that have been recognized in the financial statements and (*b*) will result in taxable or deductible amounts in future years based on provisions of the tax law. Some events recognized in financial statements do not have tax consequences. Certain revenues are exempt from taxation and certain expenses are not deductible. Events that do not have tax consequences do not give rise to temporary differences.

Valuation allowance

The portion of a deferred tax asset for which it is more likely than not that a tax benefit will not be realized.

APPENDIX III: SAMPLE FOOTNOTES AND DISCLOSURES

The purpose of this appendix is to provide users of this publication with examples reflecting how various U.S. public companies disclosed the information required by Statement 109 as amended and interpreted (before the issuance of FASB Interpretation No. 48, *Accounting for Uncertainty in Income Taxes*). Refer to Interpretation 43-9 for additional information on this topic. The source of this information was published reports as filed with the SEC in Washington, D.C.

Example 1: Southern California Edison Company

Note 5. Income Taxes

SCE and its subsidiaries are included in Edison International's consolidated federal income tax and combined state franchise tax returns. Under an income tax allocation agreement approved by the CPUC, SCE's tax liability is computed as if it filed a separate return.

Income tax expense includes the current tax liability from operations and the change in deferred income taxes during the year. Investment tax credits are amortized over the lives of the related properties.

The components of income tax expense from continuing operations by location of taxing jurisdiction are:

	In Millions		
	Year Ended December 31,		
	2005	2004	2003
Current:			
Federal	$ 255	$ (88)	$ 408
State	84	46	174
	339	(42)	582
Deferred:			
Federal	(18)	425	(134)
State	(29)	55	(60)
	(47)	480	(194)
Total	$ 292	$ 438	$ 388

The components of the net accumulated deferred income tax liability are:

	In Millions	
	December 31,	
	2005	2004
Deferred tax assets:		
Accrued charges	$ 117	$ 200
Investment tax credits	72	64
Property-related	352	196
Regulatory balancing accounts	301	321
Unrealized gains and losses	321	392
Decommissioning	163	84
Pensions and postretirement benefits other than pensions	182	125
Other	409	120
Total	$ 1,917	$ 1,502
Deferred tax liabilities:		
Property-related	$ 3,184	$ 2,915
Capitalized software costs	173	164
Regulatory balancing accounts	607	710
Unrealized gains and losses	321	289
Decommissioning	125	31
Other	327	124
Total	$ 4,737	$ 4,233
Accumulated deferred income taxes—net	$ 2,820	$ 2,731
Classification of accumulated deferred income taxes:		
Included in deferred credits	$ 2,815	$ 2,865
Included in current assets	–	134
Included in current liabilities	5	–

The federal statutory income tax rate is reconciled to the effective tax rate from continuing operations as follows:

	Year Ended December 31,		
	2005	**2004**	**2003**
Federal statutory rate	35.0%	35.0%	35.0%
Tax reserve adjustments	(2.1)	(7.3)	(2.8)
Resolution of 1991–1993 audit cycle	(5.8)	–	–
Resolution of FERC rate case	–	–	(5.9)
Property-related	(0.5)	0.4	0.1
State tax—net of federal deduction	3.2	4.8	6.0
Other	(1.7)	(0.7)	(1.9)
Effective tax rate	28.1%	32.2%	30.5%

The composite federal and state statutory income tax rate was approximately 40% for all periods presented. The lower effective tax rate of 28.1% realized in 2005 was primarily due to settlement of the 1991 through 1993 Internal Revenue Service (IRS) audit cycle as well as adjustments made to the tax reserve to reflect the issuance of new IRS regulations and the favorable settlement of other federal and state tax audit issues. The lower effective tax rate of 32.2% realized in 2004 was primarily due to adjustments to tax liabilities relating to prior years. The lower effective tax rate of 30.5% realized in 2003 was primarily due to the resolution of a FERC rate case and recording the benefit of a favorable resolution of tax audit issues.

As a matter of course, SCE is regularly audited by federal and state taxing authorities. For a further discussion of this matter, see "Federal Income Taxes" in Note 9.

Note 9. Contingencies

Federal Income Taxes

Edison International has reached a settlement with the IRS on tax issues and pending affirmative claims relating to its 1991 through 1993 tax years. This settlement, which was signed by Edison International in March 2005 and approved by the United States Congress Joint Committee on Taxation on July 27, 2005, resulted in a third quarter 2005 net earnings benefit for SCE of approximately $61 million, including interest. This benefit was reflected in the caption "Income tax" on the consolidated statements of income.

Edison International received Revenue Agent Reports from the IRS in August 2002 and in January 2005 asserting deficiencies in federal corporate income taxes with respect to audits of its 1994 through 1996 and 1997 through 1999 tax years, respectively. Many of the asserted tax deficiencies are timing differences and, therefore, amounts ultimately paid (exclusive of penalties), if any, would benefit SCE as future tax deductions.

The IRS Revenue Agent Report for the 1997 through 1999 audit also asserted deficiencies with respect to a transaction entered into by an SCE subsidiary, which may be considered substantially similar to a listed transaction described by the IRS as a contingent liability company. While Edison International intends to defend its tax return position with respect to this transaction, the tax benefits relating to the capital loss deductions will not be claimed for financial accounting and reporting purposes until and unless these tax losses are sustained.

In April 2004, Edison International filed California Franchise Tax amended returns for tax years 1997 through 2002 to abate the possible imposition of new California penalty provisions on transactions that may be considered as listed or substantially similar to listed transactions described in an IRS notice that was published in 2001. These transactions include the SCE subsidiary contingent liability company transaction described above. Edison International filed these amended returns under protest retaining its appeal rights.

Example 2: UAL Corporation

(2) Summary of Significant Accounting Policies

(o) Tax Contingencies—We have recorded reserves for taxes and associated interest in accordance with SFAS No. 5, *Accounting for Contingencies,* that may become payable in future years as a result of audits by tax authorities. Although we believe that the positions taken by the Company on previously filed tax returns are reasonable, we nevertheless have established tax and interest reserves in recognition that various taxing authorities may challenge certain of the positions taken by the Company, potentially resulting in additional liabilities for taxes and interest. Our tax contingency reserves are reviewed periodically and are adjusted as events occur that affect our estimated liability for additional taxes, such as the lapsing of applicable statutes of limitations, the conclusion of tax audits, the measurement of additional estimated liability based on current calculations, the identification of new tax contingencies, the release of administrative tax guidance affecting our estimates of tax liabilities, or the rendering of court decisions affecting our estimates of tax liabilities.

(6) Income Taxes

In 2005, UAL incurred both a regular and an alternative minimum tax (AMT) loss. The primary differences between our regular tax loss and AMT loss are certain depreciation adjustments and preferences.

In assessing the realizability of our deferred tax assets, management considers whether it is more likely than not that some portion of the deferred tax asset will be realized. During 2005, 2004, and 2003, we recorded a valuation allowance against our deferred tax assets.

The significant components of the deferred income tax provision (credit) are as follows:

	(In Millions)		
	2005	2004	2003
Deferred tax provision (exclusive of the other components listed below)	$ (7,830)	$ (640)	$ (1,017)
Increase in the valuation allowance for deferred tax assets	7,830	640	1,017
	$ –	$ –	$ –

The income tax provision differed from amounts computed at the statutory federal income tax rate, as follows:

	(In Millions)		
	2005	2004	2003
Income tax provision at statutory rate	$ (7,410)	$ (602)	$ (983)
State income taxes, net of federal income tax benefit	(416)	(28)	(48)
Nondeductible employee meals	11	9	10
Medicare Part D Subsidy	(17)	–	–
Valuation allowance	7,830	640	1,017
Other, net	2	(19)	4
	$ –	$ –	$ –

Temporary differences and carry forwards that give rise to a significant portion of deferred tax assets and liabilities for 2005 and 2004 are as follows:

	(In Millions)			
	2005		2004	
	Deferred Tax Assets	Deferred Tax Liabilities	Deferred Tax Assets	Deferred Tax Liabilities
Employee benefits, including postretirement medical and ESOP	$ 5,471	$ 29	$ 2,026	$ 30
Depreciation, capitalized interest and transfers of tax benefits	–	3,434	–	3,539
Federal and state net operating loss carry forwards	2,688	–	2,370	–
Mileage plus deferred revenue	47	–	147	–
Gains on sale and leasebacks	69	–	115	–
Rent expense	525	–	706	–
AMT credit carry forwards	294	–	294	–
Restructuring charges	4,482	–	408	–
Other	1,541	1,483	1,369	1,340
Less: Valuation allowance	(10,618)	–	(2,819)	–
	$ 4,499	$ 4,946	$ 4,616	$ 4,909

At December 31, 2005, UAL and its subsidiaries had $294 million of federal AMT credits, $2.5 billion of federal tax benefits, and $0.2 billion of state tax benefits, resulting from $7.0 billion of net operating losses, which may be carried forward to reduce the tax liabilities of future years. If not utilized, the federal tax benefits of $0.2 billion expire in 2022, $1.2 billion expire in 2023, $0.4 billion expire in 2024, $0.5 billion expire in 2025, and $0.2 billion expire in 2026. In addition, the state tax benefit, if not utilized, expires over a five- to twenty-year period.

We have determined that it is more likely than not that our net deferred tax asset at December 31, 2005, will be realized through the reversals of existing deferred tax credits.

Example 3: Goodrich Corporation

Note 1. Significant Accounting Policies

Income Taxes. Income taxes are accounted for in accordance with Statement of Financial Accounting Standards No. 109 (SFAS 109),

Accounting for Income Taxes, which requires that deferred taxes and liabilities are based on differences between financial reporting and tax bases of assets and liabilities and are measured using enacted tax laws and rates. A valuation allowance is provided on deferred tax assets if it is determined that it is more likely than not that the asset will not be realized. The Company records interest on potential tax contingencies as a component of its tax expense and records the interest net of any applicable related tax benefit.

Note 17. Income Taxes

Income from continuing operations before income taxes and trust distributions as shown in the Consolidated Statement of Income consists of the following:

	Year Ended December 31,		
	2005	2004	2003
	(Dollars in Millions)		
Domestic	$ 328.5	$ 160.8	$ 43.4
Foreign	34.6	35.9	25.4
TOTAL	$ 363.1	$ 196.7	$ 68.8

A summary of income tax (expense) benefit from continuing operations in the Consolidated Statement of Income is as follows:

	Year Ended December 31,		
	2005	2004	2003
	(Dollars in Millions)		
Current			
Federal	$ (54.1)	$ (3.5)	$ (26.9)
Foreign	(9.9)	(11.5)	2.9
State	0.6	2.7	–
	(63.4)	(12.3)	(24.0)
Deferred			
Federal	(66.7)	(49.4)	11.1
Foreign	9.8	15.3	(9.7)
State	1.0	4.0	–
	(55.9)	(30.1)	1.4
TOTAL	$ (119.3)	$ (42.4)	$ (22.6)

Significant components of deferred income tax assets and liabilities at December 31, 2005 and 2004 are as follows:

	2005	2004
	(Dollars in Millions)	
Deferred income tax assets		
Pensions	$ 214.6	$ 224.4
Tax credit and net operating loss carryovers	138.0	46.8
Accrual for postretirement benefits other than pensions	128.4	123.2
Inventories	42.2	22.8
Other nondeductible accruals	89.1	98.7
Employee benefits plans	20.5	12.9
Other	62.1	61.4
Deferred income tax assets	694.9	590.2
Less: valuation allowance	(40.6)	(11.9)
Total deferred income tax assets	654.3	578.3
Deferred income tax liabilities:		
Tax over book depreciation	(197.8)	(183.3)
Tax over book intangible amortization	(199.9)	(158.9)
Tax over book interest expense	(94.0)	(89.6)
SFAS 133	(3.2)	(38.6)
Other	(64.6)	–
Total deferred income tax liabilities	(559.5)	(470.4)
NET DEFERRED INCOME TAX ASSET	$ 94.8	$ 107.9

In accordance with SFAS 109, deferred tax assets and liabilities are recorded for tax carryforwards and the net tax effects of temporary differences between the carrying amounts of assets and liabilities for financial reporting and income tax purposes and are measured using enacted tax laws and rates. A valuation allowance is provided on deferred tax assets if it is determined that it is more likely than not that the asset will not be realized. The Company records interest on potential tax contingencies as a component of its tax expense and records the interest net of any applicable related tax benefit.

At December 31, 2005, the Company had net operating loss and tax credit carryforward benefits of approximately $138 million that expire in the years 2006 through 2015. For financial reporting purposes a valuation allowance of $40.6 million was recognized to offset the deferred tax asset relating to those carryforward benefits. The net change in the total valuation allowance for the year ended December 31, 2005 was an increase of $28.7 million.

The effective income tax rate from continuing operations varied from the statutory federal income tax rate as follows:

	2005		2004		2003	
	%	(Dollars in Millions)	%	(Dollars in Millions)	%	(Dollars in Millions)
Income from operations before taxes and trust distributions		$ 363.1		$ 196.7		$ 68.8
Statutory federal income tax rate	35.0 %		35.0 %		35.0 %	
State and local taxes	0.4 %	$ 1.3	0.7 %	$ 1.3	(0.4)%	$ (0.3)
Tax benefits related to export sales	(5.8)%	$ (21.0)	(10.2)%	$ (20.2)	(15.4)%	$ (10.6)
Trust distributions	–	–	–	–	(4.0)%	$ (2.7)
Repatriation of non-U.S. earnings under the American Jobs Creation Act	1.4 %	$ 5.3	–	–	–	–
Deemed repatriation of non-U.S. earnings	2.0 %	$ 7.2	4.6 %	$ 9.1	–	–
Differences in rates on foreign subsidiaries	(5.4)%	$ (19.7)	(21.8)%	$ (42.9)	(25.1)%	$ (17.2)
Interest on potential tax liabilities	2.0 %	$ 7.2	8.0 %	$ 15.8	33.7 %	$ 23.2
Tax settlements and other adjustments to tax reserves	6.4 %	$ 23.1	3.8 %	$ 7.4	5.2 %	$ 3.6
Other items	(3.1)%	$ (11.3)	1.5 %	$ 3.0	3.8 %	$ 2.6
Effective income tax rate	32.9 %		21.6 %		32.8 %	

In accordance with SFAS 109, APB Opinion No. 28, and FIN 18, as of each reporting period the Company estimates an effective income tax rate that is expected to be applicable for the full fiscal year. The estimate of the Company's effective income tax rate involves significant judgments regarding the application of complex tax regulations across many jurisdictions and estimates as to the amount and jurisdictional source of income expected to be earned during the full fiscal year. Evolving interpretations of new and existing tax laws, rulings by taxing authorities, and court decisions further influence this estimate. Due to the subjective and complex nature of these underlying issues, the Company's actual effective tax rate and related tax liabilities may differ from its initial estimates. Differences between the estimated and actual effective income tax rates and related liabilities are recorded in the period they become known. The resulting adjustment to the Company's income tax expense could have a material effect on its results of operations in the period the adjustment is recorded.

On October 22, 2004, the President signed the American Jobs Creation Act of 2004 (the Act). The Act provides a deduction for income from qualified domestic production activities, which will be phased in from 2005 through 2010. The Act provides for a two-year phase-out of the existing Extraterritorial Income (ETI) deduction for export sales that was ruled by the World Trade Organization to be inconsistent with international trade protocols. Under the guidance provided in FASB Staff Position No. FAS 109-1, "Application of SFAS 109, 'Accounting for Income Taxes,' to the Tax Deduction on Qualified Production Activities Provided by the American Jobs Creation Act of 2004", the deduction will be treated as a "special deduction" as described in SFAS 109. As such, the special deduction had no effect on the Company's deferred tax assets and liabilities existing at the enactment date. Rather, the impact of this deduction will be reported in the period in which the deduction is claimed on the Company's tax return.

The Act also created a temporary incentive for U.S. corporations to repatriate accumulated income earned abroad by providing an 85% dividends received deduction for certain dividends from controlled foreign corporations. The Company repatriated approximately $102 million in extraordinary dividends, as defined in the Act, during 2005 and accordingly, has recorded a tax liability of approximately $5.3 million as of December 31, 2005. In accordance with SFAS 109 and APB 23, the Company has not provided for U.S. deferred income taxes or foreign withholding tax on basis differences in its non-U.S. subsidiaries of approximately $266 million that result primarily from the remaining undistributed earnings the Company intends to reinvest indefinitely. Determination of the liability on these basis differences is not practicable because such liability, if any, is dependent on circumstances existing if and when remittance occurs.

In accordance with SFAS 5, the Company records tax contingencies when the exposure item becomes probable and reasonably estimable. As of January 1, 2005, the Company had tax contingency reserves of approximately $315.8 million. During 2005, the Company recorded a provision of $30.3 million (net of adjustments for state and foreign settlements), made payments of $19.1 million and had a $1.4 million reduction of other items including translation. As of December 31, 2005, the Company has recorded tax contingency reserves of approximately $325.6 million. The contingencies that comprise the reserves are more fully described in Note 19, "Contingencies."

Note 19. Contingencies

Tax

The Company is continuously undergoing examination by the IRS, as well as various state and foreign jurisdictions. The IRS and other taxing authorities routinely challenge certain deductions and credits reported by the Company on its income tax returns. In accordance with SFAS 109, *Accounting for Income Taxes*, and SFAS 5, *Accounting for Contingencies*, the Company establishes reserves for tax contingencies that reflect its best estimate of the deductions and credits that it may be unable to sustain, or that it could be willing to concede as part of a broader tax settlement. Differences between the reserves for tax contingencies and the amounts ultimately owed by the Company are recorded in the period they become known. Adjustments to the Company's reserves could have a material effect on the Company's financial statements. As of December 31, 2005, the Company had recorded tax contingency reserves of approximately $325.6 million.

In 2000, Coltec, the Company's former subsidiary, made a $113.7 million payment to the Internal Revenue Service (IRS) for an income tax assessment and the related accrued interest arising out of certain capital loss deductions and tax credits taken in 1996. On February 13, 2001, Coltec filed suit against the U.S. Government in the U.S. Court of Federal Claims seeking a refund of this payment. The trial portion of the case was completed in May 2004. On November 2, 2004, the Company was notified that the trial court ruled in favor of Coltec and ordered the Government to refund federal tax payments of $82.8 million to Coltec. This tax refund would also bear interest to the date of payment. As of December 31, 2005, the interest amount was approximately $52 million before tax, or approximately $33 million after tax. The U.S. Court of Federal Claims entered a final judgment in this case on February 15, 2005. During July 2005, the Government filed its brief related to its appeal of the decision with the U.S. Court of Appeals for the Federal Circuit. Coltec filed its brief related to the U.S. Government's appeal on September 6, 2005. Oral arguments were heard by the U.S. Court of Appeals for the Federal Circuit on February 8, 2006. A decision is expected by the U.S. Court of Appeals for the Federal Circuit sometime in 2006. If the trial court's decision is ultimately upheld, the Company will be entitled to this tax refund and related interest pursuant to an agreement with Coltec. If the Company receives these amounts, it expects to record income of approximately $149 million, after tax, based on interest through December 31, 2005, including the release of previously established reserves. If the IRS were to ultimately prevail in this case, Coltec will not owe any additional interest or taxes with respect to 1996. The Company may, however, be required by the IRS to pay up to $32.7 million plus accrued interest with respect to the same items claimed by Coltec in its tax returns for 1997 through 2000. The amount of the previously estimated tax liability if the IRS were to prevail for the 1997 through 2000 period remains fully reserved.

In 2000, the IRS issued a statutory notice of deficiency asserting that Rohr, Inc. (Rohr), the Company's subsidiary, was liable for $85.3 million of additional income taxes for the fiscal years ended July 31, 1986 through 1989. In 2003, the IRS issued an additional statutory notice of deficiency asserting that Rohr was liable for $23 million of additional income taxes for the fiscal years ended July 31, 1990 through 1993. The proposed assessments relate primarily to the timing of certain tax deductions and tax credits. Rohr has filed petitions in the U.S. Tax Court opposing the proposed assessments. At the time of settlement or final determination by the court, there will be a net cash cost to the Company due at least in part to the reversal of a timing item. The Company believes that its total net cash cost is unlikely to exceed $100 million. The Company reserved the estimated liability associated with these cases. The Company is in advanced stages of discussion with the IRS to settle the Rohr case and to resolve the open issues in the tax years through 1999 as described below.

The current IRS examination cycle began on September 29, 2005, and involves the taxable years ended December 31, 2000, through December 31, 2004. The prior examination cycle that began in March 2002 has reached an advanced stage of discussion with the IRS. The Company anticipates substantially all of the open issues for the consolidated income tax groups in the audit periods identified below to be resolved in 2006:

Rohr, Inc. and Subsidiaries	July, 1995—December, 1997 (through date of acquisition)
Coltec Industries Inc. and Subsidiaries	December, 1997—July, 1999 (through date of acquisition)
Goodrich Corporation and Subsidiaries	1998–1999 (including Rohr and Coltec)

There are numerous tax issues that have been raised during the examination by the IRS, including, but not limited to, transfer pricing, research and development credits, foreign tax credits, tax accounting for long-term contracts, tax accounting for inventory, tax accounting for stock options, depreciation, amortization, and the proper timing for certain other deductions for income tax purposes. The IRS and the Company have reached a tentative agreement on a substantial number of the issues raised in the prior examination cycle and the U.S. Tax Court litigation involving Rohr described above. The final settlement of these issues is subject to a further review and approval process, the outcome of which cannot be predicted at this time. If the Company settles pursuant to these discussions, the Company would anticipate reversing some portion of previously established reserves, which could be material to the Company's financial statements. The Company anticipates a final settlement in 2006.

Rohr has been under examination by the State of California for the tax years ended July 31, 1985, 1986, and 1987. The State of California has disallowed certain expenses incurred by one of Rohr's subsidiaries in connection with the lease of certain tangible property. California's Franchise Tax Board held that the deductions associated with the leased equipment were non-business deductions. The additional tax associated with the Franchise Tax Board's position is approximately $4.5 million. The amount of accrued interest associated with the additional tax is approximately $19 million as of December 31, 2005. In addition, the State of California enacted an amnesty provision that imposes nondeductible penalty interest equal to 50% of the unpaid interest amounts relating to taxable years ended before 2003. The penalty interest is approximately $10 million as of December 31, 2005. The tax and interest amounts continue to be contested by Rohr. The Company believes that it is adequately reserved for this contingency. Rohr made a voluntary payment during the three months ended March 31, 2005, of approximately $3.9 million related to items that were not being contested, consisting of approximately $0.6 million related to tax and approximately $3.3 million related to interest on the tax. Rohr made an additional payment during the three months ended December 31, 2005, of approximately $4.5 million related to the contested tax amount pursuant to the State's assessment notice dated October 20, 2005. No payment has been made for the $19 million of interest or $10 million of penalty interest. Under California law, Rohr may be required to pay the full amount of interest prior to filing any suit for refund. If required, Rohr expects to make this payment and file suit for a refund before the end of 2007.

Example 4: News Corporation

Note 2. Summary of Significant Accounting Policies

Income taxes

The Company accounts for income taxes in accordance with SFAS No. 109, *Accounting for Income Taxes*. SFAS No. 109 requires an asset and liability approach for financial accounting and reporting for income taxes. Under the asset and liability approach, deferred taxes are provided for the net tax effects of temporary differences between the carrying amounts of assets and liabilities for financial reporting purposes and the amounts used for income tax purposes. Valuation allowances are established where management determines that it is more likely than not that some portion or all of a deferred tax asset will not be realized. Deferred taxes have not been provided on the cumulative undistributed earnings of foreign subsidiaries to the extent amounts are expected to be reinvested indefinitely.

Note 18. Income Taxes

Income before income tax expense was attributable to the following jurisdictions:

	For the Years Ended June 30,		
	2005	2004	2003
		(in Millions)	
United States (including exports)	$ 2,896	$ 1,995	$ 782
Foreign	665	760	884
Income before income tax expense	$ 3,561	$ 2,755	$ 1,666

Significant components of the Company's provisions for income taxes were as follows:

	For the Years Ended June 30,		
	2005	2004	2003
		(In Millions)	
Current			
United States			
Federal	$ 51	$ –	$ –
State & local	45	38	16
Foreign	179	401	278
Total Current	$ 275	$ 439	$294
Deferred	$ 945	$ 575	$335
Total provision for income taxes	$ 1,220	$ 1,014	$629

The reconciliation of income tax attributable to continuing operations computed at the statutory rate to income tax expense is:

	For the Years Ended June 30,		
	2005	2004	2003
U.S. federal income tax rate	35 %	35 %	35 %
State and local taxes	1	1	1
Effect of foreign taxes	1	–	1
Gain for which no expense was recognized	–	1	6
Permanent basis difference on sale of investment	–	(5)	–
Resolution of tax matters	(3)	–	–
Change in valuation allowance	(1)	8	–
Other permanent differences	1	(3)	(5)
Effective tax rate	34 %	37 %	38 %

The following is a summary of the components of the deferred tax accounts:

	As of June 30,	
	2005	2004
	(in Millions)	
Deferred tax assets:		
Net operating loss carryforwards	$ 971	$ 1,523
Capital loss carryforwards	508	549
Total deferred tax assets	1,479	2,072
Deferred tax liabilities, net:		
Accrued Liabilities	316	325
Amortization and basis difference	(4,133)	(3,270)
Revenue recognition	(187)	(201)
Sports rights contracts	(118)	(124)
Other	(695)	(360)
Total deferred tax liabilities	(4,817)	(3,630)
Net deferred tax liabilities before valuation allowance	(3,338)	(1,558)
Less: valuation allowance	(1,324)	(1,541)
Net deferred tax liabilities	$ (4,662)	$ (3,099)

At June 30, 2005 and 2004, the Company had net current deferred tax assets of $155 million and $521 million, respectively, and non-current deferred tax liabilities of $4,817 million and $3,620 million, respectively.

At June 30, 2005, the Company had approximately $3.3 billion of net operating and $1.6 billion of capital loss carryforwards available to offset future taxable income. The majority of these net operating loss carryforwards, if not utilized to reduce taxable income in future periods, will expire in varying amounts between 2006 and 2023, with a significant portion, approximately $2.1 billion relating to foreign operations, expiring within the next five years, while approximately half of the capital loss carryforwards expire in five years, the remaining capital loss carryforward are in jurisdictions where they do not expire. In assessing the realizability of deferred tax assets, management evaluates a variety of factors in considering whether it is more likely than not that some portion or all of the deferred tax assets will ultimately be realized. Management considers earnings expectations, the existence of taxable temporary differences, tax planning strategies, and the periods in which estimated losses can be utilized. Based on this analysis, management has concluded that it is more likely than not that the Company will not realize all of the benefits of its deferred tax assets. In particular, this is due to the uncertainty of generating capital gains as well as generating taxable income within the requisite period in various foreign jurisdictions and the uncertainty of fully utilizing the capital losses and NOLs before they expire, through tax planning strategies or reversing taxable temporary differences in the foreseeable future. Accordingly, valuation allowances of $1.3 billion and $1.5 billion have been established to reflect the expected realization of the deferred tax assets as to June 30, 2005 and 2004, respectively. The net decrease in the valuation allowance during fiscal 2005 of $217 million was primarily due to the expiration of NOLs in a foreign jurisdiction in which the NOLs had full valuation allowances.

The Company has not provided for possible U.S. taxes on the undistributed earnings of foreign subsidiaries that are considered to be reinvested indefinitely. Calculation of the unrecognized deferred tax liability for temporary differences related to these earnings is not practicable. Undistributed earnings of foreign subsidiaries considered to be indefinitely reinvested amounted to approximately $4.7 billion at June 30, 2005. (See Note 2 Summary of Significant Accounting Policies.)

EXAMPLE 5: INTEL CORPORATION

Note 10: Provision for Taxes

Income before taxes and the provision for taxes consisted of the following:

(Dollars in Millions)	2005	2004	2003
Income before taxes:			
U.S.	$10,397	$ 7,422	$ 5,705
Non-U.S.	2,213	2,995	1,737
Total income before taxes	**$12,610**	**$10,417**	**$ 7,442**
Provision for taxes:			
Current:			
Federal	$ 3,546	$ 2,787	$ 808
State	289	(69)	223
Non-U.S.	524	390	379
	4,359	3,108	1,410
Deferred:			
Federal	(360)	(128)	420
Other	(53)	(79)	(29)
	(413)	(207)	391
Total provision for taxes	**$ 3,946**	**$ 2,901**	**$ 1,801**
Effective tax rate	**31.3%**	**27.8%**	**24.2%**

The tax benefit from employee equity incentive plans was $351 million for 2005 ($344 million for 2004 and $216 million for 2003).

The difference between the tax provision at the statutory federal income tax rate and the tax provision attributable to income before income taxes was as follows:

(In Percentages)	2005	2004	2003
Statutory federal income tax rate	35.0%	35.0%	35.0%
Increase (reduction) in rate resulting from:			
State taxes, net of federal benefits	1.3	(0.4)	1.9
Non-U.S. income taxed at different rates	(2.0)	(2.5)	(2.8)
Non-deductible acquisition-related costs and goodwill impairments	–	0.1	3.1

Tax benefit related to divestitures	–	–	(10.2)
Export sales benefit	(2.8)	(4.8)	(2.5)
Repatriation of prior years' permanently reinvested earnings	1.8	–	–
Other	(2.0)	0.4	(0.3)
Income tax rate	**31.3%**	**27.8%**	**24.2%**

The American Jobs Creation Act of 2004 (the Jobs Act) created a temporary incentive for U.S. corporations to repatriate accumulated income earned abroad by providing an 85% dividends-received deduction for certain dividends from controlled non-U.S. corporations. During 2005, the company's Chief Executive Officer and Board of Directors approved a domestic reinvestment plan, under which the company repatriated $6.2 billion in earnings outside the U.S. pursuant to the Jobs Act. The company recorded additional tax expense in 2005 of approximately $265 million ($0.04 per common share, assuming dilution) related to this decision to repatriate non-U.S. earnings. This repatriation increased the company's effective rate for 2005 by approximately 2.1 percentage points, to 31.3%. The majority of this increase, 1.8%, is reflected as a separate line item in the rate reconciliation table above, representing the rate effect of the repatriation of prior years' permanently reinvested earnings. The remainder represents the rate effect of the repatriation of the current year's earnings and is included in the rate reconciliation table as part of "Non-U.S income taxed at different rates."

During 2004, in connection with preparing and filing its 2003 federal tax return and preparing its state tax returns, the company reduced its 2004 tax provision by $195 million. This reduction in the 2004 tax provision was primarily driven by tax benefits for export sales and state tax benefits for divestitures that exceeded the amounts originally estimated in connection with the 2003 provision. Also during 2004, the company reversed previously accrued taxes related primarily to the closing of a state income tax audit that reduced the tax provision for 2004 by $62 million.

The company reduced its tax provision for 2003 by approximately $758 million due to the tax benefits related to the sale of certain businesses and assets through the sale of stock of acquired companies (see "Note 13: Acquisitions and Divestitures").

The U.S. Internal Revenue Service (IRS) formally assessed certain adjustments to the amounts reflected by the company in its tax returns for the years 1999 through 2002. (See "Note 18: Contingencies" for a discussion of these matters.)

Deferred income taxes reflect the net tax effects of temporary differences between the carrying amount of assets and liabilities for financial reporting purposes and the amounts for income tax purposes. Significant components of the company's deferred tax assets and liabilities at fiscal year-ends were as follows:

(In Millions)	2005	2004
Deferred tax assets		
Accrued compensation and other benefits	$ 212	$ 265
Accrued advertising	170	115
Deferred income	241	232
Inventory valuation	251	193
Impairment losses on equity investments	93	110
State credits and net operating losses	107	107
Intercompany profit in inventory	105	82
Unremitted earnings of non-U.S. subsidiaries	161	5
Other, net	273	92
	1,613	1,201
Valuation allowance	(86)	(75)
Total deferred tax assets	**$ 1,527**	**$ 1,126**
Deferred tax liabilities		
Depreciation	$ (806)	$ (894)
Unrealized gains on investments	(123)	(82)
Other, net	(117)	(26)
Total deferred tax liabilities	**$(1,046)**	**$(1,002)**
Net deferred tax assets		
Reported as:	**$ 481**	**$ 124**
Current deferred tax assets	$ 1,149	$ 979
Non-current deferred tax assets[1]	35	–
Non-current deferred tax liabilities	(703)	(855)
Net deferred taxes	**$ 481**	**$ 124**

[1] *Included in the "Deferred taxes and other assets" line item on the consolidated balance sheet.*

The net deferred tax asset valuation allowance increased $11 million to $86 million at December 31, 2005, based on management's assessments that it is more likely than not that certain deferred tax assets will not be realized in the foreseeable future. The valuation allowance is composed of unrealized state capital loss carry forwards and unrealized state credit carry forwards of $74 million, and operating loss of non-U.S. subsidiaries of $12 million.

During 2004, the company reclassified $445 million from deferred tax liabilities to common stock and capital stock in excess of par value. The balance sheet reclassification represented the tax benefit attributable to certain prior-year stock option exercises by non-U.S. employees and had no impact on the accompanying statement of cash flows.

U.S. income taxes were not provided for on a cumulative total of approximately $3.7 billion of undistributed earnings for certain non-U.S. subsidiaries. Determination of the amount of unrecognized deferred tax liability for temporary differences related to investments in these non-U.S. subsidiaries that are essentially permanent in duration is not practicable. The company currently intends to reinvest these earnings in operations outside.

Note 18: Contingencies

Tax Matters

In connection with the IRS's regular examination of Intel's tax returns for the years 1999 and 2000, the IRS formally assessed in early 2005 certain adjustments to the amounts reflected by Intel on those returns as a tax benefit for its export sales. Also in 2005, the IRS formally assessed similar adjustments to the amounts reflected by Intel for the years 2001 and 2002 as a tax benefit for export sales. The company does not agree with these adjustments and has appealed the assessments. If the IRS prevails in its position, Intel's federal income tax due for 1999 through 2002 would increase by approximately $1.0 billion, plus interest. The IRS may make similar claims for years subsequent to 2002 in future audits, and if the IRS prevails, income tax due for 2003 through 2005 would increase by approximately $1.2 billion, plus interest.

Although the final resolution of the adjustments is uncertain, based on currently available information, management believes that the ultimate outcome will not have a material adverse effect on the company's financial position, cash flows, or overall trends in results of operations. There is the possibility of a material adverse impact on the results of operations of the period in which the matter is ultimately resolved, if it is resolved unfavorably, or in the period in which an unfavorable outcome becomes probable and reasonably estimable.

Example 6: Charter Communications, Inc.

3. Summary of Significant Accounting Policies

Income Taxes

The Company recognizes deferred tax assets and liabilities for temporary differences between the financial reporting basis and the tax basis of the Company's assets and liabilities and expected benefits of utilizing net operating loss carryforwards. The impact on deferred taxes of changes in tax rates and tax law, if any, applied to the years during which temporary differences are expected to be settled, are reflected in the consolidated financial statements in the period of enactment (see Note 24).

24. Income Taxes

All operations are held through Charter Holdco and its direct and indirect subsidiaries. Charter Holdco and the majority of its subsidiaries are not subject to income tax. However, certain of these subsidiaries are corporations and are subject to income tax. All of the taxable income, gains, losses, deductions, and credits of Charter Holdco are passed through to its members: Charter, Charter Investment, Inc. ("CII") and Vulcan Cable III Inc. ("Vulcan Cable"). Charter is responsible for its share of taxable income or loss of Charter Holdco allocated to Charter in accordance with the Charter Holdco limited liability company agreement (the "LLC Agreement") and partnership tax rules and regulations.

The LLC Agreement provides for certain special allocations of net tax profits and net tax losses (such net tax profits and net tax losses being determined under the applicable federal income tax rules for determining capital accounts). Under the LLC Agreement, through the end of 2003, net tax losses of Charter Holdco that would otherwise have been allocated to Charter based generally on its percentage ownership of outstanding common units were allocated instead to membership units held by Vulcan Cable and CII (the "Special Loss Allocations") to the extent of their respective capital account balances. After 2003, under the LLC Agreement, net tax losses of Charter Holdco are to be allocated to Charter, Vulcan Cable and CII based generally on their respective percentage ownership of outstanding common units to the extent of their respective capital account balances. Allocations of net tax losses in excess of the members' aggregate capital account balances are allocated under the rules governing Regulatory Allocations, as described below. Subject to the Curative Allocation Provisions described below, the LLC Agreement further provides that, beginning at the time Charter Holdco generates net tax profits, the net tax profits that would otherwise have been allocated to Charter based generally on its percentage ownership of outstanding common membership units will instead generally be allocated to Vulcan Cable and CII (the "Special Profit Allocations"). The Special Profit Allocations to Vulcan Cable and CII will generally continue until the cumulative amount of the Special Profit Allocations offsets the cumulative amount of the Special Loss Allocations. The amount and timing of the Special Profit Allocations are subject to the potential application of, and interaction with, the Curative Allocation Provisions described in the following paragraph. The LLC Agreement generally provides that any additional net tax profits are to be allocated among the members of Charter Holdco based generally on their respective percentage ownership of Charter Holdco common membership units.

Because the respective capital account balance of each of Vulcan Cable and CII was reduced to zero by December 31, 2002, certain net tax losses of Charter Holdco that were to be allocated for 2002, 2003, 2004, and 2005, to Vulcan Cable and CII instead have been allocated to Charter (the "Regulatory Allocations"). As a result of the allocation of net tax losses to Charter in 2005, Charter's capital account balance was reduced to zero during 2005. The LLC Agreement provides that once the capital account balances of all members have been reduced to zero, net tax losses are to be allocated to Charter, Vulcan Cable, and CII based generally on their respective percentage ownership of outstanding common units. Such allocations are also considered to be Regulatory Allocations. The LLC Agreement further provides that, to the extent possible, the effect of the Regulatory Allocations is to be offset over time pursuant to certain curative allocation provisions (the "Curative Allocation Provisions") so that, after certain offsetting adjustments are made, each member's capital account balance is equal to the capital account balance such member would have had if the Regulatory Allocations had not been part of the LLC Agreement. The cumulative amount of the actual tax losses allocated to Charter as a result of the Regulatory Allocations through the year ended December 31, 2005, is approximately $4.1 billion.

As a result of the Special Loss Allocations and the Regulatory Allocations referred to above (and their interaction with the allocations related to assets contributed to Charter Holdco with differences between book and tax basis), the cumulative amount of losses of Charter Holdco allocated to Vulcan Cable and CII is in excess of the amount that would have been allocated to such entities if the losses of Charter Holdco had been allocated among its members in proportion to their respective percentage ownership of Charter Holdco common membership units. The cumulative amount of such excess losses was approximately $977 million through December 31, 2005.

In certain situations, the Special Loss Allocations, Special Profit Allocations, Regulatory Allocations, and Curative Allocation Provisions described above could result in Charter paying taxes in an amount that is more or less than if Charter Holdco had allocated net tax profits and net tax losses among its members based generally on the number of common membership units owned by such members. This could occur due to differences in (i) the character of the allocated income (e.g., ordinary versus capital), (ii) the allocated amount and timing of tax depreciation and tax amortization expense due to the application of section 704(c) under the Internal Revenue Code, (iii) the potential interaction between the Special Profit Allocations and the Curative Allocation Provisions, (iv) the amount and timing of alternative minimum taxes paid by Charter, if any, (v) the apportionment of the allocated income or loss among the states in which Charter Holdco does business, and (vi) future federal and state tax laws. Further, in the event of new capital contributions to Charter Holdco, it is possible that the tax effects of the Special Profit Allocations, Special Loss Allocations, Regulatory Allocations and Curative Allocation Provisions will change significantly pursuant to the provisions of the income tax regulations or the terms of a contribution agreement with respect to such contribution. Such change could defer the actual tax benefits to be derived by Charter with respect to the net tax losses allocated to it or accelerate the actual taxable income to Charter with respect to the net tax profits allocated to it. As a result, it is possible under certain circumstances, that Charter could receive future allocations of taxable income in excess of its currently allocated tax deductions and available tax loss carry-forwards. The ability to utilize net operating loss carryforwards is potentially subject to certain limitations as discussed below.

In addition, under their exchange agreement with Charter, Vulcan Cable and CII may exchange some or all of their membership units in Charter Holdco for Charter's Class B common stock, be merged with Charter, or be acquired by Charter in a non-taxable reorganization. If such an exchange were to take place prior to the date that the Special Profit Allocation provisions had fully offset the Special Loss Allocations, Vulcan Cable and CII could elect to cause Charter Holdco to make the remaining Special Profit Allocations to Vulcan Cable and CII immediately prior to the consummation of the exchange. In the event Vulcan Cable and CII choose not to make such election or to the extent such allocations are not possible, Charter would then be allocated tax profits attributable to the membership units received in such exchange pursuant to the Special Profit Allocation provisions. Mr. Allen has generally agreed to reimburse Charter for any incremental income taxes that Charter would owe as a result of such an exchange and any resulting future Special Profit Allocations to Charter. The ability of Charter to utilize net operating loss carryforwards is potentially subject to certain limitations as discussed below. If Charter were to become subject to certain limitations (whether as a result of an exchange described above or otherwise), and as a result were to owe taxes resulting from the Special Profit Allocations, then Mr. Allen may not be obligated to reimburse Charter for such income taxes.

For the years ended December 31, 2005, 2004, and 2003, the Company recorded deferred income tax expense and benefits as shown below. The income tax expense is recognized through increases in deferred tax liabilities related to our investment in Charter Holdco, as well as through current federal and state income tax expense and increases in the deferred tax liabilities of certain of our indirect corporate subsidiaries. The income tax benefits were realized through reductions in the deferred tax liabilities related to Charter's investment in Charter Holdco, as well as the deferred tax liabilities of certain of Charter's indirect corporate subsidiaries. In 2003, Charter received tax loss allocations from Charter Holdco. Previously, the tax losses had been allocated to Vulcan Cable and CII in accordance with the Special Loss Allocations provided under the Charter Holdco limited liability company agreement. The Company does not expect to recognize a similar benefit related to its investment in Charter Holdco after 2003 due to limitations on its ability to offset future tax benefits against the remaining deferred tax liabilities. However, the actual tax provision calculation in future periods will be the result of current and future temporary differences, as well as future operating results.

Current and deferred income tax benefit (expense) is as follows:

	December 31,		
	2005	2004	2003
Current expense:			
Federal income taxes	$ (2)	$ (2)	$ (1)
State income taxes	(4)	(4)	(1)
Current income tax expense	(6)	(6)	(2)
Deferred benefit (expense):			
Federal income taxes	(95)	175	98
State income taxes	(14)	25	14
Deferred income tax benefit (expense)	(109)	200	112
Total income benefit (expense)	$ (115)	$ 194	$ 110

The Company recorded the portion of the income tax benefit associated with the adoption of EITF Topic D-108 as a $91 million reduction of the cumulative effect of accounting change on the accompanying statement of operations for the year ended December 31, 2004.

The Company's effective tax rate differs from that derived by applying the applicable federal income tax rate of 35%, and average state income tax rate of 5% for the years ended December 31, 2005, 2004, and 2003 as follows:

	December 31,		
	2005	2004	2003
Statutory federal income taxes	$ 298	$ 1,288	$ 122
State income taxes, net of federal benefit	43	184	17
Valuation allowance provided	(456)	(1,278)	(29)
	(115)	194	110
Less: cumulative effect of accounting change	–	(91)	–
Income tax benefit (expense)	$ (115)	$ 103	$ 110

The tax effects of these temporary differences that give rise to significant portions of the deferred tax assets and deferred tax liabilities at December 31, 2005 and 2004, which are included in long-term liabilities are presented below.

	December 31,	
	2005	2004
Deferred tax assets:		
Net operating loss carryforward	$ 4,169	$ 3,833
Other	6	8
Total gross deferred tax assets	4,175	3,841
Less: valuation allowance	(3,656)	(3,451)
Net deferred tax assets	$ 519	$ 390
Deferred tax liabilities:		
Investment in Charter Holdco	$ (597)	$ (365)
Indirect corporate subsidiaries:		
Property, plant & equipment	(41)	(40)
Franchises	(206)	(201)
Gross deferred tax liabilities	(844)	(606)
Net deferred tax liabilities	$ (325)	$ (216)

As of December 31, 2005, the Company has deferred tax assets of $4.2 billion, which primarily relate to financial and tax losses allocated to Charter from Charter Holdco. The deferred tax assets include $2.4 billion of tax net operating loss carryforwards (generally expiring in years 2006 through 2025) of Charter and its indirect corporate subsidiaries. Valuation allowances of $3.7 billion exist with respect to these deferred tax assets of which $1.8 billion relate to the tax net operating loss carryforwards.

Realization of any benefit from the Company's tax net operating losses is dependent on: (1) Charter and its indirect corporate subsidiaries' ability to generate future taxable income and (2) the absence of certain future "ownership changes" of Charter's common stock. An "ownership change" as defined in the applicable federal income tax rules, would place significant limitations, on an annual basis, on the use of such net operating losses to offset any future taxable income the Company may generate. Such limitations, in conjunction with the net operating loss expiration provisions, could effectively eliminate the Company's ability to use a substantial portion of its net operating losses to offset any future taxable income. Future transactions and the timing of such transactions could cause an ownership change. Such transactions include additional issuances of common stock by the Company (including but not limited to the issuance of up to a total of 150 million shares of common stock (of which 116.9 million were issued through 2006) under the share lending agreement), the issuance of shares of common stock upon future conversion of Charter's convertible senior notes and the issuance of common stock in the class action settlement discussed in Note 26, reacquisition of the borrowed shares by Charter, or acquisitions or sales of shares by certain holders of Charter's shares, including persons who have held, currently hold, or accumulate in the future 5% or more of Charter's outstanding stock (including upon an exchange by Mr. Allen or his affiliates, directly or indirectly, of membership units of Charter Holdco into CCI common stock). Many of the foregoing transactions are beyond management's control.

The total valuation allowance for deferred tax assets as of December 31, 2005 and 2004 was $3.7 billion and $3.5 billion, respectively. In assessing the realizability of deferred tax assets, management considers whether it is more likely than not that some portion or all of the deferred tax assets will be realized. Because of the uncertainties in projecting future taxable income of Charter Holdco, valuation allowances have been established except for deferred benefits available to offset certain deferred tax liabilities.

The Company is currently under examination by the Internal Revenue Service for the tax years ending December 31, 2002 and 2003. The Company's results (excluding Charter and its indirect corporate subsidiaries) for these years are subject to this examination. Management does not expect the results of this examination to have a material adverse effect on the Company's consolidated financial condition or results of operations.

APPENDIX IV: INDEX OF ACCOUNTING LITERATURE AFFECTING INCOME TAXES

FASB Staff Implementation Guide, *A Guide to Implementation of Statement 109 on Accounting for Income Taxes*

FASB Staff Question No.	Description	Interpretation No.
1	Scheduling reversal patterns of existing temporary differences	18-1
2	Scheduling future originating and reversing temporary differences	21-2
3	Separate computations for each tax jurisdiction	17-1
4	Scheduling of tax contingencies	21-3
5	Temporary differences caused by a change in tax law	15-1
6	Family-owned farming businesses	15-2
7	Deferred state income taxes give rise to a U.S. federal temporary difference	13-1
8	Future percentage-of-taxable-income bad-debt deductions of a savings and loan association	31-4
9	Recognition of pre quasi reorganization tax benefits	37-1
10	Quasi reorganization that results in a net gain being credited to capital	37-2
11	Disclosures required for a post balance-sheet date change in tax status	28-1
12	Deferred tax liability for built-in gains of a S corporation	28-2
13	Adjustment of negative goodwill	30-1
14	Subsequent recognition of acquiring enterprise tax benefits	30-3
15	Deferred taxes in a "bargain" purchase business combination	30-6
16	Identified intangible assets that are not amortizable for tax purposes	9-2
17	Accounting for tax contingencies in a taxable purchase business combination	30-8

FASB Staff Question No.	Description	Interpretation No.
17A	Potential impairments caused by prior net-of-tax accounting	55-1
17B	Determining the amount of acquired tax benefits at transition to Statement 109	51-2
17C	Determining the amount of acquired tax benefits at transition to Statement 109 when information is lacking	51-3
18	Disclosure of the significant components of income tax expense	45-1
19	Intraperiod tax allocation when the enacted tax law provides for phased-in changes in tax rates	35-6
20	Withdrawn	n/a
21	Withdrawn	n/a
22	Renumbered 17A	55-1
23	Renumbered 17B	51-2
24	Renumbered 17C	51-3
25	Elections for tax purposes that qualify as tax-planning strategies	22-1
26	Alternative tax-planning strategies	22-2
27	Reasonable effort to identify tax-planning strategies	22-3
28	Change in tax status in not a qualifying tax-planning strategy	28-3

References to All Other Accounting Literature:

American Institute of Certified Public Accountants (AICPA)

AICPA Accounting Research Bulletins (ARBs)

Item	Description	Paragraph or Interpretation No(s).
ARB 43	Restatement and Revision of Accounting Research Bulletins, Chapter 2A: Comparative Financial Statements	47-3
ARB 43	Restatement and Revision of Accounting Research Bulletins, Chapter 7: Capital Accounts	37-1, 37-2
ARB 51	Consolidated Financial Statements	33-5

AICPA Statements of Position (SOPs)

Item	Description	Paragraph or Interpretation No(s).
SOP 78-9	Accounting for Investments in Real Estate Ventures	4-6
SOP 90-7	Financial Reporting by Entities in Reorganization Under the Bankruptcy Code	5-2, 9-4, 30-14, 37-3
SOP 94-6	Disclosure of Certain Significant Risks and Uncertainties	43-7

Accounting Principles Board (APB)

APB Opinions

Item	Description	Paragraph or Interpretation No(s).
APB 11	Accounting for Income Taxes	9-1, 41-3, 41-4
APB 14	Accounting for Convertible Debt and Debt Issued with Stock Purchase Warrants	36-7
APB 16	Business Combinations	51-2, 55-1
APB 22	Disclosure of Accounting Policies	App I: FIN 48 19-1
APB 23	Accounting for Income Taxes—Special Areas	18-8, 18-9, 30-5, 30-10, 31-2, 31-3, 31-5, 31-7, 31-8, 31-9, 33-1, 33-2, 33-5, 34-2, 35-5, 44-1
APB 25	Accounting for Stock Issued to Employees	30-20
APB 28	Interim Financial Reporting	5-1, 27-2
APB 29	Accounting for Nonmonetary Transactions	35-4
APB 30	Reporting the Results of Operations—Reporting the Effects of Disposal of a Segment of a Business, and Extraordinary, Unusual and Infrequently Occurring Events and Transactions	47-3

Financial Accounting Standards Board (FASB)

FASB Statements

Item	Description	Paragraph or Interpretation No(s).
Statement 2	Accounting for Research and Development Costs	30-15
Statement 5	Accounting for Contingencies	10-1, 27-1, 35-4, 35-10, 43-1, 47-3, App I: FIN 48 12-1, App I: FIN 48 23-1
Statement 13	Accounting for Leases	9-8, 21-5
Statement 34	Capitalization of Interest Costs	App I: FIN 48 15-1
Statement 52	Foreign Currency Translation	36, 9-5, 9-6, 9-7, 27-3, 31-2, 31-8, 37-5
Statement 71	Accounting for the Effects of Certain Types of Regulation	27-8, 29-1, 29-2
Statement 84	Induced Conversions of Convertible Debt—an Amendment of APB Opinion No. 26	36-8
Statement 87	Employers'Accounting for Pensions	37-5
Statement 95	Statement of Cash Flows	36-9
Statement 96	Accounting for Income Taxes	4-5, 18-1, 18-4, 18-5, 30-11, 37-1, 39-1, 43-5, 45-2, 51-2
Statement 106	Employers'Accounting for Postretirement Benefits Other Than Pensions	14-4, 20-1
Statement 115	Accounting for Certain Investments in Debt and Equity Securities	18-7, 21-6, 27-3, 35-8, 37-5, 37-6
Statement 123	Accounting for Stock-Based Compensation	30-20, 36, 36-3, 36-4, 36-9, 36-11
Statement 123R	Share-Based Payment	30-20, 35-3, 36-2, 36-3, 36-4, 36-9, 36-10, 36-11, 45-4
Statement 128	Earnings per Share	36-4
Statement 141	Business Combinations	30-1, 30-9, 30-21
Statement 142	Goodwill and Other Intangible Assets	9-4
Statement 143	Accounting for Asset Retirement Obligations	App I: FIN 48 15-1

Item	Description	Paragraph or Interpretation No(s).
Statement 144	Accounting for the Impairment or Disposal of Long-Lived Assets	20-4, 30-20, 30-23, 31-3, 33-1, 34-1, 34-2, 35-1, 35-10
Statement 146	Accounting for Costs Associated with Exit or Disposal Activities	App I: FIN 48 15-1
Statement 154	Accounting Changes and Error Corrections—a Replacement of APB Opinion No. 20 and FASB Statement No. 3	35-10, 40-4, App I: FIN 48 19-1

FASB Interpretations (FINs)

Item	Description	Paragraph or Interpretation No(s).
FIN 4	Applicability of FASB Statement No. 2 to Business Combinations Accounted for by the Purchase Method—an Interpretation of FASB Statement No. 2	30-15
FIN 18	Accounting for Income Taxes in Interim Periods—an Interpretation of APB Opinion No. 28	5-1, 5-2, 35-7
FIN 21	Accounting for Leases in a Business Combination—an Interpretation of FASB Statement No. 13	21-5
FIN 31	Treatment of Stock Compensation Plans in EPS Computations—an Interpretation of APB Opinion No. 15 and a Modification of FASB Interpretation No. 28	36-4
FIN 44	Accounting for Certain Transactions Involving Stock Compensation—an Interpretation of APB Opinion No. 25	30-20
FIN 46R	Consolidation of Variable Interest Entities—an Interpretation of ARB No. 51	4-6, 33-5
FIN 48	Accounting for Uncertainty in Income Taxes—an Interpretation of FASB Statement No. 109	10-1, 22-6, 27-1, 30-9, 35-10, 43-1, 45-2

FASB Technical Bulletins (FTBs)

Item	Description	Paragraph or Interpretation No(s).
FTB 79-16 (Revised)	Effect of a Change in Income Tax Rate on the Accounting for Leveraged Leases	9-8

Item	Description	Paragraph or Interpretation No(s).
FTB 82-1	Disclosure of the Sale or Purchase of Tax Benefits through Tax Leases	47-3
FTB 85-4	Accounting for Purchase of Life Insurance	14-5
FTB 86-1	Accounting for Certain Effects of the Tax Reform Act of 1986	27-2

FASB Staff Positions (FSPs)

Item	Description	Paragraph or Interpretation No(s).
FSP FAS 13-2	Accounting for a Change or Projected Change in the Timing of Cash Flows Relating to Income Taxes Generated by a Leveraged Lease Transaction	9-8
FSP FAS 106-2	Accounting and Disclosure Requirements Related to the Medicare Prescription Drug, Improvement and Modernization Act of 2003	14-4
FSP FAS 109-1	Application of FASB Statement No. 109, *Accounting for Income Taxes*, to the Tax Deduction on Qualified Production Activities Provided by the American Jobs Creation Act of 2004	18-9
FSP FAS 109-2	Accounting and Disclosure Guidance for the Foreign Earnings Repatriation Provision within the American Jobs Creation Act of 2004	31-10
FSP FAS 123R-3	Transition Election Related to Accounting for the Tax Effects of Share-Based Payment Awards	36-9, 36-11

FASB Staff Implementation Guides

Description	Paragraph or Interpretation No(s).
A Guide to Implementation of Statement 115 on Accounting for Certain Investments in Debt and Equity Securities: Questions and Answers	35-8

FASB Emerging Issues Task Force (EITF) Issues

Item	Description	Paragraph or Interpretation No(s).
Issue 86-43	Effect of a Change in Tax Law or Rates on Leveraged Leases	47-4
Issue 86-44	Effect of a Change in Tax Law on Investments in Safe Harbor Leases	9-1
Issue 88-16	Basis in Leveraged Buyout Transactions	30-12 30-13
Issue 90-12	Allocating Basis to Individual Assets and Liabilities for Transactions within the Scope of Issue No. 88-16	30-12 30-13
Issue 91-8	Application of FASB Statement No. 96 to a State Tax Based on the Greater of a Franchise Tax or an Income Tax	4-5
Issue 92-3	Earnings-per-Share Treatment of Tax Benefits for Dividends on Unallocated Stock Held by an Employee Stock Ownership Plan	36-6
Issue 92-4	Accounting for a Change in Functional Currency When an Economy Ceases to Be Considered Highly Inflationary	9-6
Issue 92-8	Accounting for the Income Tax Effects under FASB Statement No. 109 of a Change in Functional Currency When an Economy Ceases to Be Considered Highly Inflationary	9-6
Issue 92-9	Accounting for the Present Value of Future Profits Resulting from the Acquisition of a Life Insurance Company	30-23
Issue 93-7	Uncertainties Related to Income Taxes in a Purchase Business Combination	9-3, 30-4, 30-9, 35-5
Issue 93-9	Application of FASB Statement No. 109 in Foreign Financial Statements Restated for General Price-Level Changes	9-5
Issue 93-12	Recognition and Measurement of the Tax Benefit of Excess Tax-Deductible Goodwill Resulting from a Retroactive Change in Tax Law	27-5
Issue 93-13	Effect of a Retroactive Change in Enacted Tax Rates That Is Included in Income from Continuing Operations	27-4, 35-7
Issue 93-16	Application of FASB Statement No. 109 to Basis Differences within Foreign Subsidiaries That Meet the Indefinite Reversal Criterion of APB Opinion No. 23	4-7, 31-7, 31-8

Item	Description	Paragraph or Interpretation No(s).
Issue 93-17	Recognition of Deferred Tax Assets for a Parent Company's Excess Tax Basis in the Stock of a Subsidiary That Is Accounted for as a Discontinued Operation	33-1, 34-1, 34-2
Issue 94-1	Accounting for Tax Benefits Resulting from Investments in Affordable Housing Projects	4-6
Issue 94-10	Accounting by a Company for the Income Tax Effects of Transactions among or with Its Shareholders under FASB Statement No. 109	35-4, 35-5, 35-6
Issue 95-9	Accounting for Tax Effects of Dividends in France in Accordance with FASB Statement No. 109	4-7
Issue 95-10	Accounting for Tax Credits Related to Dividend Payments in Accordance with FASB Statement No. 109	18-8
Issue 95-20	Measurement in the Consolidated Financial Statements of a Parent of the Tax Effects Related to the Operations of a Foreign Subsidiary That Receives Tax Credits Related to Dividend Payments	18-8
Issue 96-7	Accounting for Deferred Taxes on In-Process Research and Development Activities Acquired in a Purchase Business Combination	30-15
Issue 98-5	Accounting for Convertible Securities with Beneficial Conversion Features or Contingently Adjustable Conversion Ratios	36-12
Issue 98-11	Accounting for Acquired Temporary Differences in Certain Purchase Transactions That Are Not Accounted for as Business Combinations	16-1, 30-11
Issue 99-15	Accounting for Decreases in Deferred Tax Asset Valuation Allowances Established in a Purchase Business Combination As a Result of a Change in Tax Regulations	30-22
Issue 00-15	Classification in the Statement of Cash Flows of the Income Tax Benefit Received by a Company upon Exercise of a Nonqualified Employee Stock Option	36-9
Issue 00-23	Issues Related to the Accounting for Stock Compensation under APB Opinion No. 25 and FASB Interpretation No. 44	30-20
Issue 00-27	Application of Issue No. 98-5 to Certain Convertible Instruments	36-12
Issue 05-8	Income Tax Consequences of Issuing Convertible Debt with a Beneficial Conversion Feature	36-12

EITF Abstracts, Appendix D Topics

Item	Description	Paragraph or Interpretation No(s).
Topic D-30	Adjustment Due to Effect of a Change in Tax Laws or Rates	27-1
Topic D-31	Temporary Differences Related to LIFO Inventory and Tax-to-Tax Differences	33-3
Topic D-32	Intraperiod Tax Allocation of the Tax Effect of Pretax Income from Continuing Operations	35-1, 35-2
Topic D-33	Timing of Recognition of Tax Benefits for Pre-Reorganization Temporary Differences and Carryforwards	37-4
Topic D-46	Accounting for Limited Partnership Investments	4-6
Topic D-56	Accounting for a Change in Functional Currency and Deferred Taxes When an Economy Becomes Highly Inflationary	9-6

Securities and Exchange Commission (SEC)

Rules and Regulations

Regulation S-K Non Financial Statement Requirements	App I: FIN 48 17-2
Regulation S-X Financial Statement Requirements	43-9*, App I: FIN 48 17-2

Staff Accounting Bulletins (SABs)

Item	Description	Paragraph or Interpretation No(s).
Topic 1B	Financial Statements—Allocation of Expenses and Related Disclosure in Financial Statements of Subsidiaries, Divisions, or Lesser Business Components of Another Entity (SAB 55)	40-8
Topic 5H	Miscellaneous Accounting—Accounting for Sales of Stock by a Subsidiary (SAB 51)	33-1
Topic 5S	Miscellaneous Accounting—Quasi-Reorganization (SAB 86)	39-1

Item	Description	Paragraph or Interpretation No(s).
Topic 6I	Interpretations of Accounting Series Releases and Financial Reporting Releases—Accounting Series Release 149—Improved Disclosure of Income Tax Expense (SABs 1 and 8)	43-9
Topic 11C	Miscellaneous Disclosure—Tax Holidays (SAB 1)	43-9

* Includes a discussion of certain nonfinancial disclosure requirements in Forms 10-K and 10-KSB for SEC registrants as documented in the Internal Revenue Code. This disclosure requirement results from passage of the American Jobs Creation Act of 2004.

Staff Meeting Minutes

Description	Paragraph or Interpretation No(s).
Minutes of AICPA's International Practice Task Force, December 21, 1995	27-9
Minutes of the AICPA's Regulations Committee, September 2006	App I: FIN 48 19-1, App I: FIN 48 21-1

Other SEC Guidance

Description	Paragraph or Interpretation No(s).
May 1, 1999, "Frequently Requested Accounting and Financial Reporting Interpretations and Guidance"	47-2

Index

References are to interpretation numbers and page numbers.

E

F

L

M

N

O

P

Q

R

T

U

V